D0577606

SOCIALIST DREAMS [AND] ★ BEAUTY QUEENS ★

A COUCHSURFER'S MEMOIR OF VENEZUELA

JAMIE MASLIN

Skyhorse Publishing

www.skyhorsepublishing.com

10 9 8 7 6 5 4 3 2 1

Library of Congress Cataloging-in-Publication Data available on file.
ISBN: 978-1-61608-221-5

Printed in the United States of America

Books by Jamie Maslin

Iranian Rappers and Persian Porn:
A Hitchhiker's Adventures in the New Iran

For my wonderful
Wemsy

CONTENTS

Acknowledgements

Several people deserve a special mention for their help during the creation of this book. I wish to express my gratitude to the many wonderful and varied CouchSurfers who so kindly put me up all over Venezuela; to Charles Brewer-Carias, Farrin De Fredrick, Sabrina Durling-Jones, Alan Highton, and Paul Rideough for providing many of the beautiful photographs used to illustrate this book; to my parents for their ongoing support; to Charlie Wood and Marcin Szymanek for their generosity in lending me their apartment and PC to edit the book while traveling in Kyrgyzstan; and to my long-suffering girlfriend, Emily, for putting up with my extended trips abroad and antisocial writing hours.

A particularly special thank-you must go to my editor Jennifer McCartney for first giving me the opportunity to have my writing read beyond my humble collection of friends and family; to all at the Spitzer agency, Philip Spitzer, Lukas Ortiz, and especially Lucas Hunt, whose unfailing faith in my work, encouragement, support, advice, and friendship mean the world to me; and finally, a big thank-you to my sister, Hannah, for finally making me an uncle to beautiful little Thomas. Nothing to do with the book whatsoever, but worthy of mention nonetheless.

In the interest of protecting employment, sparing blushes, and preventing slaps from wives, certain names and minor details have been strategically altered in the text. (You know who you are.)

HONDURAS
NICARAGUA
COSTA RICA
PANAMA
Caracas
VENEZU
Bogota
COLOMBIA
Quito
ECUADOR
PERU
Lima
BO

Map of the author's journey
Georgetown
Paramaribo
GUYANA
SURINAME
FRENCH GUIANA
Cayenne
BRAZIL
Venezuela
Colombia
Maracaibo
Coro
Valencia
Barquisimeto
Barinas
Cumana
Puerto La Cruz
Guayana City
Maturin
El Tigre
Anaco
San Fernando
Calabozo
Cúcuta
Puerto Ayacucho
El Caura
Parque Nacional Canaima
Parque Nacional Jaua-Sarisariñama
Parque Nacional Parima Tapirapecó
Parque Nacional Serranía La Neblina
Sierra Imataca
Boa Vista
Roraima
Trinidad and Tobago
Grenada
Aruba

Prologue

"Venezuela is an extremely dangerous country. Don't trust anyone. Including the police." We were preparing to board a flight to his hometown, Venezuela's capital, Caracas. On hearing that I spoke no Spanish and was not going there on business but vacation, he shook his head and asked incredulously, "What do you want to go *there* for?" This was a reaction I was not expecting.

On the flight the man and his family kindly told me everything that was wrong with their country–it had roughly fifteen thousand homicides a year with Caracas recently topping the list of the world's murder capitals,[1] the national institutions were rife with corruption, it suffered regular infuriating power cuts, most towns had an unofficial curfew after dark such were the dangers, and the president was a "baboon." His wife warned me that I'd have to be very careful not to get mugged, kidnapped, or arrested before my stay was over. I thought of the two grand I had hidden on me–stashed away in my shoes and socks, in different pockets, and in a money belt around my waist–and, not for the first time, felt a twinge of concern.

Venezuela might not be renowned as a popular tourist destination, but it certainly held some attraction for me. It boasted the longest Caribbean coastline of any country, the world's highest waterfall, an expansive savannah, Andean mountains, Amazonian rain forest, and even a desert. Twenty percent of the world's known bird species call it home, and within its western regions was an unexplained natural phenomenon I was determined to experience–lightning with no thunder.

I had first made up my mind to visit after casually flicking through a *National Geographic* magazine in the dusty confines of my favorite secondhand bookstore in London, Keith Fawkes Books, on Flask Lane in Hampstead. As I turned the page, a photograph gave me reason to pause and sent my heart rate soaring–and I'm not referring to a tasteful topless shot of an indigenous maiden. Rising from the page was the bizarre anvil-shaped plateau of an isolated mountain, standing alone in a sea of Amazonian mist that shrouded the forest below. This was Mount Roraima. It looked like a sacred temple. If the gods did exist then they lived in Venezuela. Even before reading the article, I knew that one day I would have to visit it.

I'd experienced the *National Geographic* effect before. A casual flick of the page in a doctor's waiting room had sent me to a remote and obscure slot canyon in Western China, twisting its way to the world's highest natural archway, Shipton's Arch; a nonchalant browse at a dog-eared copy in a dentist's office had taken me to a sacred Navajo rock formation, Naat'áanii Nééz, off the beaten track in New Mexico. In the wrong hands *National Geographic* is a dangerous magazine. So with Mount Roraima in my sights, I began to read up on Venezuela's other attractions. It looked like a place of staggering natural beauty, and in more ways than one. In addition to its stunning landscapes, Venezuela supposedly possessed the most beautiful women in the world–women who had won more international beauty pageant titles than any other country. Reason enough for a visit, methinks.

While the beauty queens merited occasional mention in the Western press, more often than not it was the country's president, Hugo Chávez, that garnered journalists' attention. From my experience, when the mainstream media routinely place adjectives before the name of a country's president–such as "populist," "firebrand," "demagogue," and "would-be dictator" in the case of Chávez–then it's a sure sign of a nation worth visiting. You never see those adjectives attributed to Western heads of state, as they're reserved for that most despicable type of leader–one with large reserves of oil.

From Chávez's theatrical speech at the United Nations, where he made the sign of the cross then clasped his hands together in prayer to protect himself from the U.S. president, or as he put it, "the devil," to his weekly national television broadcasts, which can last for up to eight hours, there *is* much to write about Mr. Chávez. But if the main export of Venezuela were broccoli instead of oil, then it is unlikely the president would regularly fill quite so many column inches here in the West. But oil it has and aplenty.

Venezuela is so awash with black gold that it has the cheapest pump prices on the planet. Drive a gas-guzzling SUV there and the cost of gas is unlikely to bother you, as at six cents a gallon you'll be able to fill up for a solitary U.S. dollar. It possesses the largest reserves of conventional "light" oils in the Western Hemisphere, but when it comes to the "heavy" stuff, it's in a league of its own, possessing a staggering 90 percent of the earth's entire extraheavy–that is, tar oil–reserves.[2] For years these heavy oil reserves would have been irrelevant, as it was too costly to extract and process them, but thanks to new extracting technologies and a high oil price, these reserves now take on far greater meaning. If the price of oil continues to remain high enough to make the heavy oil extraction commercially viable, then Venezuela easily eclipses Saudi Arabia as the world's oil reserve supremo. Attaining this status has huge implications, one of which is the control of OPEC. (Based in Vienna, the current Organization of the Petroleum Exporting Countries includes Algeria, Angola, Ecuador, Iran, Iraq, Kuwait, Libya, Nigeria, Qatar, Saudi Arabia, the United Arab Emirates, and Venezuela.)

Despite this tremendous national wealth, the majority of the population live in barrios–shantytowns where millions scrape by, often in appalling poverty. For many of them, I would soon discover, Chávez is a hero, a social revolutionary determined to reshape the country along more equitable lines. For much of the elite, he is anything but. Many see him as a megalomaniac heading a corrupt government bent on replacing private enterprise with state-controlled socialist bureaucracy. Disparity of political views often matches that of wealth. It is a country of mansions and shantytowns, of dreams and despair, of social revolution and elite resistance, and a place, I hoped, with plenty of adventures awaiting me–dangerous or not.

My plan was to spend the next few months traveling all over Venezuela in a big loop, visiting its main sites of interest, and staying with so-called CouchSurfers along the way–a concept I had heard about just weeks before when trying to find a place to stay in New York. I had put the feelers out with the limited friends I knew in the Big Apple, but struggled to find a place to crash. It was then that one of my friends recommended I try CouchSurfing.

Like Facebook, CouchSurfing is a social networking website where users have updatable profiles, with photos and friend lists; but where Facebookers predominantly post random photos, funny links, status updates, or pointlessly "poke" each other, CouchSurfers offer free accommodation, or extend offers to meet up and serve as a tour guide to other CouchSurfers who plan to visit their hometown or city. This not only gives the visitor a free place to stay, but, more importantly, provides a chance to see the destination through the eyes of a local, and visit places and people inaccessible to a standard tourist. For those offering the accommodation, it provides the opportunity to show a visitor their hometown in the best possible light and to become acquainted with new and interesting people, often from cultures very different from their own.

Simply registering on the site and contacting a CouchSurfer is no guarantee of finding a place to stay. Likewise, if you're offering to host, there is no guarantee that anyone will want to stay with you. The process is entirely consensual between both parties, and details as to the length of stay are discussed prior to an actual meeting. And before you even get a reply to a message from another

CouchSurfer, you need to have a profile that they like the look of, or at least are not disturbed by. If your profile picture makes you look like a dribbling psycho, or if you have, heaven forbid, negative feedback from past CouchSurfers, then your chances of getting a complete stranger to either visit you or welcome you into their home are about as good as mine are of winning the next Nobel Prize in Literature.

With this in mind, I hastily put together a suitable profile, complete with happy innocuous pictures of me on past travels, and wrote a suitably upbeat and inoffensive profile statement:

I love to travel to places that challenge and inspire me, and to meet people who do likewise.
My big love is the great outdoors and anything to do with the natural world. I teach wilderness survival skills in my spare time and am a bit of a tree geek—having just qualified as a tree surgeon.

I selected the "traveling at the moment" option so as to avoid people mistakenly contacting me for a place to stay in my hometown, London, then selected Caracas as my first destination and narrowed the search to those who could speak English. I was now ready to meet some like-minded travelers. Or so I thought.

First up on the Caracas list was a girl of thirty, whose profile didn't exactly match what I considered to be the true spirit of the site which promotes "cross-cultural encounters" and has the slogan Participate in Creating a Better World, One Couch at a Time.

Her profile stated that you could stay on her couch:

[I]f and only if. . .You are not backpacking across South America with no money in your pocket. Transportation system here doesnt work and you have to take taxis, which are expensive . . . You are not on a tight budget, going out to eat and party is expensive too and I live large!

She then went on to state that "*you MUST bring me some present, something from your country . . .*" On her reference section she had written an endorsement of someone who had stayed with her and why she liked him.

> *Something we have in common: we dont like backpacking. Poshpacking is our thing so i like him inmediately. I really admire Joost's endurance to travel so far so long. I thought i was a hard core traveller . . .*

Poshpacking–how very hard-core, sweetie.

I quickly decided she wasn't my type of person and skipped to the next profile. I ended up messaging a load of people saying that I would be coming to Venezuela soon and wanted to meet locals wherever possible, so if they could put me up, then thank you very much. These messages I tried to tweak slightly to reference something in their profile in order to personalize them a bit. I was the lucky recipient of numerous replies, but unfortunately for me, everyone I'd contacted seemed to either be out of town on the dates I would be there, have relatives staying and therefore no room, or be otherwise unavailable to put me up.

I messaged a load more.

This time I got four offers. One from a pretty girl in her twenties called Penelope, who wanted to meet up for a coffee and show me around, and three from people willing to put me up at their place. The first was from a sixty-five-year-old British widower called Austin, who lived with twelve cats and had spent the last thirty years in the country; the second from a young Venezuelan student called Jonathann; and the third from a German in his early thirties called Hans, who was currently living and working in Venezuela as a journalist. Hans signed off his message to me with a slightly confusing disclaimer:

> *And due to a weird experience I had two weeks ago I'd like to add that I'm open minded and someone else's sexual orientation is not my cup of tea but I'm not interested in men.*

I commenced a gracious e-mail exchange with all concerned and hoped to spend a couple of nights with each of those offering accommodation. Austin, it turned out, was going to be in neighboring Colombia on the day would I arrive, but would be getting back the day after, so I planned to stay with one of the other two first. Jonathann contacted me soon after bearing bad news; due to unforeseen circumstances, he could no longer host me. So it looked like it would have to be Hans.

In the messages I received from both Austin and Hans, they provided, without any prompting on my part, warnings on Caracas's dangers. "I don't want to alarm you," wrote Austin, "but Caracas is not a safe city so you have to be very street wise. You need to get a confirmed place to stay for the first night and you must take one of the airport black taxis." He went on to write, "You should know that Venezuela has been very close to a civil war . . ." Hans was likewise vocal on the dangers and implored me to take an official cab from the airport, "Many robberies have been reported on the route to Caracas, so DONT go with pirate taxis, please."

In addition to the dangers, I was also given advice on the difference between the official exchange rate and the black market rate for the Venezuelan currency, the bolivar. This was of great importance and turned out to be a huge help. The official exchange rate was 2.15 bolivars to every U.S. dollar. However, the unofficial black market rate was roughly 6.5 bolivars to the dollar. So unless you wanted to see your money disappear quicker than a politician's preelection promises, it was essential to exchange your cash on the black market. The downside to this was twofold; not only did you have to deal with the shady characters doing the black market transaction, but you had to carry a vast quantity of money on you, since any traveler's check, cash withdrawals, or credit cards transactions would charge you the official rate. The fixed official exchange rate, along with a strict control on converting bolivars to dollars, is in place to stabilize the currency's value, encourage domestic investment, and prevent capital flight abroad.[3] As a foreigner, of course, using this rate makes the country ridiculously expensive.[4]

Thanks to this confusing practice, I had boarded the flight to Caracas, a city I had repeatedly been warned was extremely unsafe, carrying over two thousand U.S. dollars spread about my person. Keeping this safe and changing it on the black market were not my only concerns, for despite Austin's instructions that I have a confirmed place to stay when I arrive, I had yet to hear back from Hans–which meant I also didn't have his address or phone number. I had sent him a message three days before my departure with a request for these and to take him up on his suggestion of sending a friend of his, who was a cabby, to pick me up, but by the time I boarded my flight, I had still received no answer. If nobody materi–alized, I would resign myself to catching a cab, of the official variety, to the center of town and booking into a cheap place to stay.

As my plane descended into Caracas, the sun had yet to break the horizon, but it was already getting light, giving me a spec–tacular predawn glimpse of the area's tropical surroundings. The airport was located right up against the crashing waves of a sandy palm–fronted Caribbean coast, and behind, rising up from the shoreline like a giant barricade against the ocean, were towering green mountains, beyond which, I assumed, lay Caracas.

After passing through the monotony of customs, I was greeted with a most welcome sight. The words

JAMIE MASLIN

on a handwritten sign held up by a cheerful–looking man. Hans had come through after all. I shook the hand of my driver, who intro–duced himself as Ricardo, and a second later we were approached by a money changer, but Ricardo waved him off. In very broken English he simply said, "Hans change money later." That was fine by me.

Ricardo walked me to his car, graciously opening the door, and with a wide smile welcomed me to Venezuela.

And so my journey began.

CHAPTER 1

Bloodsuckers, Boob Jobs, and Bizarre Names

Dawn had just broken, and a lazy soft pink light diffused across the landscape as we drove to the center of Caracas. I love this time of day more than any other, and especially when traveling. Everything seems so still, but at the same time there's a tangible optimism in the air, like the moment before the curtain rises on a big theater performance, and although it might not live up to your expectations, the anticipation at the start is still the same. Minutes earlier I had been tired and lethargic from an uncomfortable night on a plane, but now I felt energized and excited to the point of agitation to be here in a new unexplored country, at the beginning of a long and no doubt fascinating adventure.

Forested peaks soon gave way to chaotic sprawling barrio shantytowns, which clung to the undulating terrain like limpets to a rock, and rose up precariously on top of each other in the most haphazard manner imaginable. Being so early in the morning, there was barely a soul about, with the inhabitants tucked up in bed unseen behind their home's ramshackle walls. Red-painted slogans in support of Venezuela's president, Hugo Chávez, adorned many of the dwellings. Along the highway we passed several billboards with the image of Chávez striking optimistic and magnanimous poses. We drove in near silence due to my lack of Spanish and Ricardo's of English. It was just what I needed to get my thoughts together and prepare for what I had been led to believe would be an extremely challenging city.

Caracas is situated in a valley dominated by the towering Mount El Ávila, which rises 7,400 feet to the north of the city, isolating it from the Caribbean coast beyond. This handy landmark serves as a useful navigation tool as I would soon discover. As we got closer to the center of the capital, the barrios yielded to monolithic skyscrapers, gleaming like beacons in the low morning light. Freeways twisted every which way, spreading out like tributaries of the Amazon into Caracas's myriad districts, housing the city's four million inhabitants. As it wasn't yet five o'clock, few had roused themselves yet, imparting a strange serene and peaceful atmosphere to the city, which I knew could be anything but. Was this the calm before the storm? I wondered.

We pulled into centrally located run-of-the-mill residential area, Bello Monte, comprising countless forgettable apartment blocks, and came to a halt on a steep incline outside a weathered-looking six-story tower. By the time of our arrival, life was just beginning to stir in the streets outside. Morning deliveries of crates of fruit, cartons of milk, and crusty loafs of bread were off-loaded at local shops. A few early risers purchased newspapers from a small kiosk across the road and nursed small cups of espresso coffees at a welcoming café opposite, slowly bringing the area to life.

A moment later, Hans came out to meet us. In person he was smaller than I imagined, although there was a definite suggestion of intensity about him as he greeted us with a smile–his profile picture had been lit from one side, leaving half his image mostly dark.

There are certain subjects that social norms in other parts of the world might deem inappropriate to launch into after just meeting someone, but if Hans was anything to go by, in Venezuela, politics wasn't one of them. After retracting his palm from our first handshake, he thrust into it a piece of paper he'd just acquired through his job as a journalist, which, he said, was a list of government officials who had lost money obtained through corruption that had been stashed away secretly in a recently collapsed foreign bank. Alongside the individual's names were the amounts each had apparently lost. Whether this was a reliable list or not, I have no idea, and Hans freely admitted that he couldn't verify it.

"Corruption is out of control in Venezuela," he said.

After squaring up the fare with Ricardo, Hans reached into his pocket and handed me two hundred bolivars on loan, adding that he'd arrange for me to exchange some money on the black market in the next few days and that I could pay him back then. I thanked him. We headed into his block, which had an intricate security system–one key for the front gate, one for the lobby, one to activate the lift, and two to open his front door. If you chose to use the stairs, then you needed yet another key to access the given floor.

Hans's apartment was a small dusty one-bedroom place with basic living and kitchen area. On the living room wall hung a big map of the world. Wedged into a good-sized bookcase was a substantial collection of books–comprising mainly of travel guides and hard-hitting political works with a Venezuelan and anti-Chávez theme. By the window was a slightly droopy houseplant that had clearly seen better days and in the sink resided a pile of dishes, now coated in a water-resistant oily residue, whose precarious structure brought to mind a leaning tower. In the bedroom, two unmade single beds had been pushed together to form a double. The bathroom, consisting of a toilet and tiny shower cubicle, was accessible through the bedroom, making any nighttime call of nature slightly awkward since I'd be sleeping in the living room. We dropped off my cumbersome backpack before heading to the café opposite for a rousing caffeinated beverage and to get to know each other.

Hans had, like Austin, been in neighboring Colombia for the last few days and only just got back. He had replied to my message to confirm I could stay, but had only sent this after I'd boarded my flight. Over a strong aromatic espresso and a breakfast of flaky pastries filled with ham and cheese, Hans told me about himself and his experiences in Venezuela. He had grown up under communism in East Germany before the fall of the Berlin wall and had come to Venezuela because of his interest in President Hugo Chávez's socialist "Bolivarian Revolution," and to further his journalistic career. He was no fan of Chávez, however, and told me, "Living in Venezuela is like living in *Alice in Wonderland*, it just doesn't make any sense. The country doesn't function on any level, so how can Chávez talk of exporting his revolution abroad when nothing works at home?"

Like the family at the airport, he was keen to impress upon me just how dangerous the city was and that I should be aware of my surroundings at all times. He, too, mentioned the country's horrific murder rate, the latest figures for which stand at sixteen thousand per year. In Caracas it equated to roughly two hundred homicides a year for every one hundred thousand citizens[5]–New York City by comparison has about six murders per one hundred thousand.[6]

"Law and order needs to be the government's top priority," he said. Then he added, "Don't ask the police for anything, and if you see them coming, cross the road to the other side." They were, he said, thoroughly corrupt and useless at fighting crime. However, more worrying than their inefficiency at fighting crime was their actual involvement in it.

"Our county's justice minister, Tarek El-Aissami, recently admitted that 20 percent of all crime in Venezuela was committed by the police themselves!"

Hans's lack of faith in them was widespread. In a recent survey, a massive 70 percent of those polled said "police and criminals are practically the same."[7] In a fourteen-month period from January 2008 until March 2009, the Venezuelan police were implicated in a staggering 755 murder cases. Not police killings in the line of duty, of which there were far more, but actual homicides.[8] The conversation now moved onto Chávez and what Hans saw as his demagogue tendencies. He said he thought Chávez was creeping towards becoming a dictator. While telling me this, he got concerned that the guy behind was listening in on our conversation. In a hushed whisper, Hans told me that he was worried the guy was a "Chavista," as supporters of President Chávez are known, and that if he heard him criticizing Chávez, then he might "launch into a prepared dialogue on the merits of the revolution."

Thus briefed, Hans explained he had an amateur photography class to get to, handed me a map, and said that under no circumstances should I look at it on the street, as to do so would be an invitation to getting robbed. If I needed to look at it, then it was safest to do so in a café or somewhere discreet where I wouldn't be noticed.

Bloody hell, I thought, *how dangerous is this place?*

He subtly pointed out areas on it that I must not venture into, recommended a public park as my first stop, and told me to memorize the layout as best I could. We arranged a place to meet up this afternoon, in an area circled on the map called Sabana Grande.

Despite Hans explaining how to catch a bus to the park, I was keen to stretch my legs after the flight. I set off on foot into an increasingly hot morning.

By the time I reached Caracas's main thoroughfares, the place was heaving. Commuters and students rushed to work and school packed into cars and buses while others poured from metro stations onto the congested sidewalks. The city's street vendors were now fully up and running with the day's trading, many of whom sold tasty-looking Venezuelan culinary delights such as fried corn flour turnovers known as empanadas, and the ever-popular arepas, or cornmeal pancakes. There was no shortage of customers filling up with breakfast on the go, and I joined them. I went for an assortment of empanadas–shredded beef, a fishy paste of some sort, and a black bean and cheese combo. I watched the vendor drop them into a big bronze frying pan filled with oil and then place them into a colander lined with paper towel, which soon became saturated in its quest to reduce the fat content of these artery-clogging delicacies.

I passed a strange hodgepodge of architectural styles, of which the color gray featured heavily, and none of which I could describe as being uplifting. Characterless tower blocks and skyscrapers abounded. It was as if the city's planners picked the worst that the last four decades of building design had to offer, then arbitrarily threw them together with a garnish of plastic-fronted fast-food outlets and tacky-looking beauty salons.

I suddenly came across an enthused group of men and women, ranging from those in their late teens to others well into their forties, all of whom were wearing red T-shirts and baseball caps, passionately giving a presentation to a small crowd seated in the shade under a small marquee. It was immediately clear that those giving the talk were "Chavistas" involved in a community presentation. I took a seat to check out what was going on. Despite the fact that I spoke no Spanish, it was clear from the slide show that it was on the people's constitutional rights, access to education, and socialism in general. Social community actions like this are a common sight in Venezuela, some of which are independent, others of which are sponsored by the government, the best examples of the latter being the social programs known as missions. These provide services and funds to poor communities and function as a sort of grassroots parallel government that sidesteps official bureaucracy. There are many different types of missions, specializing in programs ranging from education to health care, from housing to culture, whose main objectives are to deliver tangible benefits to normal citizens. They are a demonstration of raw democracy in action and serve to include those who until Chávez's presidency were deemed inconsequential in their own country–the poor.

About half of those gathered seemed genuinely interested in the presentation, and the other half more interested in the free bottled water being handed out. A middle-aged Chavista lady approached me with a bottle of water and a form of some sort to complete. This was a chance to try out one of the few Spanish phrases I had learnt and had been repeating to myself since boarding my flight.

"No hablo español," I said, followed up with an optimistic, "Habla inglés?" She shook her head and moved on to another person a few seats down, who was better placed to read and fill out her form, handing him the bottle of water in the process. It was blisteringly hot and I eyed the water enviously. It was clear I couldn't fill in any of the woman's paperwork and was, in essence, just a sightseer, but I politely gestured to her for a free bottle. She handed me one, and with it I ambled on up the street.

I discreetly brought out my map to locate the park, only partly following his advice–deciding that purposefully going into a café to look at it was wholly unnecessary, and even bordered on paranoia. After locating it on the map, I discovered it was a twenty-minute stroll down the road.

It was called Parque del Este and was the capital's premier park, with over two hundred acres, containing a range of attractions that included rock gardens, lakes, an aviary, cactus gardens, a snake house, and a spectacular collection of trees and plants. The park was a delightful oasis of calm away from the crowded streets outside. People sat chatting, picnicking, reading books, exercising, and generally enjoying the brilliant morning sunshine. I reclined next to some vibrant red flowers, where a humming bird hovered, darting from bloom to bloom. Savoring the last of my water, I gazed high above at a large pair of birds of prey, circling upwards, riding on the rising thermals. I tried to imagine what their view of the city was like and wondered what my Venezuela trip would bring. Despite the warnings I had received so far about the country, and the pronouncements from Hans that it "doesn't work," I felt optimistic.

I ended up spending the best part of the day browsing through the park, and before I knew it, it was time to go and meet Hans. He'd recommended catching a subway to our rendezvous point, but after looking at the map, I decided to walk it. The thought of working out the subway system at rush hour with no Spanish seemed something of an unnecessary challenge on day one, so I went for the easier option, and despite being told it would be safer not to walk, I set off again on foot.

It was by now late afternoon, and the light's departure heralded the arrival of a storm. Lightning stretched its many forking arms across a purple-tinged sky as thunder roared, echoing through the city streets and around towering skyscrapers. I sheltered beneath the awning of a café as the rain created a crescendo of tiny drumbeats above my head. I became a passive spectator, watching as the world transformed into a reflective mosaic of water and shimmering light. Purposeful strides gave way to outright urgent dashes from the city's occupants, as they sped towards every available shelter. The torrent lasted just a few minutes, the reverberations of the now-distant thunder far longer.

Thanks to the newly fresh air, it was a pleasant, if slightly long, walk to reach my prearranged meeting place with Hans, which was a crowded subway station called Plaza Venezuela, located in the thriving shopping district of Sabana Grande. Hans arrived, with typical German efficiency, a minute before he was due.

We headed for a drink together, and en route Hans subtly pointed out an interesting attribute shared by many Venezuelan women–that is, how ridiculously large their breasts are. Not just a little larger than average, mind you, but huge inflated silicone balloons.

I pretended not to have noticed, but in truth it was impossible not to as I'd been walking past women all day with great big "Pamela Andersons" displayed prominently in the skimpiest of tops. Many of those with the biggest boob jobs were slim and petite in all other respects. "Look," said Hans, as we passed a clothing store, "even the mannequins are big up top!" and indeed they were.

Beauty, and as a consequence cosmetic surgery, is big business in Venezuela. In fact, it's something of a national obsession. There are more beauty salons listed in the Caracas yellow pages than pharmacies, and the city has one beauty salon for every two cafés—and it has plenty of cafés. There are respected schools for aspiring beauty queens, and Venezuela has an unparalleled record in international beauty pageants, having won five Miss World titles, five Miss International titles, and six Miss Universe titles.

Boob jobs are so popular they are advertised on Venezuelan TV, and banks offer special lines of credit to fund them. Amazingly, many girls receive implants for their fifteenth birthday as part of their traditional quinceañera, or coming-of-age celebrations, something that President Chávez has spoken out against. During a marathon TV address lasting a staggering eight hours, Chávez took to task parents who might give their daughters such a present, stating, "Now some people think, 'My daughter's turning fifteen, let's give her breast enlargements.' That's horrible. It's the ultimate degeneration." He went on to blame Western beauty icons such as Barbie dolls for the popularity of the operations. Sadly, with cosmetic surgery being so popular, individuals unqualified to perform the operations have set themselves up as surgeons, often with horrendous results.

We dropped in at a thriving café for a freshly squeezed pineapple juice and to catch up on each other's day. Despite waiting at a counter bar directly in front of a member of staff, we received no acknowledgment that we existed. Hans shook his head in annoyance.

"The service is terrible in Venezuela, if you don't yell at them, they ignore you."

Hans yelled.

We got a juice each.

Over these, Hans told me of his encounters with Venezuelan women and that he'd been dismayed that all too often they expected him to pay for everything.

"If you are white in Venezuela, you are automatically considered higher up the ladder than a nonwhite, but many people will simply be after your money."

This, he said, was the case not just on dates but often when going out with male and female friends too. In fact, he said that even male Venezuelan friends would often be shy to dip into their pocket on a night out, and that often he wondered if people were after something, or had an agenda when befriending him.

I wondered whether he was paranoid.

Next, Hans told me something fantastic about the names that some Venezuelan parents give to their rather unfortunate children. These, I would put into two categories: naively unfortunate and downright dumber than dumb. Those that fell in the former category were the result of the peculiar Venezuelan practice of combining the first names of the mother and father in order to create a unique made-up baby name. The results were questionable. Take, for example, the names Anna and Jesus (pronounced Hessus in Spanish), which combined gives you the rather inappropriate, although not uncommon, Anus.

Truly the name of an asshole if ever there was one.

But odder still were the names inspired by the most unlikely of arbitrary sources. These included popular sports shoes, fast-food restaurants, infamous political figures, and superheroes. Hans had previously written an article on this strange cultural phenomenon and, as part of his research, had surreptitiously acquired lists of patients' names from doctors and dentists. These had included Superman, Ladi Diana, Max Donald, Stalin, Nick Carter Backstreet Boyz, Genghis Khan, US Navy, and my favorite, Air Jordan.

It must have made for some interesting James Bond-esque introductions, "The name's Gonzales, Nick Carter Backstreet Boyz Gonzales."

After finishing our juices, we caught a bus back to Hans's apartment. Here we reclined on the sofa with a cup of sweet-smelling fruit tea. Just like this morning when Hans and I had first met, he was keen to dispense with general chitchat and wanted to delve into that emotive and divisive ground of hard politics, and in particular President Chávez. "What do you think of Mr. Chávez?"

he asked me, as if to test whether we were on the same page politically. We weren't. Having read about Chávez and Venezuelan politics for several years, we proceeded to discuss him at length and generally disagreed on all but the basic outline facts of his rise to power.

Hugo Rafael Chávez Frías was born in a mud hut in 1954 near the small western Venezuelan village of Sabaneta. He is of indigenous, African, and Spanish descent and, due to the extremely poor conditions of his parent's village, was raised by his paternal grandmother in Sabaneta itself. At seventeen he joined the country's oldest military academy, graduating as a sublieutenant. The academy subsequently permitted him to do graduate studies at the Simón Bolívar University in Caracas, where he studied political science. While there, he became highly politicized and, along with his fellow students, developed a socialist political philosophy they termed Bolivarianism–named after the venerated Venezuelan general Simón Bolívar, who liberated the country and much of Latin America from Spanish colonial rule in the 19th century. Bolivarianism draws on the ideas from several other high-ranking participants of the fight for Venezuelan independence, as well as renowned socialist leaders, revolutionaries such as Che Guevara, and even Jesus Christ, whom Chávez has called "the world's greatest socialist."

Chávez describes Bolivarianism's central tenets as including economic and political sovereignty, an equitable distribution of the nation's oil revenues, anti-imperialism, economic self-sufficiency, fostering an ethos of national civic service, and political participation of the populace at a grassroots level. He often stresses this form of socialism as distinct from previous manifestations, particularly that of the former Soviet Union, stating, "We must reclaim socialism as a thesis, a project, and a path, but a new type of socialism, a humanist one, which puts humans and not machines or the state ahead of everything."

While still developing his political ideas at university, Chávez became a semiprofessional baseball player and in 1969 reached the

Venezuela National Baseball Championships. After university he joined the military, becoming a paratrooper. He served for seventeen years, obtaining the rank of lieutenant colonel.

In 1989 a wave of protests and riots spread throughout Caracas, sparked by the then president Carlos Andrés Peréz's implementation of International Monetary Fund "free market" reforms that included the privatization of state-owned companies, reduction of customs duties, tax reform, and the removal of petroleum subsidies. The latter led to huge increases in the price at the pump as well as the cost of public transport. In what became known as "Caracazo," which roughly translates as "the Caracas smash," the security forces brutally crushed the protests, leading to as many as three thousand deaths.[9]

Chávez's discontent at the government's reforms and brutality led, in 1992, to him launching an unsuccessful military coup against Peréz. The plan was for army units under his control to seize key military, political, and communications sites, and to put Peréz under arrest. Things didn't go according to plan, and soon Chávez and his small group of rebels were holed up in a museum unable to transmit orders to their supporters throughout the country. When it was clear the coup was doomed to failure, Chávez decided to give himself up but on the condition that he could appear on national television and address the nation. This was granted. He used the broadcast to tell the Venezuelan people that he had only failed "for now," or in Spanish "por ahora." The appearance served to catapult him from relative obscurity into the spotlight, and for many of the county's poor, he became a folk hero and figurehead in the fight against the Peréz government's rampant corruption–something present and widespread in Venezuelan politics long before Chávez's presidency.

Chávez was sent to prison, but a year into his sentence Peréz was impeached. The new president, Rafael Caldera, pardoned Chávez, who served in total just two years behind bars. After his release, he launched a presidential campaign and was successfully elected president of Venezuela in 1998, with 56 percent of the vote. Four years later, Chávez was briefly removed from power by a Washington-sponsored coup, which led to his kidnapping and imprisonment on an island off the Venezuelan mainland. The coup lasted just forty-seven hours and was defeated thanks to a popular uprising. In total Chávez and his supporters have won fourteen out of fifteen elections over the past twelve years,[10] three of them presidential, the results of which were verified by international observers from the Carter Center and the Organization of American States.

Despite his success in these elections, Hans was quick to paint Chávez as almost bordering on a dictator, due to him winning a referendum on changing the constitution to allow future presidents to run for office as many times as the people were willing to elect them. This, Hans claimed, was a sure sign that Chávez and Venezuela were heading towards a dictatorship, despite the people being given a democratic vote on it.

I had read the same argument numerous times before, by others in the mainstream media keen to paint Chávez as such, and so was fully aware of similar systems that operated in Western countries.

"So would you consider Britain or indeed your home country Germany as heading towards dictatorships?" I asked dryly.

I received a confused look, so elaborated.

"Neither of those countries have limits on how many terms a prime minister or chancellor can serve. And until recently the French president could likewise be reelected indefinitely, so does that mean France was a dictatorship up until 2008 when the law was changed?"

"You've come here like many other leftist intellectuals, with misguided preconceived notions of Mr. Chávez!" he said with disgust.

I didn't consider myself a leftist, or that I had preconceived notions, but quietly liked the inference that I was an intellectual, so took it as something of a compliment. In a sense it was all a bit awkward, as I'd only met the guy this morning but already he seemed genuinely annoyed at me. Since I still hoped to stay here for a couple of nights, I decided it best to try and smooth things over.

"Well, let's agree to disagree, mate."

It seemed to do the trick, and moments later we were chatting about some friends of his who ran a center for street kids in the barrios. This, Hans said, he could arrange for me to visit. I agreed.

We spent the rest of the evening watching *Pathfinder*, a peculiar and particularly bad movie on DVD, whose basic premise was that a group of Vikings landed in pre-Columbus North America and decided to go on a bloody rampage slaughtering all Native Americans in sight before being overcome themselves by one of their own who had been raised by the natives years before. It was a strange film, to say the least, and one in which the Vikings spoke in their native tongue, but the Native Americans conversed in English. We endured about half of it before giving up and crashing out.

Hans brought me a single mattress from his bedroom and gave me a sheet–it was simply too hot for anything else. We bade each other good night and I got into bed.

Minutes later, it began.

At first it was a just a mild itch around the ankles. This didn't last long. In a matter of minutes the irritation had crept over every exposed area of my flesh and multiplied tenfold in intensity. Gentle rubbing gave way to forceful clawing actions as the itching quickly progressed from a mild irritation to outright torment.

Some little bastards were biting me, and biting me good.

I got up and delved into my backpack, retrieving some super-strength DEET insect repellent, which I applied all over, including on my face. It had no discernable effect, and within seconds I was scratching wildly again. My inability to ignore whatever it was that was eating me only made me more agitated. In desperation I tried to enter into a sort of Zen-like meditative calm where I was unmoved and no longer reacted to the pesky buggers. This was all very well in theory, but in practice the irritation simply built up in me like a pressure cooker, until I exploded out of this superficially serene state into a flurry of random frustrated scratching.

I turned on the light to see if I could spot whatever it was that was feasting on my blood, but could see nothing. In my guidebook I had read about tiny infuriating Venezuelan sand flies, called *puri-puri*, which loved to feast on foreigners' "exotic" blood, and itched like hell. I wondered if it was them, or possibly bedbugs. Despite the temperature, I put on a long-sleeved shirt, pants, and socks, then wrapped my hands up in a T-shirt and tried to sleep with this protective layer in place. It was swelteringly hot, but after a while, fatigue won out and I eventually succumbed to sleep.

CHAPTER 2

"Papers, please!" (Without the Please)

If there's one person venerated in Venezuela above all others, it's the country's liberator from Spanish colonial rule, Simón Bolívar. This morning, Hans and I planned to visit his museum and birthplace in the historic part of Caracas.

Although small in size, the historic part of the city was delightful, being so very different from the other areas of the Caracas I had seen yesterday. Its main hub was a leafy square complete with ornamental streetlamps, manicured shrubbery, and several fountains embellished with shiny golden cherub statues. In the center was a majestic and towering metal statue of Bolívar, rearing up triumphantly on horseback. The square conveyed a tranquil ambience, mottled by a kaleidoscope of light filtering through the swaying leaves of several large specimen trees. It was a lovely spot to relax, although we could hear the shouts and cheers of a large crowd somewhere nearby. Little did I know that later in the day I would be arrested and put in jail–however, that morning I was still oblivious to my impending misfortune.

Around the perimeter was a collection of colonial buildings painted in soft pastel colors, including one that had been a former notorious prison, which was now used by the Ministry of Foreign Affairs. Despite the area's current atmosphere, Hans explained that for a while it had been a "no-go area" for anyone opposing the government, as the square had become something of a focal point for Chávez supporters.

"They wouldn't even let the elected mayor take up office here because he opposed Chávez. And to diminish his power and prevent him using one of the area's trophy buildings, the government transferred much of his department to a different district!"

Around the corner from the square was the former residence of Simón Bolívar, and just a few paces farther was a museum dedicated to him. Walking to the museum, we came upon a rollicking folk dance festival. Many of those gathered were wearing the red T-shirts and caps of ardent Chávez supporters.

(Many people wear red every day to show they are proud to support Chávez and the PSUV. The shirts are acquired by going to campaign headquarters or providing support during a campaign, although any red shirt is generally considered a sign of a Chávez supporter. As one of my Venezuelan friends recently remarked to me, "The wealthy don't wear much red these days.") A makeshift stage was erected at the end of the street on which competing couples danced. Those performing ranged from about seven years old up to retirement age. All seemed to be having a great time as the crowd contributed enthusiastic claps, cheers, and hollers. Traditional Venezuelan folk dances combine influences from Spain and Africa, as well as indigenous dance moves and rituals, reflecting the three demographic groups that make up the population.

The dance on stage was known as the joropo, Hans explained, a term which can also refer to an entire genre of music to which Venezuela's unofficial national anthem, "Alma Llanera," belongs. It is customary to have a rendition of this to conclude social gatherings and parties. To dance the joropo, males wear slightly modified cowboy gear comprising of a "ten gallon" hat, jacket, boots, and dress pants, while females wear more traditional Spanish flamenco-looking outfits with frilly hems and necklines.

I may like to shake my ass a bit on the dance floor from time to time, and in my more deluded moments like to think I'm reasonably good at it, a flight of fancy generally liberated by several pints of inebriating liquid, but, in truth, I'm hopelessly clumsy when it comes to dancing, and especially so when compared to just about every able-bodied Venezuelan–and probably a few disabled ones too. It must be in the blood or maybe the water, as even the youngest of them could move in perfect hypnotic rhythm. In fact, out of all those competing, it was the youngsters whom I found the most impressive to watch, such was their skill at so tender an age.

Venezuelans learn to dance when very young, the boys perhaps spurred on by their mother's common rallying cry, warning them that those who can't dance will never get a girlfriend. It seems to do the trick as I never met a Venezuelan who couldn't dance, and well at that. The most popular are the Cuban salsa and a Colombian folk dance called the cumbia, which originated as a courtship dance amongst slaves. But for a lot of Venezuelan teenagers, it's a bizarre, although strangely appealing, form of dancing known as reggaeton, which is the dance of choice. I got my first encounter with this in another section of the crowd when Hans and I moved on towards the outside of the house of Simón Bolívar: A circle had formed around two individuals who were "dancing" to some fast-paced modern Latino music supplied by a portable stereo. I say "dancing," but a more accurate description would be "having sex with your clothes on"–much to the crowd's delight. The two individuals partaking in this were not just getting up close and personal in what might be considered a "dirty" dance but were actually a whisker shy from performing sex acts to music. The male dancer fell to his knees while the girl gyrated her genitalia–in perfect rhythm I grant you–in his face. I didn't know quite what to make of that, but those gathered whooped and hollered approvingly. We left for the relative quiet and civility of Simón Bolívar's birthplace when the guy started to mime taking his young dance partner from behind.

Casa Natal de Bolívar was the place where on July 24, 1783, Simón Bolívar, the great liberator of Venezuela from Spanish colonial rule, was born. Although the original house had been destroyed by an earthquake, what stood there today had been lovingly recreated. Despite it not being original, I found the place quite atmospheric such was the legacy Bolívar left. His endeavors dramatically changed the history of vast swathes of Latin America, liberating areas which comprise the modern countries: Bolivia, Colombia, Ecuador, Panama, Peru, and Venezuela.

Simón Bolívar was born into a wealthy Caracas family that arrived from Spain some two hundred years before. Orphaned from a young age, he was raised by his uncle. At sixteen years old he left for Spain and France to further his education. While in Europe, the young Bolívar studied the works of Rousseau and Voltaire, two eminent political philosophers whose works influenced key players in the French and American revolutions. He married a young Spanish girl, who accompanied him back to Venezuela, only to die of yellow fever soon after. Despite having many female companions throughout the rest of his life, he never remarried.

After the death of his wife, Bolívar returned to Europe where he lived for a while in Napoleonic France, during which time he met with leaders of the French Revolution. From France he went to the United States to study the political configuration of the country after the American Revolutionary War. He then returned to Caracas in 1807, keen for a bit of revolutionary liberation for his homeland, and it wasn't long before he had made the acquaintance of several like-minded individuals.

Bolívar believed that for people to be free, they had to unite against all invaders, regardless of their disguise. He joined the military, serving under Francisco de Miranda, who in 1806 began the independence struggle. Six years into the campaign, Miranda was betrayed by some of his supposed comrades and arrested by the

Spanish, who shipped him off to Spain where he died in jail. With Miranda's arrest, Bolívar took control of the military and spearheaded the revolution. Following several failed endeavors to defeat the Spanish in Venezuela, he fled first to Colombia, then Jamaica, and finally Haiti, before returning to have another crack at the Spanish.

Thanks to the Napoleonic Wars recently ending, Bolívar managed to hire British mercenary veterans of the Napoleonic campaigns to join his existing army. After an arduous march across the Andes, his army surprised and defeated the Spanish at the Battle of Boyacá, and with it Colombia gained its independence. In total he led his forces in thirty-five successful battles that ultimately liberated the whole of northwest South America and part of Central America, which was unified under the name Gran Colombia. The people of Venezuela paid the heaviest price for freedom, with their country seeing the majority of the fighting and a quarter of the population dying as a result of the struggle.

Although initially a combined republic, it wasn't long before the first cracks began to appear in the union due to escalating sectarian tensions. In 1828 Bolívar took control of Gran Colombia as dictator, and with it his popularity began to plummet. An assassination attempt followed, and soon after, in extreme bad health, he resigned. He died shortly afterwards in 1830 in Santa Marta, Colombia, deeply disillusioned, depressed, and penniless, at only forty-seven years old. Before his death he remarked that "the three greatest fools of history have been Jesus, Don Quixote and me" and noted that "[Latin] America is ungovernable; those who served the revolution have plowed the sea."

On dying, Bolívar's prediction came true, and the union of Gran Colombia began to disintegrate. Venezuela became an independent nation, and despite being instrumental in the country's liberation from Spanish rule, the new leaders of the country decided to ban Bolívar's remains from returning to his homeland. It wasn't until twelve years later that the authorities rescinded, and his remains were brought from Colombia to Caracas. Today he is venerated, not only in Venezuela but in much of Latin America.

There wasn't really a lot to look at in Bolívar's birthplace, save for some paintings by Tito Salas depicting a heroic Bolívar in battle as well as during other momentous occasions in his life as a freedom fighter.

As we exited the house this time through a crowd of dancers of African descent, who were wearing big elongated hats and had, for some reason, "blacked up" their faces further, we arrived at the Museo Bolivariano, or Bolívar Museum. To get in, we had to not only write our name in an entry book but also give our passport number to the member of staff stationed there.

"Just make it up," Hans told me quietly and explained that you were required to give your passport number for all manners of pathetic reasons in Venezuela, including just about any purchase over a few dollars in value.

"I even had to give my passport number when buying a pair of underpants! Can you believe that?"

Hans explained that he always made the number up as he didn't like this encroachment on his civil liberties. I couldn't have agreed more and made up my mind to do so from now on. The claimed reason for this obsession with ID is to prevent businesses from evading taxes. By forcing them to attach an ID number to every sale makes it much harder to hide the price of goods sold when they have to present the purchaser's info when filing tax returns.

The museum was mildly interesting and contained a number of personal artefacts of Bolívar's as well as independence memorabilia. These included handwritten letters, swords, muskets, shaving kits, and medals. Hans was especially keen to show me one personal item in particular, namely, Bolívar's boots–not because of their design or material used, but because of their diminutive size, meaning that the towering giant of Latin American history depicted in the colossal statue in the square was, in reality, something of a shorty.

"I do not admire Bolívar," Hans stated under his breath. "In fact, you could say he was a pedophile and a coward."

"Why?" I asked.

"He deserted his men and was presented with young girls as trophies when he won battles."

This was not an opinion it would have been wise to advertise here amongst the crowds of ardent Bolívar fans, so I inquired no more and headed to the museum's first floor, where the coffin that carried his remains from Colombia to Caracas was located. In addition to this was the funeral ark that transferred his ashes to their current resting place at the Panteón Nacional, or National Pantheon of Venezuela.

After a good look around, we headed out through the hordes of dancers until we reached some streets, which, although congested, were not nearly as impassable as those in the historic part of town.

Hans explained that his contact who could change my dollars on the black market had offices nearby, but he was having some trouble contacting him. I must have looked concerned as he responded, as if to reassure me, "Don't worry, we'll arrange something." I hoped so.

"How do you know this guy?" I asked.

"He's a very wealthy man who owns several Dali paintings, one of which a museum in Germany asked him to loan them. Because I'm German, he contacted me to use some of my journalistic contacts back there to check out the place's credentials," Hans said, following up with, "He always has a need for foreign cash."

His contact sounded an interesting fellow. I hoped to get to meet him.

While casually strolling down the street, Hans spotted four policemen from the notorious Policía Metropolitana–a feared anti-Chávez force allied with the capital's anti-Chávez mayor–who appeared to be questioning someone up ahead.

"Uh-oh, they're going to stop us," Hans said, even though they were still a good thirty feet ahead. Moments later one of them caught sight of us, making it too late to cross the road.

The policeman fixed an unblinking stare on me, which contained an all-too-obvious sadistic glint that betrayed his delight in spotting two likely victims whom he could wield his little bit of power over.

He barked something at us in Spanish, while the others threw us menacing glares. All of them carried guns. Not being able to speak or understand the lingo, I just shut up and let Hans do the talking.

"He wants to see our passports," Hans stated flatly.

"I don't have mine."

"Just show him your copy instead."

"I don't have one of those either."

"Why not?" Hans asked, as if it was common knowledge that you had to carry such material at all times in Venezuela. I told him I didn't know it was necessary, having not read any reference to this in my guidebook. I apologized to him for the unforeseen hassle this might cause and explained that in Britain there were no such laws requiring you to carry ID.

The senior policeman, who was doing the talking, was a short, fat, stumpy cretin with a face that only a fist could love, which brought to mind that all-too-common animal slang used for his profession, which seemed perfectly justified in his case. He had a slightly infected eye that was bloodshot red in color, and an attitude which stank nearly as bad as his breath.

Hans presented a photocopied version of his passport to him, which the policeman eyed contemptuously. He then explained to the cop that, unfortunately, I had no similar documentation on me. This provoked a protracted discussion between the two of them, during which Hans periodically turned to me to translate what was being said.

It didn't sound good.

The cop said if I didn't have a passport, then he'd simply arrest me. While Hans tried valiantly to reason with him, his junior colleague proceeded to force his fingers into my jeans' pockets and rummaged through their contents, much to my growing, and poorly disguised, discontent. Out came my wallet and some loose change. He methodically thumbed through the wallet's banknotes, taking his time and savoring the process, before glancing casually my way with a questioning, slightly self-congratulatory expression, which he accompanied with an inquisitive raised eyebrow.

This little procedure was supposed to appear superficially innocent and curious, but was, in reality, anything but, and was actually him saying, "Well, look what we have here! There's money in your wallet, and since you're in a spot of bother, maybe the money could help get out of the bother, by . . . well it's not for me to say." Hint. Hint.

My loose change was handed back, and my wallet held out for me to take. I reached out and grasped hold of it, but he maintained his grip for a second longer than necessary and fixed my gaze with the same suggestive expression as before. I grabbed it back, stuffing it into my pocket with a sardonic smile and a stare of my own that told him, in no uncertain terms, to fuck off!

They could see that I was a tourist, as evidenced by my gringo appearance and complete lack of Spanish skills. In a city with such ridiculous crime levels, surely they had better things to do rather than trying to extract bribes from foreigners.

Hans reluctantly told me the only way out of this was for him to go and fetch my passport from his apartment (a journey that in total would take the best part of a couple of hours) or to pay a bribe, of course.

Hans joined me as I was led, luckily without cuffs or physical coercion, towards a series of uninviting gray buildings and decaying tower blocks. I shook my head in disbelief at what a pointless waste of everybody's time this was. We arrived at a door leading into one of these bleak dwellings. It had no windows or signs to announce that it was anything to do with official police business. Hans looked concerned, but told me he'd be back as soon as possible. He left, and I was escorted inside.

Inside it was hot with clammy putrid air and an oppressive uninviting atmosphere. It was far from an official police station, being more a makeshift location where cops hung out, ate food, watched TV, intimidated their detainees away from the public's prying eyes, and generally avoided the more taxing and inconvenient fight against crime outside.

I was in a large room with a decrepit wooden table in its center, complete with several battered metal chairs. Nearby was a crackling archaic television set, and in the far corner what looked like the beginnings of a corridor leading to areas unseen. I was ordered with some aggressive Spanish dictum and a stumpy pointed finger to sit at the table and remain there. The only other features of the place were a small shrine to the Virgin Mary, an old oven, and a "missing persons" picture taped to the wall, which was a photocopied mug shot of a young boy. I didn't hold out much hope of the police finding him if this was how they spent their days.

I figured I had at minimum of a couple of hours to kill so resigned myself to keeping quiet and trying to relax. Sitting at the table with me was a cop lounging around devouring food from a Tupperware container. He chewed with his mouth open, giving me an unwelcome view of his masticated mulched-up meal. Another policeman came and joined us at the table, eating a bread roll in a similar manner–like a pig. A cop by the door actually spat on the floor.

Charming.

Now that Hans had gone, the senior cop began to exert his authority. Despite knowing full well that I couldn't speak Spanish, he approached the table and began to yell at me in his native tongue. I got the impression this was as much to show off to his subordinates and act the big man–despite being a short ass–as it was to try and intimidate me. A classic case of "small man syndrome" if ever I saw one.

He went through my pockets, going one step further than his colleague had outside by actually taking the banknotes out of my wallet and casually dropping them one by one onto the table. He gazed at them for effect as they floated down. With the landing of the last one, he looked from it to me with a suggestive smile. The implication was clear, but his chances of me willingly giving in and paying him a penny were zero, especially since Hans was now making his way back to his apartment.

He forcefully yanked a metal chair from under the table, causing a high-pitched screech. He spun it around, straddled it like a horse, and looked me eye to eye.

Arrogant shit.

More grandstanding followed as he mouthed off at me. Two of the other cops liked the look of this and joined in, so for the next several minutes I had to sit still and put up with these morons baiting me. I felt like a caged animal being prodded with a long stick, knowing all too well that I could do nothing about it. Despite this impotency, I couldn't quite rise above it mentally and found myself constructing fancifully imaginary meetings between me and the lead cop under very different circumstances, ones in which I could squarely stick a right-hander on his fat little face. It helped pass the time.

Sadly, pigs weren't the only animals I had to deal with in here, as all the while I got an earful from them, I attempted to fend off a squadron of dive-bombing mosquitoes. It wasn't easy, and every time I reacted with an unsuccessful swat of my hand, the police would snigger. My exposed arms in particular took the brunt of the attack.

By this stage I had made a mental note of the head policeman's name, not in order to complain to his superior, as he was likely of the same professional calibre, making such actions pointless, but in order to mention the little shit in my future writings. His badge read, "Orta O."

When Señor Orta tired of yelling at me, he did something rather odd, which even his colleagues looked perplexed by. Without warning he loosened his belt to which his revolver was strapped, unbuttoned his pants, then slid them down past his underwear, exposing a sweaty, jock-strapped crotch.

Not a pleasant sight.

Using his pants like a bellows, he now proceeded to fan his nether regions.

Was he trying to imply I was about to get fucked? I hoped not.

Reaching down, my antagonist thoughtfully rearranged his "family jewels"–which looked decidedly wanting in the size department from where I was sitting (my condolences to Mrs. Orta)–then did himself up again. Porky's little games weren't over yet, as after pacing back and forth past me several times, he slammed his handcuffs on to the table and began to mime cuffing me to the overhead beam. Grabbing the chair next to mine, he positioned it directly beneath the beam and beckoned me to stand on it so I could be cuffed up here.

Surely he was joking.

I shook my head, but wondered whether he was serious, and I was about to experience a bit of literal hanging around until Hans reappeared.

It seemed to rile him that I hadn't looked outwardly concerned by his threat or complied with the instruction to get up on the chair.

He upped the ante.

Grabbing a small pocketknife from his pocket, he came face-to-face with me, his breath assaulting my face like a pervasive toxic mist. Through gritted teeth he pointed at me, then drew the blunt side of the knife across his own throat.

I got the implication.

As if this wasn't enough, Mr. Orta now picked up an empty juice carton from the table and sliced the top off it with his knife. Again he ran the blunt side of the blade across his neck, but this time mimed catching imaginary blood in the carton, which he then pretended to imbibe.

Was this guy for real? Despite his threats, I can't say I was particularly intimidated by him or the situation. I was more annoyed and slightly disappointed, as it was now that I really began to see what Hans had said about law and order, and that "the country doesn't work." If this was the reception a law-abiding tourist got in Venezuela, then the country's police force had some big problems.

After a while, Señor Orta got bored with me and headed outside with the others, relinquishing sole jailer duty to a younger officer, Jemenez E, who up until now had been preoccupied with the television set in the corner. With the others gone, he gestured for me to join him. He was watching *Troy*, starring Brad Pitt and Sean Bean, which was dubbed in Spanish. Jemenez proved himself to be a decent guy, indicating that I should swat something on my ear. I did, and in the process killed a mosquito, which exploded into a squishy pulp of red in my hand.

I nodded a gracious thank-you.

After what seemed like half a day, but was in reality a couple of hours, Señor Orta stuck his head inside the building and made a come-hither gesture. Outside was Hans and my passport.

I was free to go.

I told Hans of Orta's pathetic antics and mimed the knife-to-neck scenario. Hans was appalled and immediately berated the stumpy little prick for his behaviour. It was hardly a surprise when the runt denied it with a surprised "I don't know what you're talking about" shrug. As Hans and I left, he translated for me what he'd said to Orta as a parting gesture.

"No wonder the country has fifteen thousand murders a year, if you waste your time harassing clearly innocent tourists. You're a disgrace!"

I learnt soon after of a local saying in the barrios: "It is better to be left with the muggers than with the Policía Metropolitana." I could well see why.

CHAPTER 3

Feline Frenzy

Hans looked at his watch impatiently. We'd waited over half an hour at one of the city's main subway stations for a female friend of his to arrive.

"Venezuelans are always late," he said, with a disgruntled shake of the head.

"That can't gel with your German reputation for efficiency," I ventured, hoping to ease his angst.

He looked at his watch again.

"Wait here, I'm going to see if she's outside."

I sat myself on a waist-high wall leading to some stairs. A moment later, a subway employee was hollering at me to get down.

After a few minutes, a pretty twenty-something girl turned up and looked around as if she was supposed to be meeting someone. Due to my lack of Spanish, I decided to remain mute. Hans returned and I was introduced to her as Celeste, a Spanish teacher from the barrios who spoke a little bit of English.

God knows what inspired Hans, but for some unknown reason he decided to break the ice with Celeste by telling her that I wanted to see a photo of her naked. She looked at me with a look of bemusement. I shook my head to indicate that I had said nothing of the sort and had no such desire–though on further reflection concluded that yeah, I guess I wouldn't mind seeing such a photo after all.

We traveled to the apartment of Gustavo and Deanna, who ran the school for street kids.

Their apartment was a humble place decorated with colorful works of art–watercolors, pastels, pencil drawings–many done by the kids they worked with. Some of them were very good.

"You can meet the artist in a minute. He's joining us for dinner," said Deanna.

Not long afterwards he arrived. His name was Jesus, who was a friendly and animated college student in his early twenties with good English. "I'll show you some more of my work sometime if you like," Jesus offered.

While Deanna kneaded some dough for a batch of home-made pizzas in the kitchen, we settled down in the sitting room to hors d'oeuvres of crackers smeared with generous quantities of pesto and beaded glasses of cooling homemade iced tea. Over the food we discussed my earlier encounter with the police. All were appalled, although none particularly surprised. Jesus had experienced quite a bit of trouble with the police himself.

"One night the police pulled me and my friends over. As we wound the window down to answer their questions, one of the police casually tossed a small packet into the car. They then said that they would search the car for drugs, and if they found any, they would either issue a fine or make an arrest. We had no choice but to pay a bribe."

During the conversation I discovered that the police were not allowed to put their hands into suspect's pockets, which of course had happened to me twice. Jesus told me that a friend of his had been badly beaten up in the street one night by a group of police officers in a completely unprovoked attack, in which the police seemed to be acting out of sadistic pleasure alone. I considered myself lucky to have only had the suggestion of my neck being slit.

After our meal, Deanna and Gustavo offered to take me to see the work they did with the street kids in the barrios. I was keen to see their organization but also the barrios themselves. I had been told they were unsafe unless accompanied by a local, or someone like Deanna and Gustavo, who were well-known and respected there, so I accepted their offer immediately.

We met the next day at a subway station situated near two huge 53-story, 730-foot skyscrapers, both part of the Parque Central complex, one of which, Deanna explained, had suffered a terrible fire in 2004. The whole upper third of the east tower had been a towering inferno, which raged for seventeen hours, destroying twenty floors and making the fires in the World Trade Center on 9/11 look small by comparison.

"Part of the building was being used to store documents on corruption, which were all conveniently destroyed in the fire," she said with a smile.

It had been repaired now but must have been one hell of a sight when it was on fire–being the tallest building in Venezuela and for a long time the tallest in South America.

We jumped on a bus opposite some artistic murals of a saluting President Chávez, set to a backdrop of the Venezuelan flag. It was a cramped, hot, and bumpy ride to the outskirts of the barrio after which we walked in on foot. The barrios were a strange reality to enter after strolling around more affluent and prosperous areas of the city. Here life was stripped bare. Wants were replaced by needs–the primary one being shelter. Handmade ramshackle dwellings, many little more than shacks with tin roofs, were precariously stacked upon each other, on topography no building inspector would ever sanction, their collective enormity enveloping many of the city's undulating hills. A labyrinth of alleyways spread out from the main arteries of the streets, twisting like slot canyons in a mountain range and remaining stubbornly faithful to the natural contours of the land. Many of the buildings were unfinished, some in a state of virtual collapse.

I wondered how they fared during earthquakes.

This is how millions of the country's poor live, often in homes with no running water or sanitation. (The majority of the inhabitants in these areas are of indigenous or African descent, whereas, by contrast, in the richer middle- and upper-class areas the inhabitants are predominantly white, being, by and large, of Spanish decent.) Plastering the outer walls of many of these homes were stencil paintings and posters in support of President Chávez, who, being of mixed race, shares the barrio resident's heritage. Before him, these areas were depicted on maps as greenery, as if the poor and their homes simply didn't exist. And for many of the country's lighter-skinned elite and previous governments, they didn't. They were best left forgotten about.

But not anymore.

For under Chávez great change has come to the barrios. Through social programs, the lives of many of the country's poorest have been transformed. Educational projects have achieved almost 100 percent literacy in Venezuela–something previously unknown in the country's modern era. Today the poor study subjects such as math, art, and history, learn musical instruments, and their rights under the constitution. They are provided with subsidized food, free breeze-block bricks to construct their homes, and free universal health care, installing in vast numbers a confidence and optimism unthinkable before Chávez.

Chávez funds these social programs through revenues from the country's vast oil wealth, something which had previously stayed in the pockets of the elite, and much of which ended up abroad. In the years prior to him taking office, the country experienced the most rapid descent into poverty that Latin America has ever known. In 1980, 18 percent of the population was below the poverty line, by 1995, three years before Chávez became president, that number had soared to 65 percent. Under Chávez poverty has fallen by half and extreme poverty by two-thirds.[11]

While walking through the barrio, we were greeted with many approving waves and gracious smiles from the locals, who were clearly familiar with Deanna and Gustavo. Despite the smiles and the soothing morning sunshine, a rawer side to life was always on display. Bullet holes peppered many of the buildings. We passed a metal gate so riddled with them that it was almost falling off its hinges. I wouldn't have wanted to be here, especially at night, without an escort.

We stopped to say good morning to a friendly man in the street, who introduced himself to me with a warm handshake. After some general chitchat, we bade him good day and headed deeper into the barrio. Deanna told me that he was a drug dealer and money lender; a nice guy, but miss a payment and, well, you didn't want to miss a payment.

Up ahead children played barefoot and topless in the street, throwing a basketball at a hoop. I gestured for them to pass me the ball. A kid with frizzy hair and a wide smile tossed it over. I hadn't played basketball for many a year and had never been any good at it, but I slowly dribbled the ball nearer the hoop and took a shot. To my absolute delight, it descended into the basket with a satisfying swoosh. It was a very lucky shot, so I quit while I was ahead and waved good-bye to the little 'uns.

We arrived at Deanna and Gustavo's center, located opposite a building that looked to be in a state of near collapse and was covered from top to bottom in flags, posters, and banners expressing support for Chávez. The center was a small building in the heart of the barrio covering two floors. Upstairs was a typical, although basic, arts and crafts classroom, full of random stacks of textured paper, paintbrushes soaking in jars of water, colored pencils and pens, rolls of sticky tape, and huge containers of paints. The walls were adorned with pictures of famous Venezuelan baseball players cut out from magazines, and the whole place was imbued with the unmistakable smell of squeezy pots of glue. The scent transported me right back to art lessons at school.

In here was a group of five boys in their early teens and a very short and hunched middle-aged man. I was introduced around then shown the actual work carried out. The children were given jobs making decorative notebooks, which were then sold to fund the center and provide an income for the kids. Some were guillotining paper, others the cardboard used for the covers, while others still were producing the patterned paper used to cover the books. This looked the most interesting and creative task, which consisted of submerging a thick sheet of absorbent paper into a bath filled with a solution of water, soluble glue, and gasoline. Once the paper was submerged, random splatters of paint were flicked from a paintbrush onto the water's oily surface. These merged, forming wavy concentric patterns. The paper was then slowly raised to the surface through these patterns, which were imprinted upon it. This was then hung up to dry. After being given a demonstration of the process by one of the kids, I was encouraged to try it myself. I found it relatively easy and quite good fun, as every attempt produced a unique one-off pattern.

Deanna explained that the aim of the center was to give kids a practical skill with their hands that translated into something constructive and useful, but also profitable for them. The center had been open for eighteen years and had seen hundreds of children come and go. A while ago some of these budding artists were lucky enough to be flown to Florence in Italy after the city's mayor visited the center. In Florence they were taken to an art institute where they learnt additional techniques for producing the patterned paper.

Deanna explained that they didn't get as many volunteers as they would like to, and that one of the reasons for this was that Venezuela was so dangerous. She told me of a Swedish girl who had volunteered with them for a while and had ended up getting engaged to a local guy from the barrios. Not long after the engagement, her fiancé had been murdered, shot some fifty times. The girl left for home soon after.

* * *

Unfortunately for me, Hans had still not managed to get in touch with his contact who could exchange money on the black market, so I contacted the other CouchSurfer, Austin, who'd offered me accommodation, and asked whether he knew anyone that could help. He did.

Hans and I therefore agreed that I'd head off to stay with Austin, but before I continued my journey up the coast, I would drop by at his place to pay him back for his generous loan. This was working on the assumption Austin's confidence of exchanging currency on the black market was not misplaced. If it was, then I was going to get well and truly shafted by the official exchange rate. In one store I had seen a regular tub of Häagen-Dazs ice cream retailing for forty-nine bolivars, which at the official rate was a mind-boggling twenty-two dollars. A smidge expensive methinks, even for an ice cream lover like me. While in the Caracas area, I had also hoped to meet up with CouchSurfer Penelope, who had offered to go for a coffee, but since I'd received no response to the last two messages I'd sent her, I concluded it was a no-goer.

Austin e-mailed instructions on how to make it to his place, which was on the outskirts of Caracas in an area called El Hatillo.

> *Go to Altamira and with the mountains to your back walk south past the Canadian Embassy 200 meters to the Metrobus stop for El Hatillo. This service only operates until 10 in the morning and again from 4 in the afternoon. Get off at Farmatodo (a chain chemist store).*

When chatting to Austin on Hans's phone–my cell didn't work in Venezuela–we'd agreed a suitable time, and Austin had said he'd be waiting at the chemist store to pick me up.

I caught the bus as suggested, which was a clanger built in the 1970s, whose "bigger is better" gas-guzzling engine let out a strangely appealing throaty rumble as we headed southeast towards El Hatillo. With gas being so ridiculously cheap in Venezuela, the country is awash with cars and buses from this period, which would be considered grossly inefficient elsewhere, but in a land where water is twenty times more expensive than gasoline, it's hardly reason for concern, at least from a cost point of view.

I'd ridden in the back of the bus for the best part of twenty minutes when it pulled into a stop on the side of a heaving main road heading up a steep hill. Due to paying inadequate attention to my surroundings, I only noticed an enormous drugstore sign emblazoned with the word "Farmatodo" as the bus began pulling off again.

Shit. I shouldered my backpack and scrambled to my feet, while yelling at the driver to stop. He continued to accelerate, so I lunged towards the still-open rear door intending to jump, only to be whiplashed back a split second later by the backpack's strap, which was caught between seats. As the bus pulled into traffic, I struggled desperately to free the strap and yelled once more to the driver, this time accompanied by several cries from other passengers attempting to help. After much fumbling, I got it free at the precise moment the driver decided to hit the brakes. I landed face-first in the aisle, helped on my way by the weight of the pack. I hastily clambered upright, and with little in the way of composing myself, but more than a little embarrassment, threw myself off the bus. As it chugged into the torrent of traffic, disappearing into areas unknown, I breathed a big sigh of relief.

Austin was nowhere to be seen, so I sat outside in the drugstore's congested parking lot and waited for him in the sunshine, beneath a rather peculiar billboard. On it was a busty underwear-clad woman with a naughty glint in her eye who, by the looks of it, was manhandling a macho-looking stud standing next to her. This grabbing of the fella's "old chap" was thankfully left to the imagination, as obscuring the delicate area was the word *orgasmos,* with the letter *O* represented by an agape lipstick-covered female mouth. Behind the cavorting couple were an assortment of men and woman in varying states of carnal ecstasy. Beneath the *orgasmos,* in smaller type, were the words *la historica secreta del orgasmo.*

I figured it was some kind of sex show. It crossed my mind to go and see it, purely from a journalistic standpoint you understand, but unfortunately for me, and you the reader, the next performance occurred after I left the city.

I waited and waited for Austin but there was no sign of him, so after an hour and a half I decided to first go in search of a phone booth and to attempt to call him, just in case there had been some unforeseen problem.

I looked up the Spanish word for telephone in the back of my guidebook and zeroed in on a woman in a low-cut top, high heels, and short skirt to ask where one was located. I tried to turn on the suave, which was none too easy considering all I hoped to say was, "Un teléfono público?" On hearing my feeble attempt at Spanish, she asked if I spoke English. This was more like it. The lovely lady pointed me in the right direction and minutes later I was dialing Austin's number.

I got through first time and was a little less than generous in offering him the benefit of the doubt than perhaps I should have been.

"Austin, it's Jamie," I said bluntly. "I'm just wondering where you are?"

"I waited as arranged, where were you?" Austin responded.

"How long did you wait?"

"For over half an hour outside the Farmatodo chemist, where I told you to get off."

After a bit of extrapolation, it became apparent that we'd been waiting at different "Farmatados."

Ten minutes later, Austin arrived in his car to pick me up. He was a robustly built sixty-five-year-old with a balding head, bushy white beard, and welcoming smile. Almost immediately, we were laughing and joking together and quickly forgot about the earlier confusion. On the way to his home we stopped briefly to pick up a mountain of cat food for his twelve feline companions. I wondered how I'd find sharing a place with so many cats, which, it's got to be said, have never been high on my list of preferred pets.

Austin's place was located on the outskirts of town in a semi-rural area, complete with farmers' fields and lush green undulating hills. He lived with his son Oscar, who was currently out at college. Their apartment was surrounded by coiled razor wire, and to enter the compound, you had to pass an electronic security gate. Three separate security locks followed, of both codes and keys, to access the apartment. Inside, it was a lovely place with a spacious open-plan sitting room, separated from an equally large study by a sliding glass door which led to a balcony. The view from here was wonderful, and looked out across textured green peaks, palm and pine trees, and the cheerful red roof tiles of surrounding homes. Austin gestured that I'd be sleeping on the couch, and then went to get us a snack.

Immediately on following him into the kitchen, I was overpowered by the smell. Here the twelve cats had free rein and were sitting everywhere, including the stove, the fridge, in open cupboards, the counter, and even on "clean" plates. Cat hair was everywhere. The smell was so bad that I escaped to the adjoining room where unfortunately the cat's litter trays were located. Austin explained that the cats lived in these two rooms, and that they never left the apartment. For the life of me I couldn't work out why on earth he would want to keep cats in the kitchen, of all places.

Just off from the litter room was a small bathroom that looked like it hadn't been used in a very long time. It was covered in dust and dirt, and residing inside were motorcycle wheels and tires, as well as old striplights, which were propped up against the sink. Its only other feature was a shower cubicle with an open pipe for a showerhead.

"This is the bathroom you can use," Austin said.

I tried to look appreciative and upbeat, but didn't relish the thought of trying to clean in there.

I breathed a sigh of relief when we made it back to the sitting room, and more so when we adjourned to the balcony outside. Austin was completely unaware of the stench in the kitchen, having lived with the cats for so long that it had become unnoticeable. But to a first-time visitor it was immediately obvious. In the interests of diplomacy, I decided to remain mute.

My parents had encountered a similar situation when house hunting, where they'd viewed a house for sale whose owners had fourteen dogs, a cockatoo, and a chameleon, which were allowed to do as they pleased in the property. The estate agent had warned my folks beforehand of the nauseating smell, but said that the owners themselves were totally oblivious to it. If one ignores the stench, however, the house itself turned out to have potential, so my parents ended up making an offer, while figuring into the equation the cost of getting the place professionally stripped and steam cleaned, twice. In the end the owners rejected the offer but in a bit of unintended humor said that if my parents upped their bid slightly, they'd graciously throw in the carpets!

As we sat out on the balcony, Austin told me he was an expat Brit who had lived in Venezuela for the last thirty years after coming to South America with the intention, as he put it, of "marrying a beautiful woman." This he had done, but sadly, he was a recent widower.

He'd had a varied career, which included being vice president of the British Chamber of Commerce for several years. One of his other positions had very nearly made him extremely wealthy, when, as the number four at a company, he'd acquired a substantial stake in the business. This had been worth over one hundred million U.S. dollars at the peak of the dot-com boom, but due to contractual obligations, he'd been unable to cash out at that time. When he had, his stake had diminished to half a million.

"That must have been devastating," I said, thinking aloud.

"No, not at all," he said. "I've worked hard all my life and never really had problems with money. You have to be thankful for what you have in life."

He told me a friend of his had just made the best part of four million dollars on a "lost" Van Gogh painting he'd bought for only eighty thousand, but despite this, his friend had commented to Austin, only half jokingly, that it was a shame he hadn't made as much as a buyer of a da Vinci painting known as *La Bella Principessa*, which had also recently been discovered. Before its still-contested verification (Leonardo had supposedly immortalized one of his digits on the canvas), the da Vinci had been purchased by a Swiss collector for nineteen thousand dollars, but it was now valued at over 150 million.

I was intrigued at how Austin was acquainted with people flogging Van Goghs here and there, especially after hearing of Hans's acquaintance who apparently owned several Dalis–not something I would have expected from a couple of CouchSurfers.

Austin explained that his friend was an art expert, and in particular a Picasso specialist, who had been hired by a wealthy landowner in neighboring Colombia to verify a number of supposed Picassos that a drug baron was offering him as part payment for his property. Paintings like this were used by such individuals in much the same way as you or I would use a check. Thrown into the bargain was a potential Van Gogh painting of some cedar trees that had apparently been stolen from Holland by the Nazis.

After verifying the Picassos, the landowner gave Austin's friend the option of purchasing the supposed Van Gogh for eighty thousand dollars. He trusted his professional judgment enough to agree to this and bought the painting. Because reparations had already been paid by Germany to Holland after the Second World War, if the painting turned out to be legit, then he stood to make a pretty penny–which is exactly what happened.

For lunch Austin kindly prepared a creamy lamb and vegetable curry, served with soft rice and washed down with a cooling and delicious fresh watermelon juice. As generous and kind as this was, I had to subtly remove several cat hairs from the meal.

Soon after we'd finished eating lunch, Austin's spirit seemed to suddenly depart him.

"Since my wife's death I have suffered from depression, and as a result sleep a lot, which is what I'm going to do now. I'm sorry not to be a better host."

He recommended that I go for a walk in the center of El Hatillo and mentioned several nice craft stores and an interesting church there. I was given a set of keys, told to get a bus to town–the direction of which he vaguely gestured–and moments later he withdrew to his bedroom. I headed outside.

A weathered bus pulled up next to a mound of construction sand being used for a building site across the street. I hopped on and, with a bit of gesturing to the driver, managed to decipher the surprisingly small fare for the ride, which I paid for with some of the bolivars Hans had lent me. We set off and headed in the direction Austin had gestured. Fifteen minutes later, it arrived at the end of the line. There was a small shopping mall with a supermarket in the basement, and not much else. It quickly became apparent that I'd caught the bus in the wrong direction. What the hell–I figured I might as well have a look about the place. As the mall looked of little interest, I continued up the road along to see what I could find.

It wasn't long before I had walked into the leafy district of La Lagunita, where vast opulent mansions complete with multiple garages, tiled driveways, landscaped gardens, and satellite dishes big enough to coordinate a moon landing, were located around a huge exclusive golf course. I chuckled to myself on seeing the golf course, recalling something Chávez had said about the sport during a television broadcast. "Let's be clear," he said, "golf is a bourgeois sport," before going on to make fun of the golf carts used in the game, which he claimed were evidence of the sport's inherent laziness.

The area contained a pornographic display of wealth after seeing the barrios, almost obscene in its brazen salutation to accumulation. High metal fences jacketed in razor wire and surging with electricity kept the occupants of these open prisons in a state of permanent siege. Several had security guards, others had dogs that growled as I walked past. I wouldn't want to live in the barrios but neither would I here. The houses were impressive but depressing in their implicit acknowledgement of the underlying fear in the country, maybe subconscious and lurking beneath the surface, but real enough nonetheless.

As I walked, I pondered the contradictions of Caracas. For sure, every big city has its rich and poor, but I'd seen no place where the difference was so stark. I tried to imagine what people from the barrios felt about places like this. Did they look at the residents and imagine that they'd got there through hard work or ingenuity, and aspire to emulate them? Or did they view them with resentment and envisage them as part of a lucky sperm club who'd either inherited their good fortune or made it through the exploitation of the general populace through their forebears' colonial conquest? I imagined they probably thought the latter, and if they did, then for the most part, I concurred.

On arrival back at Austin's place, he was awake. We sat on the balcony as the sun went down, nursing a tangy fresh pineapple juice each. Not long afterwards, his son, Oscar, and his friend, Victor, arrived. Both were clean-cut, respectable-looking college students dressed in the ever-popular Venezuelan casual getup of horizontally striped polo shirts and blue jeans. They spoke excellent English. With their arrival, Austin excused himself and went to bed for the night.

I liked Oscar immediately, being softly spoken with a sharp intellect and an understanding, unlike Victor, that a conversation consisted of more than just one person speaking over everybody else. I kind of admired Victor's manic enthusiasm, but my god, the kid liked to hear the sound of his own voice and was none too interested in the resonance of anybody else's.

"That's an interesting point," Oscar or I would try to interject when Victor paused momentarily to inhale.

"Yes, it is," or "I know." He would quickly nod before continuing in his unique broken-record style of oratory, "And another thing . . ."

When the subject turned to politics, as it so very often does in Venezuela, he just went on and on and on, almost to the point of it being amusing–although not quite. It didn't matter if you were in agreement with his point or not, he just wanted to do all the talking. With this in mind, whenever he stopped for a gulp of beverage, I would turn the conversation to Oscar and specifically ask him something.

Neither of them liked El Presidente, but I expected nothing less as generally speaking, the rich in Venezuela don't and the poor do. Victor remarked of Chávez, "He's not up to the job." We moved onto the subject of oil reserves being something of a double-edged sword for the country.

"With the exception of Norway, no other country with vast oil reserves is particularly rich, in the sense of a majority of the population having a high standard of living as opposed to a large percentage living in poverty," said Victor. This, he argued, was down to nations without resources being forced to develop good "systems of governance and industry" as a priority, whereas those that had ample resources didn't have this pressure.

It was an interesting point, as oil had certainly played a key role in the lack of industrial and agricultural development within Venezuela. Before the discovery of oil in the early 20th century, Venezuela's economy had been agricultural, with the production of coffee, cotton, sugar, tobacco, and cocoa generating the bulk of the nation's wealth. This soon changed to an economy based on the production of oil and the services and commerce associated with it. By the 1920s Venezuela had become the largest exporter of oil in the world, and had seen its agricultural sector decline to a third of

GDP. By the 1950s it was down to 10 percent, and by 1998 it stood at just 6 percent.

The prominence of oil and a lack of robust industry meant that no significant entrepreneurial class emerged. Because the state regulated the oil industry and the majority of economic activity was in this sector, the country's power base shifted from the once-powerful landowning elite to the state. And since foreign oil companies controlled domestic production up until 1974 when the country's oil industry was nationalized–nominally, that is, as in truth it was still in thrall to the overseas oil companies–neither did any Venezuelan oil magnates emerge.

The phenomenon of specific economic sectors declining as a result of increased growth in another sector is something economists refer to as the "Dutch disease"–named after the repercussions the Dutch economy suffered after natural gas was discovered off its coast.

In Venezuela the shrinking agricultural and industrial sectors were then unable to satisfy huge increased demand for consumer goods, leading to mass importation–something which exacerbated decline in these economic sectors further. To make matters worse, in the 1970s and 1980s Venezuela adhered to a fixed or pegged exchange rate with the U.S. dollar that made the bolivar artificiality high and served to make imported goods dramatically cheaper than domestic ones. An additional knock-on effect of the near eradication of domestic agriculture was that a vast percentage of the rural population moved to urban areas. For a twenty-year period from 1958–1978 when oil prices were high, this oil-dependent model produced the highest per capita GDP in Latin America. During these boom years, rich Venezuelans on vacation in Florida acquired the nickname of Give Me Twos, a reference to their exorbitant spending habits. But when oil prices went down, the reverse occurred. With the steady twenty-year decline in oil prices in the early 1980s, poverty in Venezuela soared to the highest levels in all of Latin America.

One of Victor's theories to tackle poverty in the capital was simply to change the location of the capital itself.

"If the government, and all the institutions that come with it, moved to a new capital, then, it is likely a lot of the poor would follow due to the employment it would create," he said.

Apparently this had been done with some success in Brazil in the sixties, when the capital had been changed from Rio de Janeiro to Brasilia. I wondered if this theoretical moving of the poor was just a case of out of sight, out of mind.

Just like politics, crime was proving to be another oft-discussed subject in Venezuela. Both Victor and Oscar had been robbed, Oscar three times and Victor fifteen times, who had been mugged with knives, guns, and by gang intimidation.

"My area borders a barrio, so I often go to sleep to the sound of gunfire," Victor said. He was, perhaps not surprisingly, adamant that when he finishes his studies, he would live abroad. Oscar, on the other hand, wanted to stay in Venezuela, despite his father's encouragement to move overseas.

"The country has a lot of potential, and if it's going to succeed, then it needs educated people to stay."

In general he was far more optimistic about the country's future than Victor.

We chatted late into the night, and by the time I hit the sack, I was more than ready for sleep. This was easier said than done as thanks to the small size of the sofa, my legs had to remain in a state of suspended elevation on the armrest. Mercifully though, it was fully free of the infuriated flies/bugs that had so terrorized my nighttime hours at Hans's place.

CHAPTER 4

The Truth Behind the Headlines

One of the most important and dramatic events in modern Venezuelan history occurred just four years into Chávez's presidency, when in 2002 a bloody coup attempt to remove him from power was launched. The events of that day as well as those leading up to it and the subsequent fallout have shaped the course of the nation and its relations with the wider world, the United States in particular. For many Venezuelans these events are an unhealed wound in the consciousness of the country. Understanding the true history of the coup is essential in order to understand many of the tensions in the country today, as well as those between Venezuela and the United States, and of the distorted portrayal of Chávez and the country so prevalent in our Western media.

When Chávez was first elected in 1998, there were few in Washington's corridors of power who believed his revolutionary rhetoric would materialize into tangible reality once in office, and so there was something of a wait-and-see policy regarding Chávez from the Clinton administration. With previous Venezuelan governments being servile puppets of the United States, the general consensus was that more of the same could be expected from Chávez, regardless of any earlier electioneering talk of a "Bolivarian" revolution.[13]

In fact, in Venezuela itself much the same assumption was made, with Chávez winning his first election not through the overwhelming support of the poor–as he has done in subsequent elections–but of the middle classes.[14] The middle classes voted in large numbers for Chávez, primarily because they were desperate to see someone tackle the country's rampantly corrupt and inefficient political system. This was something they blamed for their diminishing affluence, which had declined for the last twenty years. It was only when Chávez's policies began to lean increasingly leftwards that the middle classes deserted him, and it was only after efforts by the country's elite to depose of Chávez undemocratically that his policies began this increasing lean.[15]

So what first caused Venezuela's elite to vehemently oppose Chávez and to subsequently launch a coup against him? In essence the country's old governing elite found themselves systematically removed from their traditional institutional positions of power, not just in the arena of politics but right across the board, in areas such as the economy, culture, and the judiciary.

This democratic process began with Chávez drawing up a cabinet containing no connections to the old elite. Previously the tradition had been for the government's top ministers to be selected from the specific sector related to the post–a defense minister from the military, an economics minister from the corporate world, a culture minister from the media, and so on. By contrast, Chávez's cabinet was almost entirely comprised of the country's left wing. His next act that further diminished the old governing elite's power was drafting a new constitution. Before this could take place, Chávez was required to call a referendum asking the public whether or not a constitutional assembly should be configured to redraft the historic document. This proved extremely popular with the public, garnering a vote of 92 percent in favor. Another vote was taken to elect members of the constitutional assembly, in which Chávez and his supporters won 125 out of 131 seats. After four months of deliberations, a new constitution was thrashed out and a vote taken to approve the document, which was passed with a 72 percent majority. The result was a constitution, not only approved by the people, but written in large part by them, with all citizens having been invited to participate in its creation. For many observers it is considered one of world's most advanced constitutions, with prominence given to the population's human rights as well as their rights to education, health care, nutrition, housing, justice, and a fair salary. Other key elements of the constitution are given over to the rights of historically marginalized groups such as the indigenous population and women.

The constitutional assembly, which Chávez and his supporters now dominated with all but 6 out of 131 seats, appointed a temporary legislature called "Congresillo," which was tasked with making several new institutional appointments to be ratified at a later date once a new national assembly had been elected. These appointments included a new supreme court and national electoral council, two institutions previously controlled by the old governing elite.

Despite these changes, it was the new constitution's requirement for all elected officials to take part in a "megaelection" in order to "relegitimize" their positions that saw the old ruling class practically wiped out democratically from the upper echelons of institutional power. These elections consisted of some thirty-three thousand candidates standing for over six thousand offices, including mayors, state governors, national assembly deputies, city council members, even the presidency itself. Of the 165 seats on the national assembly, Chávez and his supporters won 104. Of the 23 state governorships, they secured 17. Chávez himself was reelected with 59.8 percent of the vote. With supporters of Chávez enjoying a comfortable majority in the national assembly, they were able to ratify the appointments made by the temporary transitional legislature. At the end of this process, the country's old governing elite had been virtually purged from power.

With Chávez and his supporters controlling a two-thirds majority of the national assembly, they passed forty-nine law decrees, two of which in particular made the old ruling class see red. These, along with the elite's elimination from the country's institutional seats of power, served as some of the main motivation domestically for fomenting a coup against the president. The first of these law decrees was a new land law known as Ley de Tierras, which promised to redistribute huge fallow plantation properties of over five thousand hectares in size to the nation's landless citizens. Crucially, these properties would only qualify for redistribution if they had sat idle for in excess of two years. The second was a hydrocarbons law, which doubled the royalty taxes paid by foreign oil majors on new finds within Venezuela. The foreign oil companies had become used to keeping 84 percent of their sales revenues from the oil they pumped up from Venezuela's land and waters, but under the new law this would drop to a mere 70 percent[16]–leaving 30 percent that could fund much-needed social projects for the millions that live in poverty. Such actions for the betterment of the country's poor were seen by the establishment as a direct threat to their traditional privilege and wealth.

In a final act that many analysts believe was the catalyst domestically for the launching of the coup attempt, Chávez began proceedings to take control of the state-owned oil company, PDVSA. Despite this supposedly being under government control, its management was actually subservient to the foreign oil majors, with the ruling elite running the company like a private business for the benefit of a select few rather than the collective good of the country. Chávez referred to it as a "state within a state" and announced his intention of replacing the existing board with his own people in order to redistribute the nation's oil wealth to its citizens, stating, "Venezuela's wealth does not belong to a minority." On April 4, 2002, the management employees of PDVSA responded, instigating a strike that closed down large sections of the company.

For the United States and its CIA, having a society develop distinct from the traditional probusiness subservience of the region's governments posed the mortal "threat of a good example," which, if left unopposed, would serve to inspire other nations to free themselves against the odds. This alone would have been enough for them to warrant deposing of Chávez, especially since at times Venezuela has been the largest supplier of foreign oil to the United States, but there was an additional reason for them wanting to get rid of him, and fast. According to renowned American investigative journalist Greg Palast, who predicted the coup live on radio before it happened, it was not only the raising of taxes on oil companies that made the, by now, Bush administration determined to remove President Chávez, but events occurring much further afield. Palast writes in *The Best Democracy Money Can Buy*,

> *It is from* [OPEC's secretary general] *Rodriguez that I learned the April 12, 2002, coup was enacted before the plotters were ready, and why. Iraq and Libya were trying to organize OPEC to stop exporting oil to the United States to protest American support of Israel. U.S. access to Venezuela's oil suddenly became urgent. The April 12 coup against Chavez was triggered by U.S. fears of a renewed Arab oil embargo without the Venezuela fail-safe in place. Chavez had to go, and right now.*

The Venezuela fail-safe was Venezuela's ability and willingness to pump far more oil than its OPEC quota allowed, in order to break the embargo, something the country had done to stop the Arab oil embargo in the seventies but which now, with Chávez as president, Venezuela would have been unwilling to do for Washington.

And so the coup was launched.

Spearheading the domestic campaign against Chávez were two prominent individuals: Pedro Carmona, chief of the country's confederation of business and industry, and Carlos Ortega, leader of a trade union with long-standing links to the traditional political establishment. In the months preceding the coup, both men flew to the United States to conduct meetings with members of the Bush administration.

The coup began with a relentless media campaign against Chávez. With 95 percent of Venezuela's TV, radio, and print owned by the far right, daily attacks on Chávez became the constant theme. Much of the privately owned media began encouraging the public to take to the streets to demonstrate against Chávez; and on April 11, 2002, an anti-Chávez march–whipped up by the hysterical media coverage, some of which compared Chávez to Hitler and Mussolini[17]–set off in downtown Caracas for the headquarters of the state-owned oil company. At the same time a second march of pro-Chávez supporters centered around the presidential palace, Miraflores.

Ostensibly the two marches were to be kept far apart, but the organizers of the anti-Chávez demonstration had a different agenda and began following a prearranged plan in which they redirected their march towards Miraflores, herding their group in the direction of the pro-Chávez marchers. Despite many within the anti-Chávez march protesting this route change, the organizers were unyielding and insisted on the change of plan. To rally the demonstrators towards the palace, Venezuelan television station RCTV broadcast a call from Carlos Ortega encouraging marchers to head there. It was the beginning of a sinister and deadly plan in which the marchers were merely pawns to be sacrificed in a rich man's game. As the anti-Chávez protesters approached the government supporters, gunfire began ringing out from unseen snipers, who carried out a cold-blooded massacre of random marchers; nineteen were killed, many from a head shot, and sixty-nine wounded.

It was a textbook CIA tactic as used in previous agency coups where an atrocity is carried out and then blamed on the subject targeted for deposition in order to enrage the public against them–the classic example being the ousting of Mossadegh in Iran, where a wave of shootings and bombings was carried out by the CIA and then blamed on Mossadegh through gray propaganda.

The propaganda part of the plan against Chávez was now enacted by the Venezuelan media. Not long afterwards, deceptively edited film footage was broadcast on Venezuelan television station RCTV and other private broadcasters showing Chávez supporters firing handguns from a city bridge. This was the proof, so the media claimed that Chávez's supporters had carried out the massacre and had been caught red-handed in the act.

"Thank God there's this evidence," a commentator states over the footage.

But the footage from the bridge was far from what the media attempted to portray it as. For what was selectively aired merely showed Chávez supporters firing handguns–something that many Venezuelan's carry–into the distance. Despite the footage not showing at whom they were firing, the media was categorical; they were "shooting at people marching below." Crucially though, below was not shown. Footage that emerged later which was taken from a slightly different angle makes it crystal clear that there weren't any marchers below the bridge and that the road was deserted. In the extended footage the Chávez supporters are seen ducking and lying down, clearly trying to avoid being shot themselves. They are shown firing both upwards and downwards, defending themselves against snipers shooting at them from the top of buildings and antigovernment police units firing at them from below. (To watch footage of this, see *The Revolution Will Not Be Televised*, by Irish filmmakers Kim Bartley and Donnacha O'Briain, and *The War on Democracy*, by John Pilger–both available on Google Videos.)

Not long afterwards, footage was aired of a statement from military chiefs denouncing Chávez and blaming him and his supporters for the massacre, "Venezuelans! The president of the republic has betrayed the trust of his people. He's massacring innocent people with snipers. So far . . . six people have been killed and dozens wounded in Caracas. This is intolerable. We cannot accept a tyrant in the Republic of Venezuela."

But what those watching the television didn't know was that this statement had been prerecorded long before any of the marchers had been shot. Caracas-based CNN correspondent Otto Neustald revealed that the day before the coup he had received a telephone call from a friend with close ties to the opposition who had stated, "Otto, tomorrow the eleventh there will be a video of Chávez, the demonstration will go towards Miraflores, and there will be deaths, and twenty high-ranking officers will pronounce themselves against the government and will demand Chávez's resignation."

By 8:00 pm that evening the head of the army, General Efrain Vasquez Velasco, announced on television that he also had turned against Chávez, stating, "Until today I was loyal to you, Mr. President." With the head of the army against him, it wasn't long before the presidential palace was surrounded by tanks. At roughly 10:00 pm after the signal from the state television station had been cut by the plotters, members of the army's high command entered Miraflores to issue Chávez an ultimatum; resign or the palace would be fired upon. Chávez refused to resign. In the early hours of April 12, with but five minutes until the renegade army officers' deadline expired, Chávez agreed to be kidnapped by the army in order to prevent a second massacre, this time of those inside Miraflores. As his abductors led him away, palace officials and ministers broke out in spontaneous song, singing in solidarity with their president. Despite his refusal to quit, the media announced triumphantly to the nation that Chávez had resigned.

And so with Chávez gone–spirited away to an island military base to have his fate decided–the coup plotters began their celebrations. On the morning of the twelfth amid a presidential palace packed to the rafters with the country's business elite, Pedro Carmona, dressed in a decorative sash and ribbons, declared himself president–receiving a congratulatory hug from Ignazio Salvatierra, president of the bankers' association. Wasting no time, Carmona began to systematically undo the forty-nine laws so abhorrent to the country's business leaders and plantation owners, as well as to the foreign oil companies. As he set about dissolving Venezuela's supreme court and congress and sacking the attorney general and other government officials, the rich white folk in attendance began chanting like demented fools, "Democracia! Democracia!"

In the United States the lapdog corporate media followed their Venezuelan colleagues' lead, broadcasting the same manipulated footage of Chávez supporters on the bridge and spewing the same lies that the footage was proof Chavistas had carried out the slaughter.

White House spokesperson Ari Fleischer endorsed the corporate media version of events:

> *We know that the action encouraged by the Chavez government provoked this crisis. According to the best information available, the Chavez government suppressed peaceful demonstrations. Government supporters, on orders from the Chavez government, fired on unarmed, peaceful protestors, resulting in 10 killed and 100 wounded. The Venezuelan military and the police refused to fire on the peaceful demonstrators and refused to support the government's role in such human rights violations. . . . The results of these events are now that President Chavez has resigned the presidency. Before resigning, he dismissed the vice president and the cabinet, and a transitional civilian government has been installed. This government has promised early elections.*[18]

To the plotters it now looked like the coup was a success. However, their celebrations would be short-lived, for what they hadn't bargained on was the reaction of the country's poor. The following day when word began to get out to the masses that the resignation of Chávez was a sham–confirmed by Chávez's wife through a call to an independent radio station still on the air–the barrios erupted. Up to a million people marched down from the city's hilltop shacks and surrounded the presidential palace, demanding Chávez's return. Crucially for Chávez and his supporters, one of the country's elite paratroop regiments stationed in nearby Maracay had remained loyal to the president (the elected one) and refused to comply with the coup regime, issuing a statement to that effect. As word spread of their resistance, other battalions began to make public pronouncements of loyalty to Chávez. The tide was turning.

In what must rank as one of the dumbest decisions of the coup plotters, they had not seen fit to replace Chávez's personal presidential guard but instead decided to keep them on, deeming it unnecessary to replace them with guards of whose loyalty they were assured. The result was predictable. With the palace surrounded by Chávez supporters baying for the coup plotters' blood, the presidential guard seized their opportunity. Swinging into action, they retook the palace, arresting those who hadn't already managed to flee.

In custody, Chávez had been oblivious to events occurring outside and was for a while convinced he would be executed. But as the coup began to disintegrate, two of the leading plotters flew to the island of La Orchila where he was being held and, in a last-ditch attempt to salvage the coup, tried to convince Chávez to sign a resignation letter. He refused and they left empty-handed, only to return unexpectedly a few moments later, tails between their legs–their pilot having decided to make a quick exit in the plane without them, leaving the plotters stranded with Chávez on the island. I'd have loved to have been a fly on the wall for that one as it must have made for a decidedly awkward moment for the two conspirators, especially since Chávez's next airborne visitors would be a squadron of loyal paratroopers flying in to take him back to the palace and restore him to power.

Chávez arrived back at Miraflores by helicopter at 4:00 am–just forty-seven hours after his kidnap–amid scenes of jubilation from the thousands gathered there, many of whom were in tears. By 4:30 am he was addressing the nation:

> *I send a message from the depth of my heart to Venezuela and the world that this palace is of the Venezuelan people . . . The people have retaken this palace and they will not be removed!*

It wasn't long after Chávez was back in the presidency that evidence began emerging of Washington's involvement in the botched coup. Despite the White House having stated, "We know that the action encouraged by the Chávez government provoked this crisis," and asserting that "government supporters, on orders from the Chávez government, fired on unarmed, peaceful protestors," it is now clear Washington knew this was bullshit from the start. Secret CIA intelligence briefs issued before the coup to the top 200 decision makers in the U.S. government reveal, at the very least, that the Bush administration knew full well what had really happened. The documents–obtained through the Freedom of Information Act by lawyers Eva Golinger and Jeremy Bigwood–were issued between March 5 and April 8, 2002, three days before the coup itself. The document from April 1 states,

> *Disgruntled officers within the military are still planning a coup, possibly early this month.*

The subsequent brief titled "Conditions Ripening for Coup Attempt" issued April 6 states,

> *Dissident military factions, including some disgruntled senior officers and a group of radical junior officers, are stepping up efforts to organize a coup against President Chavez.*

The document goes on to state that

> *the plotters may try to exploit unrest stemming from opposition demonstrations slated for later this month or ongoing strikes at the state-owned oil company PDVSA.*

This, of course, is exactly what did happen. Considering that the Bush administration endorsed as authentic the opposition's claims that Chávez caused the killings and had resigned–which their own intelligence briefs show they clearly knew were false–they not only acted as accomplices to the plotters but actively served to cover up the crime for political expedience. After the furor following the release of the CIA briefs, a White House spokesperson initially claimed that the administration had not warned Chávez of the plot because this would have amounted to "interference" in the internal affairs of Venezuela. This story, however, was hastily changed to the White House claiming that actually they had warned Chávez after all–something the government of Venezuela vehemently denies. Either way, it doesn't account for the lies they told in stating that Chávez himself was responsible for the killings.

Despite the CIA documents being written so that they read as passive observations on forthcoming events, as opposed to direct involvement in them, this does not discount a deeper CIA involvement in the coup. As author Gregory Wilpert points out, "It is important to note that the security briefs are prepared by the intelligence section of the CIA, not its operational arm. That is, the CIA covert operations arm could have had a hand in the coup, even though the security brief presents events in Venezuela from an observer's and not a participant's perspective."

And there is indeed evidence of the United States playing a greater role in the coup. For other recently released documents reveal that groups instrumental in fomenting the coup were being funded indirectly by the U.S. government. In the run-up to the coup, the United States funnelled millions of dollars to opposition groups through *USAID* and the Orwellian named *National Endowment for Democracy*–a group that passed out money to organizations whose leaders were later bestowed with cabinet positions in Pedro Carmona's brief dictatorial government. A document from the U.S. State Department lays bare such funding:

> *It is clear that NED [the National Endowment for Democracy], Department of Defense (DOD), and other U.S. assistance programs provided training, institution building, and other support to individuals and*

organizations understood to be actively involved in the brief ouster of the Chavez government.

Eva Golinger, who was instrumental in obtaining many of the classified documents, states in an interview in *The War on Democracy*, "During the six-month period prior to the coup in April 2002, the U.S. government invested more than two million dollars into financing these organizations that they knew at least six months before were planning to overthrow the government." In a laughable response to the allegation, the former U.S. assistant secretary of state Roger Noriega states in the same film, "Just because it happened after we provided support to these group doesn't mean it happened because we provided support to these groups."

Other evidence of more direct involvement in the coup comes from Wayne Madsen, a former officer of the U.S. spy agency the National Security Administration. Madsen has stated that during the coup the "US Navy provided signals intelligence and communications jamming support to the Venezuelan military," and that "the National Security Agency (NSA) supported the coup using personnel attached to the US Southern Command's Joint Interagency Task Force East in Key West, Florida." [19]

Chávez has, on numerous occasions, personally given an interesting account of an incident he claims occurred three days before the coup, at an official reception being held for a departing Chinese military attaché. In attendance at the reception were representatives from the Venezuelan and foreign militaries, including U.S. officer David Carzares. While making small talk and politely nibbling on the assorted canapés, Carzares is said to have requested to speak to Venezuelan officer General Gonzalez. Unbeknown to him, there were two General Gonzalezes, and as luck would have it–although not for him–he was taken to the wrong one. Querying Gonzalez, he is said to have asked, "Why haven't you contacted the ships that we have on the coast and the submarine we have submerged in La Guaira? What has happened? Why has no one contacted me?

What are you waiting for?" To which a confused Gonzalez simply replied, "I'll find out," before relaying the information straight back to Chávez and passing on Carzares's business card, which he had been given by him so he could get in touch.[20]

A further bit of evidence which adds weight to this account is that after Miraflores had been retaken by the presidential guard, a Venezuelan Air Force report submitted to short-lived dictator Carmona was discovered in the palace. In it are details of U.S. ships entering Venezuela's territorial waters.[21] Other evidence exists of U.S. colonels signing their names in at the Caracas military headquarters on the day of the coup, of a U.S. registered plane being stationed on the island where Chávez was held–something that under normal circumstances would not be expected given that the island is a military base–and of the U.S. ambassador coming down to have his photo taken with the murderous coup plotters.[22] And in the immediate aftermath of the coup, there are suggestions that the U.S. government spearheaded efforts to have the dictatorship of Pedro Carmona formally recognized. According to the then foreign minister of Mexico Jorge Castañeda, a person who crucially has been a frequent critic of Chávez, "There was a proposition made by the United States and Spain, to issue a declaration with Mexico, Brazil, Argentina and France recognizing the government of Pedro Carmona."[23]

And yet another CIA document, this time issued on April 17, 2002, reveals that just days after the coup, the United States was again actively trying to undermine Venezuelan democracy, this time through a "U.S. backed initiative to send an OAS [Organization of American States] democracy mission to Venezuela." The document went on to make clear just what exactly the "democracy mission" would do, referring to "OAS efforts that might legitimize the coup plotters" and "an OAS mission to constrain his [Chavez's] ability to retaliate against his foreign or domestic opponents."

But perhaps the best evidence of U.S. involvement in the coup is the CIA's past record in Latin America. As American historian and author William Blum has written of the botched coup,

> *How do we know that the CIA was behind the coup that overthrew Hugo Chavez? Same way we know that the sun will rise tomorrow morning. That's what it's always done and there's no reason to think that tomorrow morning will be any different.*[24]

From orchestrating coups to rigging elections, from backing death squads to carrying out assassinations, from crushing popular movements to installing brutal dictators, the CIA's bloody history in Latin America is rarely mentioned in the Western mainstream where a vacuum of knowledge surrounds these epic crimes that have extinguished countless lives, destroyed numerous democracies, and seen the aspirations of the region's poor majority systematically snuffed out in the interests of Western big business and the United States–which are often one and the same. Blum's book *Killing Hope: US military and CIA Interventions since World War II* methodically chronicles such operations. In Latin America these interventions have occurred in Guatemala, Costa Rica, Guyana, Haiti, Ecuador, Brazil, Peru, Dominican Republic, Cuba, Uruguay, Chile, Bolivia, Grenada, Suriname, Nicaragua, Panama, El Salvador, amongst others.[25]

There were numerous fallouts and ramifications from the botched coup. The more significant being a further chilling in relations with the United States; the opposition losing another of their former institutional power bases, this time in the military; the Venezuelan television station RCTV not getting its license renewed, amid much international furor; and Chávez increasing his social policies apace, eventually declaring that he would build "socialism of the 21st century" in Venezuela.

The reporting in the Western media of the case of RCTV not getting its license renewed is a classic example of the sort of misinformation and out-and-out propaganda against Chávez so prevalent in the West. The common claim is that Chávez ruthlessly closed down the broadcaster, silencing it for being critical of the government–an action it is often claimed serves as proof positive that Chávez is a virtual dictator, adamant on crushing all dissenting opinions. Rarely, however, is a truthful account given that pays even lip service to the categorical fact that RCTV was deeply complicit in the coup to remove Venezuela's democratically elected leader, or that the station was not closed down at all but simply did not get its license renewed after it expired five years post the coup.

U.K.-based media watchdog *Media Lens*, commenting on RCTV's actions in the run-up, during and after the coup, states,

> *For two days before the April 11, 2002 coup, RCTV cancelled regular programming and instead ran constant coverage of a general strike aimed at ousting Chavez. A stream of commentators delivered fierce criticism of the president with no response allowed from the government. RCTV also ran non-stop adverts encouraging people to attend an April 11 march aimed at toppling the government and broadcast blanket coverage of the event. When the march ended in violence, RCTV ran manipulated video footage falsely blaming Chavez supporters for the many deaths and injuries.*[26]

RCTV's actions also included broadcasting an appeal from Carlos Ortega urging the demonstrators, in contravention of the law, to march on Miraflores; refusing to broadcast the news in the aftermath of the coup when up to a million enraged citizens[27] hit the streets to protest at the ousting of Chávez, during which time RCTV acted as if nothing out of the ordinary was occurring by running cartoons, old movies, and soap operas instead; the station's owner, Marcel Granier, meeting at the presidential palace with dictator Carmona to offer him his support; and refusing to broadcast the news when Chávez was flown in and rightfully regained the presidency.

In a telling statement from one of the coup plotters after it looked like their operation had been a success, Vice Admiral Victor Ramirez Perez stated on television, "We had a deadly weapon: the media. And now that I have the opportunity, let me congratulate you." In another telling admission caught for prosperity on film, one appreciative coup leader remarked, "I must thank Venevision and RCTV." Later on during national assembly hearings held into the coup, RCTV's news director testified that his bosses had given him clear orders: "Zero Chávez, nothing related to Chávez or his supporters. . . . The idea was to create a climate of transition and to start to promote the dawn of a new country."

U.S. media watchdog FAIR pointed out, "Were a similar event to happen in the U.S., and TV journalists and executives were caught conspiring with coup plotters, it's doubtful they would stay out of jail, let alone be allowed to continue to run television stations, as they have in Venezuela." (RTCV was allowed to continue its satellite and cable broadcasts.) Not that you'll read much of this in *The New York Times* or the like. *The New York Times*, coincidently, endorsed the coup when it looked like a success, only to backpedal afterwards, issuing an apology.

Despite Chávez initially taking rather a cautious approach on returning to the presidency–with him reinstating the former directors and managers of the state-owned oil company PDVSA–he soon began to rethink this approach when further attempts to oust him occurred. These came in 2003 in the form of a manager-led shutdown of the oil industry and in 2004 in a recall referendum. Both of these attempts failed, with the managers subsequently being replaced and Chávez winning the referendum hands down–the results of which were verified by election observers from the Organization of American States and the Carter Center. Such attempts only served to further consolidate Chávez's power base and, along with the 2002 coup, convinced him to push further with reforms, which, had it not been for these attempts to oust him, may not have even occurred.

For many of Chávez's supporters, the coup was a lifting of the veil, revealing for the first time just how far those opposing Chávez would go to get rid of him, serving to reinvigorate the poor majority's participation in the political process and alerting many to the need to actively defend and organize against such attacks on their democracy, from enemies both foreign and domestic.

CHAPTER 5

Pole Dancing

Sunlight began to slowly illuminate the living room of Austin's apartment through the balcony doors, gently bringing me to a state of consciousness with stiff back and neck. Austin arrived soon after and pointed to a towel he'd left out for me the night before that I could use for showering. He then headed off to the kitchen, which I'd made up my mind to only venture into if absolutely necessary. As I picked up the towel, it unraveled, releasing a shower of cat hair in its wake, highlighted by the hazy morning sun. Examining it close-up was like looking at an animal pelt–it was absolutely caked in the stuff. I made up my mind to use a T-shirt to dry myself instead.

Before opening the kitchen door, I inhaled deeply, then quickly made my way through to the small bathroom just off from the cat's litter room. I negotiated my way past the motorcycle tires and wheels, then stripped off to my birthday suit and placed my clothing in the sink to avoid getting it dirty. As I faced and turned on the exposed pipe of the shower, there was a momentary delay, followed by an almighty retching sound as an air pocket cleared within it. A second later it exploded into life, hitting me with significant force square in the face with a deluge of thick rusty red liquid. It obviously hadn't been used for a very long time. The red color soon cleared, and after a brief wash I attempted to dry up with my thin cotton T-shirt–never an easy task–before heading back to the sitting room.

There were certain things that Austin and I had to organize today. Austin had to go to the bank and I had to exchange some currency. Luckily for me, Austin arranged a meeting with an acquaintance of his who could change my dollars for the black market rate. This turned out to be an interesting transaction on the third floor of a tower block in the center of the city. The premises for this looked nothing like a business address to me, being more akin to a small discreet apartment where money changing and the like was carried out. Stationed outside the front door sat two sour-faced security guards in suits, waiting to check the credentials of those desiring to enter. After a brief word with Austin, they opened up then promptly shut the door behind us. We were led through to a back room where, after the briefest of pleasantries, we got down to business.

I received some cash for my two thousand dollars, which I stuffed into the relative safety of my socks–none too easy given the quantity of bills–in order to prevent pickpockets from getting their hands on it once in the street, and the rest I got by way of check. This, the helpful black marketeer explained, I could cash at a bank across the road, but I had to be very careful doing so. I mustn't, he explained, under any circumstances use a regular cashier. They could not be trusted as they might have an accomplice pretending to be a customer waiting for an innocuous signal from the cashier, perhaps a straightening of a tie or a scratch of the neck, which would indicate I was carrying significant money. The accomplice would then follow me outside and rob me. To get around this, he arranged for one of his staff to speak personally to the manager and for him to deal with me in a back room.

He was as good as his word and all went according to plan. Not long after, I was able to be good to mine too, when Austin stopped off at Hans's so I could pay back his loan. Both his and Austin's kindness in arranging an exchange for me were an extremely big help and saved me a lot of money in the long run. With some bolivars in my pocket, I was now ready to set off and explore the rest of the country.

* * *

While waiting at a surprisingly airportlike bus terminal, complete with check-in-style desks and revolving carousels for security-tagged luggage, it dawned on me that the passenger ahead of me having his boarding pass checked was slightly overdressed for a tropical country. Surely a puffer jacket, pair of gloves, hat, and blanket were wholly uncalled-for?

How wrong I was.

If you want to experience winter in the Tropics, simply buy a ticket for a long-distance Venezuelan coach. God knows why, but they are equipped with the coldest, most inappropriate air-conditioning systems known to mankind, which seem to have only one setting–frostbite. The coaches are so bitterly cold that I would not, in all honesty, be the least surprised to discover that some unfortunate soul has died of hypothermia on one. What the logic behind their insanely cold interiors is, I have no idea. And if the Venezuelans I asked were anything to go by, then the locals were similarly perplexed. Later on in my trip around the country, I met a fellow traveler who was a keen mountaineer–he was adamant that he'd never spent a night on a mountain as cold as the one he spent on a Venezuelan coach. Not that the actual air temperature was as cold as fifteen thousand feet up a snowy peak, but when you climb a mountain, you generally expect it, and so go prepared with a down-filled sleeping bag, gas stove, and the like. But if you're unfamiliar with the modus operandi on Venezuelan coaches, and make the mistake, like my mountaineering friend, of catching an overnight bus wearing nothing but a clammy T-shirt and shorts, then a torturous night shivering in the fetal position awaits.

I wasn't quite so underdressed, in that I was wearing jeans in an attempt to blend in with the locals, none of whom I had seen wearing shorts in Caracas despite the roasting weather. Nonetheless, I was still damn cold and was as pleased as Punch when the coach pulled up in the town of Puerto la Cruz. As I had been so cold for the last five hours, it came as something of a shock when the door let out a loud pneumatic hiss and opened into a sauna-hot Venezuelan day. I stepped into the blissful warmth with a felinelike stretch, and it wasn't long before my core temperature was smiling again.

I was now standing opposite the ferry terminal for the country's most popular vacation spot, and my final destination for today, Margarita Island. The island was 390 square miles in size, had a population of around 420,000, and boasted some of Venezuela's best beaches. Thanks to its duty-free status, it was also something of a shopping mecca. I had arranged to stay there with a thirty-year-old CouchSurfer called Miguel, who worked on the island taking tourists out on boat trips. We had exchanged a couple of messages on the CouchSurfing website and then talked on the phone to formulate a plan on how to meet. Our arrangements were, at least to my mind, a little on the vague side. Miguel had been adamant that there was little point in him giving me his address as he lived in an obscure location that I would be unable to find even with a taxi. My best bet, he said, was to catch a bus to the largest town on the island, Porlamar, and to call him from there. He would take a bus to meet me and bring me back to his place.

Unfortunately the next ferry wasn't due for a couple of hours, so I strolled to the center of town to go in search of some food. There was no shortage of cafés to choose from, selling such traditional Venezuelan treats as fried plantains (savoury bananas), pork rinds, empanadas (fried corn flour turnovers), and arepas (cornmeal pancakes). I was whiling away my spare time, before the ferry arrived, on the veranda of a beachfront café. Here I washed a couple of juicy cheese-filled arepas down with several ice-cold

Venezuelan *Polar Ice* beers, amid the ambiance of the promenade's gently swaying palms and the glistening waters of the Caribbean beyond. By the time I'd finished, I was feeling suitably relaxed but surprisingly tipsy.

To make sure I didn't miss the ferry, I gave myself a good thirty minutes leeway, but in the end this proved unnecessary as it turned up over an hour and a half late. As the ferry's doors opened, a stampede of foot passengers and vehicles poured out, with everyone jostling for position, keen to make up for lost time or to catch the next connecting bus. When the signal for boarding went, I bustled my way on with the rest of the eager crowds in search a good seat for the three-and-a-half-hour journey. I acquired one by the window and moments later spotted a European-looking couple in their fifties looking for a place to sit. I tried to listen in on their accent to decipher where they were from but it was near impossible to hear above the surrounding commotion. They settled on the seats behind me. I listened more closely now. Were they Russian? Rummaging through their stowed luggage, the man triumphantly produced two bottles of champagne. I smiled at him in the forlorn hope of copping a free glass. Seconds later, about a dozen or so of their friends joined them, congregating in the aisle chatting and occupying the other available seats nearby, including the one next to me. Here a significantly worse-for-wear middle-aged woman with blurred eyes and what looked like an alcohol-induced smile sat.

"Señor, what is your country?" she asked.

"Britain. What's yours?"

She ignored the question and, touching my forearm, said, "You're very handsome."

She half-hiccupped half-burped.

Charming.

"Thank you," I replied, stifling a laugh as the ferry pulled away.

The explosive pop of a champagne cork exiting a bottle at high speed elicited a raucous cheer from the group of unidentified foreigners. In an instant my admirer's attention had gone from me to the alcohol on offer. A handful of little plastic cups were filled and handed out. When the frisky fifty-something next to me was passed hers, the gentleman doing the passing turned to me with a "Señor, would you like a glass?" followed up by "What is your country?"

I quickly let it be known that a glass of champagne would be a delightful accompaniment to my journey, and, after telling him where I was from, asked the same of him.

"Where do you think?"

"Russia, maybe?"

"Close. We are from Poland," he said with a glowing smile.

For the next few minutes I circulated amongst them, making small talk over several champagnes. When these ran dry, a couple of bottles of Chilean red wine were produced. This was turning out to be a very nice ferry ride, indeed. The Poles were on the last couple of days of an organized tour which had taken them to the famed Angel Falls, as well as on a boat trip along the Orinoco Delta, something they highly recommended. At one point on their journey they had unofficially crossed into Brazil, something which, apparently, was quite easy to do in certain isolated places without a passport. After some general chitchat, interrupted periodically by the inebriated woman waddling over to tell me again that I was handsome and trying to persuade me to have a little waltz with her, I decided to sit down. By this stage I was feeling quite inebriated myself. In order to avoid my not-too-secret admirer, I switched seats and ended up next to a Polish professor of chemistry.

After discussing his trip and hearing the basics of his job, the conversation ground to an uneasy halt. A sort of awkward silence descended in the space between us, inducing pained involuntary smiles and ponderous glances at the floor. I hastily tried to come up with something to break the deadlock, my anxiety building with every uncomfortable passing silent moment. Think of something to say! Think of something to say! We'd exhausted each other's trips and professions, so what now? How about Poland? I didn't know much about the place but knew there were plenty of Polish migrant workers in the U.K. Maybe there was something worthy of comment here.

Eureka! That was it. Suddenly I remembered something I'd read in the newspaper about the Polish community in England. However, the problem was that my alcohol-numbed mind didn't pause sufficiently to ponder whether it was a likely topic to reignite a cordial conversation before my stupid intoxicated mouth opened wide and started blabbing.

"I hear a lot of Poles regularly flout Britain's fishing laws," I blurted out with zero acuity of mind.

"Is that right?" the professor replied, looking most perturbed.

Shit. I cringed inwardly as it dawned on me that this was not the best of openers. But I'd started now so had little choice but to go on.

"Yes," I continued, "I've read they illegally catch the protected carp from Britain's rivers and ponds, and eat them, particularly at Christmastime, when I believe it's something of a delicacy in"–I trailed off–"Poland."

"Well, I am sorry for that," he replied, as if I were holding him personally responsible for the dwindling carp stocks of Britain's waterways.

I willed the ground to open up and swallow me down like a Pole with a tasty mouthful of Christmas carp. When it didn't, I faked tiredness and said I was going to have a nap. I made up my mind to stay clear of daytime boozing sessions from now on.

The sleep did me good and I awoke feeling like a new man as we arrived after dark in the island's main port of Punta de Piedras, significantly later than expected. While waiting for the vessel's exit doors to open, I strategically stood near the Poles in the hope that they'd ask where I was heading to on the island and then offer me a lift. I subtly asked their tour representative, who was a pretty multilingual woman of about my age, for advice on the best way to make it to the main town of Porlamar.

My plan worked a treat, and it wasn't long into our conversation that the tour rep had a brain wave and suggested that I come along with them. Her group wasn't going to Porlamar; in fact they were splitting in two with half going to a distant resort called the Dunes and half heading elsewhere on the island, but she offered to get the driver of the Dunes group to drop me at Porlamar afterwards, on his way back again to the ferry port. The Dunes was a good distance past my destination, so it would be a far longer journey, but the lift was still a massive help as I would avoid the hassle of trying to work out the multiple local buses with no Spanish skills or having to pay an extortionate fee for a taxi. If my money was going to last for the duration of my trip, then I couldn't be splashing out on cabs unnecessarily.

Chaos reigned as we disembarked the ferry. Agitated drivers revved their engines as they waited to roll down the vessel's huge clanging metal ramp, only to find themselves grinding to a halt a moment after departure as they plunged into a congested bottleneck of horn-beeping vehicles–the exhaust fumes mingling in the dusty, headlight-illuminated night air. Foot passengers milled around nearby in varying states of confusion, attempting to locate onward transport or people waiting to meet them, making me glad to have my own lift already lined up.

In the interests of not losing my free ride, I stuck close to the Poles as we waded through the crowds searching for their minibus drivers. We found the one going to the Dunes resort, who was parked around the corner listening to Metallica on the vehicle's stereo. The guide introduced me to the driver and explained the new plan to him. He was a local from the island who spoke good English and was A-OK with dropping me off. I hopped into the passenger seat and through the window thanked the tour rep for her help. With this she headed off in search of the other bus. When the rest of the tour group boarded, the driver promptly turned off Metallica, replacing it with what I took to be his standard-issue tourist compilation CD. This was comprised of Latino salsa rhythms and easygoing Caribbean oil drum beats, fostering images of hammocks swaying gently beneath beachfront palms and piña coladas sipped by the poolside. The Poles loved it.

As we drove away from the port, it became immediately apparent that something big was going down on the island. There was a huge military presence on either side of the road, giving the place a foreboding atmosphere in the dark. Lining all the highways were twitchy-looking armed soldiers spaced out at uniform intervals, many of whom peered suspiciously towards us as we passed.

"What's going on?" I asked the driver.

"Chávez is hosting a conference on Margarita with leaders from South America and Africa. They're all here, Morales, Gaddafi, Mugabe, you name it. The island is packed and security very tight."

This sounded interesting, but the driver knew little more about it other than the conference name, the *Africa-South America Summit*. I hoped to find out more later and wondered if I might even catch a glimpse of any of the leaders.

Although the military was here because of the conference, several areas of Venezuelan civil life have seen increasing involvement by the military since Chávez was first elected–something I sure as hell wouldn't want to see in my home country and which instinctively raises my hackles. Chávez has awarded many key positions in his government to military officers both active and retired and has supported the election of former officers to mayoral and governor positions. The military itself has taken on some typically civilian duties, the most prominent of which was a project in 2000 called Plan Bolívar, which assigned military personnel to social projects aimed at alleviating poverty. After a corruption scandal in which several officers were removed from their posts, Plan Bolívar was scrapped. Chávez has also pushed for greater involvement of the civilian population in the military with his establishment of Mission Miranda, a citizen defense force aimed at fighting any future foreign invasion. Such blurring of civilian and military roles has led to allegations of Chávez in effect running a military government and of a creeping "Cubanization" of the country, a reference to the committees set up to defend the Cuban Revolution. Chávez defends such programs, by claiming a desire to create unity between the civilian population and the military, and likes to quote Mao Zedong when doing so, "The people are to the military as the water is to the fish." Considering Mao was a mass-murdering psychopath, methinks he's probably not the best of people for Chávez to cite on this subject; not if he wants to convince skeptics like myself that is.

As we drove to the northeastern tip of the island going through sparsely populated areas, the driver and I chatted on and off for the one hour and fifteen minutes it took to reach our destination.

A colonial-style archway manned by security welcomed us to the Dunes resort. After a rudimentary check, we drove in past costly-looking chalets and manicured palm-lined gardens before pulling up at an expensive-looking main reception building. Here the Poles were met by a new rep, who took over tourist duties. I bade them farewell and remained inside the minibus with the driver. A second later, an irate-looking man approached the vehicle and began talking to the driver through the open window. By his tone and body language I took the man to be the driver's immediate boss. Straightaway it became apparent that something was up. I recognized the word *inglés*, so they were talking about me.

"You'll have to get off here," the driver stated firmly, out of the blue.

"No. You're taking me to Porlamar. Remember?" I responded, incredulous.

"I'm going back to the ferry. I can take you there if you like but not Porlamar."

"Listen, we had an arrangement. You'd drop the group off here and then take me to Porlamar on your way back to the ferry. Why else would I have ridden with you for the last hour into the middle of God knows where, only to go all the way back again to where I started from, over two hours later?!"

"You'll have to get off here," he repeated, unwilling to debate the issue.

What the hell! The guy had been all "sugar and spice" on the journey here and was well aware of the arrangement, even going so far as to point out the turning we'd be needing later on. Clearly his boss had put a wrench in the works, so I pleaded with him instead, which proved pointless as he spoke as much English as I did Spanish.

I could feel my annoyance building up inside me and really felt like disposing with what little diplomacy I had left and having a blazing row instead. I tried to calm myself down and think. Maybe I could get the Pole's new rep to override the boss man and insist that the driver stick to the bargain.

"Hold on," I said.

Jumping out of the vehicle, taking my pack with me just in case the driver decided to pull a fast one, I pushed through the doors of reception and headed towards the check-in desk where two of the Poles were talking with their new rep.

"Excuse me," I said to the rep, "I wonder if you can help me sort out a little problem I have with the driver of your group?"

I turned to gesture through the glass doors at the minibus outside and was greeted by the sight of the driver's boss jumping into my seat and slamming the door behind him. A nanosecond later the bus screeched off. I made a move to give chase but gave up not two paces in. It was clear I was already too late.

"Assholes!" I spitted out after them, only to find my voice unintentionally amplified by the acoustics of the reception area. An uneasy silence filled the immediate vicinity as all eyes turned to me in the posh resort. The Poles and the rep looked my way apprehensively, hardly putting them in the right frame of mind to assist me. I approached with as friendly a smile as I could muster under the circumstances and explained my situation to the tour rep. He wasn't interested and seemed unable to grasp the basics of what had happened.

"Where did you say you came from?" he asked.

I explained again that I had met his colleague on the ferry and that she had arranged for me to get a lift to Porlamar with the group's driver on the way back.

"No," he stated, shaking his head, "I don't think she would have done that."

I tried to get him to call her but it was no good, he didn't give a damn. And what was the point anyway, the driver had left so I was stuck here. I asked him if there were any buses nearby. There were none. I shook my head in disbelief at how quickly my situation had deteriorated. If I hadn't already arranged to meet Miguel, I would have gone "bush" and tied my jungle hammock between two trees for the night. I decided to call him to make a plan and wondered whether he had a car and could pick me up. This was rather optimistic on my part after he'd told me he would catch a bus to meet me in Porlamar.

Thanks to this pointless detour and the ferry being late it was now pushing 10:00 pm, making it several hours past the time I said I would call–and I was still miles from our arranged meeting point. I asked the rep if there were any pay phones in the resort.

"No," was his one-word reply.

Since it had been the holiday rep's colleague who had offered me the lift in the first place and one of the company's drivers who had screwed me over, I figured he owed me one, so asked to borrow his cell. He claimed it was out of credit. I didn't believe him but managed to contain my discontent behind a mask of civility.

The only option was to try and borrow the reception's phone but I suspected they would deny this since I wasn't staying there. I near pleaded with the rep for him to use his influence to persuade them. After all, he had a whole tour group staying here so must have had some serious leverage with them. Reluctantly he agreed and began to initiate a dialogue in Spanish with the receptionist that I was immediately suspicious would be none too helpful, or at best neutral to my cause, but to which he could then claim afterwards–once they'd refused him that–"I tried." Since it was an expensive resort, the receptionist spoke good English, so I quickly interjected after the rep had started the conversation and continued on his behalf, making sure to associate my plight with him and the other paying guests in his group. I concluded my impassioned speech with a wholly fictitious "It would be a big help to us both," gesturing to the rep, and in so doing implying that, by doing me a favor, they'd be doing a big customer of theirs one too. They passed me the phone and I got through first time.

"Jamie, I thought you were no longer coming!" exclaimed a surprised Miguel.

After telling him my tale of woe, he told me the bad news that I already suspected–he didn't have a car. My only option would be to catch a cab. There was no point meeting in Porlamar anymore as it would be better to go direct to his town of Los Robles. The cab would cost much more from the Dunes than it would have done from the ferry terminal and take just as long. If I'd caught a budget-sparing bus at the ferry, I would, in all probability, already be at Miguel's. I was not best pleased, but I was where I was. This time I insisted on taking Miguel's address despite him maintaining that the taxi driver would have no idea how to find his street or house, both of which were apparently hidden away somewhat. He said to get me dropped off in the center of Los Robles and to call him once there.

I can't say I was overly happy with this "arrive at night in an unknown area and phone" option, but what could I do? I got reception to order a taxi for me, and before I knew it, I was making my way along an unlit back road towards Miguel's place, driving through some of the island's undeveloped semiwild and hilly interior–something which, due to the reflective effect of the car's window in the dark, I could only get glimpses of when sticking my face up against the glass.

We arrived in Miguel's town, the center of which contained a square, a small church, lots of basic single-story residential housing and not much else. The place was all but deserted, save for a few "tough guy" adolescent types playing basketball in the main square. The cabby spoke no English, and after several futile attempts of me reading the Spanish for *public telephone* from my phrase book, he pulled over to have a look at the text himself.

He dropped me across the road from the only pay phone in the square and charged me an extortionate rate in the process. As he pulled away, I began searching through my pockets for some spare change to use in the telephone, at which point I discovered it was of the card-only variety and didn't accept coins.

Shit.

So here I was, stranded at night in the middle of a town I knew nothing about, in a country everybody had been quick to impress upon me was mighty dangerous, with zero Spanish skills, nor any way of contacting the person I was supposed to be staying with. I was carrying a dirty great backpack which, along with my gringo appearance, announced "tourist" to the world like a neon sign for would-be muggers.

Things weren't looking too rosy.

The guys playing basketball stopped what they were doing and started to look my way. I decided it best to walk off with purpose as if I knew exactly where I was going while hastily formulating a plan. I bypassed the ballplayers and headed towards the church on the other side of the square. The way I saw it, my priority was using a phone, any phone. If I couldn't, then the only other options were to wait around in the center of town on the off chance that Miguel came looking for me and miraculously stumbled upon me–before someone of ill intent did–or to sleep rough. There were no hotels, hostels, boardinghouses, or other variations on this theme. Since the only phone in town was useless without a card, I figured I had to try and speak, by way of my phrase book or mime, to a local and offer to pay for the use of their phone card or cell, if they had one.

Around the corner from the church stood a group of guys in their late teens hanging out by a little kiosk–the only place open at this time–selling canned drinks, potato chips, and candy bars, manned by a guy only slightly older than them. They weren't really the demographic I was hoping to ask for assistance and were probably statistically the most likely age group to attempt to mug me, but they were all I had. I headed over.

They looked my way long before I reached them. I approached the one I took to be the alpha male of the group with a confident "Hola," followed up by "Habla inglés?"

"No," was his slightly bemused response.

I looked around the rest of the group and repeated the question, receiving the same as before.

"Un teléfono público?" I asked, to which they pointed back to the one in the square. I mimed slotting a card into the phone, then waved my hands as if to say, "I don't have one." It seemed to do the trick, at least they seemed to understand what I meant. Turning to the guy working the kiosk, I did my best to ask whether he sold such cards, "Teléfono público, err, card?" I said, miming slotting a card into a phone. He shook his head.

Up next was the tricky bit. I tried to mime, "I'll give you money if you let me use your cell." This I attempted by pointing at myself, then at the alpha male, before rubbing my thumb and fingers together in order to effect money, finishing up with a mime of texting on a cell phone–not that I wanted to text but it seemed the best way to establish that I wasn't talking about the public phone. It took a few attempts until they twigged what I wanted, at which point the guy at the kiosk came good and offered me his cell–for free. I showered him with a thousand thank-yous and got through to Miguel first time. Minutes later I recognized a 3-D version of his profile picture striding across the street. Boy was I pleased to see him.

He recognized me as well–not particularly difficult given that I was the only gringo in town and happened to be carrying a whopping great backpack. With a big smile and a man hug/chest bump, he welcomed me to Margarita. Like Hans, Miguel looked quite different in the flesh when compared to his mug shot. He was taller and slimmer than I imagined and looked older than his twenty-nine years, with slightly receding mousey hair and a weathered coffee-colored face. He wore a perpetual dry smile and had the easygoing satisfied countenance you might expect from someone who lives on a sun-drenched Caribbean island. We ambled down a couple of unlit streets in a rather dilapidated area to get to his place, which was just past an abandoned lot no more than five minutes from the main square. Blocking the entrance to his home was a huge sliding metal gate secured with a chunky padlock. Stuck atop the property's high walls were jagged shards of broken glass. This was much more basic than the places I'd stayed at so far, but it was a welcome sight after a tiring day by road and sea.

With Miguel's unlocking and sliding of the clanging metal gate, several dogs inside began barking wildly. We entered into a small courtyard. To our right was a single-story house and up ahead towards the back of the courtyard were a couple of additional dwellings, one of which Miguel pointed out as his room. We opened the door to the main house and entered into a very basic kitchen where we were met by his other housemates, their two cats, and five dogs–the only type I recognized being an Alsatian.

He lived with his sister Stefany, her husband Alfonso, their two adult sons Gabriel and Jorge, and friend Luis, all of whom rented the place together. The men wore nothing but their shorts, of the cutoff denim and surf variety–a wise decision in tonight's sweltering heat. Alfonso spoke a few words of English, but only Miguel and Stefany were proficient enough to hold a conversation, so all introductions went through them. After going through the basics, I was offered a seat at the kitchen table and some food. Miguel dished up spaghetti served with little pieces of chicken wing and a thin tomato and onion sauce. Over my meal he explained that most of the household were hitting the sack soon as they had to get up early to take tourists from the mainland on snorkeling trips to a Robinson Crusoe–style desert island paradise called Cubagua Island, situated about seven miles off the coast of Margarita.

"You should come along too. If you get up early, you can join Alfonso on his boat. I can't take you on mine as my boss will be on board, who won't allow free rides for friends, but there is no worry on Alfonso's," explained Miguel, adding, "It will be a lot of fun."

I accepted immediately.

Luis, Miguel explained, would also be joining me on board for a freebie as he was not working. Alfonso wasn't sure if he would be able to get us a free lunch, as this was cooked by a chef on board who had strict supplies based the number of paying customers, so recommended we buy some food, just in case. He was, however, certain he could get us free alcohol, all day long. To hell with my earlier decision to stay clear of daytime boozing sessions–it sounded a mighty fine plan to me.

After eating my fill, Miguel pointed out the bathroom and showed me to the room in the main house where I would be sleeping. It contained an old foam mattress, a small weathered desk, and a cupboard. Mercifully, it also had a ceiling fan. I can't say it was clean or attractive but it was home, for now, and definitely appreciated.

CHAPTER 6

Surrender Your Booty!

Luis spoke not a word of English, so I just followed his lead as we headed out of the house in our beachwear. We needed to catch two different buses to get to the marina, the first of which went to my illusive destination of the night before, Porlamar. On the second bus, which was crowded way beyond capacity, Luis became infatuated with a Penelope Cruz look-alike. She had an ultraconfident man-eater air about her and was fully aware of the effect she was having on poor Luis, who, with the occasional flirtatious glance, she reduced to a near dribbling wreck. When she exited the bus a few stops down, Luis flashed a cheeky grin my way, then pointed to his eyes with forked fingers before directing them at her, as if to say, "Look at that!" Most of the males on the bus were doing exactly that, save for a fellow on board with his missus who had to maintain "eyes front" as Penelope strutted her stuff catwalk-style down the road.

Heading down the highway, we passed several cars whose rear windshields were scrawled with the slogan Viva Chávez. Lining the route were colorful murals in support of the president alongside depictions of Che Guevara and the emblem of the Africa-South

America Summit: an image of the two continents joined together along their original tectonic split. Over breakfast earlier, I had managed to decipher a little more about the summit from Miguel. It was being held to bolster ties between the two continents, particularly on matters of trade and security. Nearly thirty leaders were attending, many of them flying directly from the UN General Assembly in New York. The summit on Margarita had overlapped the New York conference, which some saw as an indication of its ambitions to be an alternative forum for the two continents.

We pulled into the port and, after stocking up on cheese and ham sandwiches from a nearby shop for lunch, headed towards a large weathered motor yacht about sixty feet in length at the end of the jetty. It had seen a few voyages, evident from the peeling paint on some of its flaky woodwork and the rusty orange stains on its otherwise white hull. On board were five uniformed crew members and a rather theatrical-looking Alfonso, who was dressed up like Johnny Depp from *Pirates of the Caribbean*. He beckoned us on board with a swashbuckle of his sword. I gave him a gracious nod. He reciprocated and gave me a welcoming slap on the back. While Luis chatted to Alfonso, I reclined on a flat bit of the deck catching some rays. It was a glorious morning with calm waters and just a suggestion of breeze–perfect weather for our voyage.

Fifteen minutes later, a bus full of tourists rocked up, totaling about fifteen people. Alfonso sprang into character, welcoming them on board with a bottle of rum in one hand and more pirate theatrics. The tourists got into the spirit of things and were laughing and joking with him as they boarded, creating a fun atmosphere of anticipation. The vacationers were all Venezuelan with the exception of a chubby balding corporate type in his fifties, who, Alfonso managed to translate for me, was Russian. He strode on board wearing a pair of eighties-style sunglasses, a smart-collared shirt–partially unbuttoned on the lower rungs to allow his hairy beer gut to breathe–and an expensive-looking chunky Rolex. Walking on, arm in arm with him, was a platinum blonde glamour-model type in her twenties sporting a miniskirt and equally skimpy top. Luis grinned at me, as if reaching the same conclusion as to what the girl saw in him, and it wasn't his personality.

We got underway soon after, at which point the crew began taking orders for complimentary drinks. I couldn't quite believe my luck as I was handed the first of what would be many free ice-cold bottled beers and sat back with a big smile on my face as we cruised through the turquoise Caribbean waters to our first destination, a partially sunken ferry that had hit a reef. The wreck was a twisted rusting carcass, now covered in seabirds, particularly pelicans, of which there were over twenty. Face masks, flippers, and snorkels were handed out for those, like me, who fancied a dip. Luis remained on board nursing his beverage. About half the passengers ventured into the bath-warm waters in their swimwear–in my case shorts, which I'd worn just for this purpose.

The sheer quantity of debris beneath the water was astonishing. Above the surface it seemed a reasonable size, but when underwater it looked huge. There was metal everywhere. Shoals of exotic fish gracefully patrolled around decaying twisted lumps of machinery and darted through the rusting exposed portholes of this ghostly nautical skeleton, making for a fascinating, and at times slightly eerie, half an hour. I finally clambered out of the water and enjoyed another beer in the hot sun as we headed to our next stop: the island of Cubagua.

The island was a little slice of paradise. It had white-sand beaches dotted with occasional swaying palms and was surrounded by clear waters shimmering in the brilliant sun. There was next-to-no-proper infrastructure, with the exception of a big red-and-white-striped lighthouse and some small rustic fisherman's dwellings. Although virtually deserted today, the island was once a hub for pearl diving and had been the location of the first Spanish settlement in Venezuela. It was discovered by Christopher Columbus in 1498 and sustained a thriving community in the town of Nueva Cádiz until an earthquake destroyed it in 1541.

We moored up in the island's main bay where the more adventurous of the group–myself included–dived off the boat and swam ashore. The others caught an outboard dinghy into a small jetty and within minutes were lying prostrate on sun loungers laid out in readiness for their arrival. Here they were attentively served alcohol. I decided it rude not to join in with this important group activity, and so for the next couple of hours did nothing more taxing than drink bottled beer and iced rum and Coke, as the Caribbean waters lapped gently on the shoreline and myriad seabirds provided an ample source of curiosity in the clear blue sky above. It was a hard life but someone had to do it. I could get used to CouchSurfing.

After a while Luis pointed to another boat approaching the bay and gestured for me to follow him down the beach in its direction. Pulling up in a small dinghy was Miguel, who was leading passengers from the main boat ashore. He was doing his whole animated tourist guide routine, so could only exchange minimal pleasantries with us in the form of a subtle nod of the head. His group was much more purpose driven than Alfonso's chilled-out boozing assemblage, and was led by Miguel straight to a bog filled with thick mud. Following his lead, they began caking themselves in the stuff, having obviously been told of its medicinal or beautifying effects. This looked a laugh, so Luis and I dived in, literally. We came out covered from head to foot in the thick sludge, so much so that only our eyes and teeth remained uncovered. Within seconds I could feel the pleasant sensation of the mud contracting and cracking on my skin as it dried and lightened in the baking sun.

Miguel waved us over to take part in some posed group photos, at which point Alfonso brought a splattering of his troop over to join the fun. Accompanying him were the Russian and his lovely lady. The girl waded into the mud with Alfonso, while her other-half remained on the sidelines watching. When she got up to her waist in the mud, she requested, much to Alfonso's delight, that he help her apply the stuff to her upper back, shoulders, and even part of her neckline. Alfonso couldn't believe his luck and dutifully began smearing her with an attentive application. Her sugar daddy watched with a look that tried to convey nonchalant amusement, but which couldn't quite hide his unease at the far younger, charismatic, and handsome Alfonso getting to grips with his "bit of stuff." As if this wasn't enough, when it was time to wash the mud off, Alfonso helped her do so in the sea, this time rubbing his hands up her toned thighs and even fleetingly on her taught G-string exposed buttocks–something she and he appeared to be rather enjoying.

We ended up spending the best part of the day on the island, in which I generally took it easy, got quite drunk, and enjoyed the tranquility of the scenery. By the time we boarded the boat and headed back to Margarita, it was late afternoon. During the journey the crew marshaled us all to the rear of the boat for some sort of presentation when suddenly the surreal sound of the opening salvo from the *Village People's* "YMCA" struck up on the boat's speakers. Suddenly the doors of the lower deck burst open to reveal Alfonso dressed up as a camp biker, complete with leather hat, jacket, and pants, and sporting a fake handlebar moustache. Everyone laughed. As the track played, he began singing and dancing striptease-style as the rest of the boat clapped and sang along enthusiastically. Off came his hat and jacket to a rapturous cheer. He bent over, jiggled his ass from side to side, and then with a dramatic flicking motion pulled off his pants, which split along a Velcro seam, revealing a skimpy pair of Speedos underneath. Before the applause had subsided, he grabbed an alms box and went from person to person asking for tips. I reached into my pocket for a note, but when Alfonso got to my seat, he gave me a subtle wink and a shake of the head to tell me to abstain. Luis was familiar with the routine and left his wallet firmly where it was.

Back on terra firma we all caught the same chartered minibus, which stopped at various expensive resorts to drop off the satisfied-looking tourists. By the time we were on the road heading back to Los Robles, it was getting dark.

One of the things about CouchSurfing around a country is that in order to get a confirmed place to stay at your next destination, you need to check your e-mails regularly in case you've received an offer of accommodation or one has cancelled on you. There was no computer at Miguel's place, so on the journey back to Los Robles I asked about the Internet. When we arrived in town, the guys dropped me off outside a small Internet café around the corner from the town's main square and only a few blocks away from their house.

I logged on and received bad news from the CouchSurfer Erick, who had previously offered to put me up at my next destination in my loop around the country, Ciudad Bolívar. He could no longer accommodate me due to work commitments. This was a bit of a hassle as I had already contacted the other "surfers" in the area and come up with nothing. It looked like I was going to have to take the boring option and book into a hotel instead. I spent a good hour and a half online, and by the time I'd finished, it was pitch-black outside and the streets near deserted.

On my way back to Miguel's place something very uncharacteristic happened to me. I got lost. Extremely lost. I was convinced I knew the simple route back so paid only minimal attention as I strolled along on autopilot, rounding what I thought was the final corner that should have brought me face-to-face with Miguel's house, only to find that a completely different building stood in its place. The discovery really threw me, and for a while I stood perplexed as to where on earth I'd gone wrong.

As I remembered it, the route was straightforward, although not literally. To my recollection, it was past the church, turn left out of the main square, pass an abandoned lot containing a big mango tree and a tethered donkey, hang a left onto Miguel's road, round the corner, and hey presto, you were there. But I wasn't. How this happened I simply couldn't work out, as I was sure I had the route correct after walking it the night before with Miguel and then in reverse with Luis this morning. I retraced my steps back to the start of the lot. Looking around, I had no idea if the area was considered unsafe by Venezuela's standards, but it was certainly far from salubrious. In the dark it was now impossible to see the donkey or the mango tree.

Right, I thought to myself, *approach this logically*. There were several streets that backed onto the lot, so I figured it must have been a simple case of me getting Miguel's one confused. I decided to walk up all of these in a process of elimination. As I headed up the first one, I approached a group of guys playing cards and drinking beer at a white plastic table out the front of their home. I immediately became aware of how much I must have stuck out like a tourist, strolling around in the dark miles away from the nearest resort. Perhaps not surprisingly they all looked my way. I passed several other groups of people sitting out socializing, presumably to avoid the stifling heat indoors. After a couple of minutes it became apparent that this wasn't Miguel's street, so I turned back, receiving more curious stares on the return leg.

I repeated the process with the other streets and then in desperation decided to try the streets at the end of these, several of which were unlit. In the end I crisscrossed a good bit of the neighborhood, many parts multiple times. Not only was I no closer to locating Miguel's house, but by now it must be apparent to some of the people I had repeatedly walked past that I was lost. As a precaution against getting mugged, I minimized the cash in my wallet, stashing the excess into the discreet Velcro-sealed back pockets of my shorts.

I tried desperately to recall the route, but the more I thought about it, the more it seemed like my first route was correct. I decided to head back to the darkness-enveloped lot and try it again. It wasn't that I was expecting Miguel's house to miraculously appear where a different one had earlier been, but I hoped going back there would somehow jog my memory. It didn't. What it did was give me genuine cause for concern. As I walked along the edge of the lot, I spotted a group of guys in their late teens hanging out up ahead. As I got closer, I spotted the faint silhouette of a rifle held at waist height so that the butt was resting on the ground.

Shit.

Adrenaline flooded my system, racing around my veins as my heart began pounding heavily in my chest. *Am I about to get mugged?* I wondered. The group spotted me now, making an about-turn on my behalf all too obvious, so I had little choice but to continue towards them. I attempted to appear unfazed, and as if I knew exactly where I was going–easier said than done after walking around hopelessly lost for the last half an hour. When almost on top of them, I spotted, to my relief, that the gun was an air rifle–not that I'd have wanted one of those blasted in the face at close range, but it didn't quite hold the same sway over me as the high-velocity version.

Strolling past the group without incident, I wondered if I would get a rude awakening in the back of the head with a pellet. It never materialized, but it was enough to convince me to go back to the Internet café and try to find someone willing to let me use their phone.

This proved surprisingly easy, and in no time Miguel had met up with me outside the café. It was on exiting the square that I saw where my navigational error had occurred. On the right-hand side just before the lot that had been so fundamental to my navigation was a short unlit street leading in the opposite direction around the corner to . . . another entirely separate abandoned lot–the correct one. And of course just up the road from here was Miguel's house.

It was a great relief to pass through the gate and join the guys, who were sitting around in their shorts relaxing in the kitchen with a beer. Having spent the day with me, Alfonso was keen to ask me some questions and got Miguel to translate. Of particularly interest to him were my previous travels, especially when he heard I had visited Iran.

"Is it very dangerous?" he asked.

I explained that despite its image in much of the West, it was, in fact, an extremely safe country to travel in (if you ignore road traffic accidents) and that Venezuela was far more dangerous given its crime and murder rate. He seemed surprised at first but then annoyed, not at me but his own misconception.

"So it is just the bullshit lies of North America!" he exclaimed with disdain, through Miguel.

From out of nowhere the dogs in the courtyard erupted into aggressive barking. A moment later there was a crash at the padlocked gates. In an instant everybody was on red alert and had jumped up and run outside to investigate. Luis quickly scaled the house's single-story roof, perhaps with the intention of seeing down the street. I joined the others at the gates. Stumbling across the road away from the house was a drunk clutching his partially pulled-down pants, who, upon reaching the bushes opposite, began to relieve himself. From the pool of liquid just inside the courtyard it was clear he had been doing likewise through the metal gates and had then fallen over when the dogs inside scared the hell out of him. He was very lucky his junk hadn't ended up as the Alsatian's supper.

Back inside I asked the guys what they thought of Chávez. They liked him, although none would commit to calling themselves Chavistas–something generally reserved for his more politically active supporters. Miguel told me some of what he saw as Chávez's achievements. He mentioned the advances in health care and education as well as two government schemes he was potentially interested in taking part in one day. The first was the government's sponsorship of cooperatives, whereby if a group of people came up with an idea for a cooperative business–that is, a jointly owned venture run for the mutual benefit of those involved and often the community at large–they could approach the government for start-up loans to get the business off the ground. Once the relevant forms had been filled in, the funding would be all but guaranteed. This bypassed banks, who would normally only lend to wealthier customers with an approved credit history, or who would charge extortionate rates for those without one. The promotion of cooperatives is something that is enshrined in the country's constitution, which vows to "promote and protect" them. The scheme is generally considered a great success with there being only 763 cooperatives registered when Chávez first came to power, with there now being over 200,000. On the downside, at least for the government anyway, was that, according to Miguel, a lot of people formed such cooperative groups with no intention of really getting them off the ground, and only did so to receive the government grant. If the business then failed, they would not have to repay the money. A 2006 census backs this up, suggesting that as many as half of the registered cooperatives could be "phantom cooperatives" or ones that do not function properly–either way that still leaves a good 100,000 functioning cooperatives that have transformed people's lives for the better, something which before Chávez's presidency would have seemed impossible. Creating a phantom cooperative was something Miguel said he did not agree with and would never do himself, saying that he would only consider starting one if convinced the business had potential.

Another scheme he told me of was one whereby if you raised a nominal amount of capital to buy a house, the government would then put up the rest of the money to subsidize the purchase. You could then pay a mortgage to the government at a far more agreeable rate than available from a commercial bank. For those on a low income, the government provided a subsidy of roughly U.S.$9,000 to help with the purchase. One of Miguel's good friends had recently taken part in the scheme and was now the proud owner of his own apartment, something which, without government assistance, he wouldn't have had a chance of doing. This allows people without credit ratings or sizable deposits to escape continuous tenancy.

We spent the rest of the night chatting away, swapping stories on each other's travels and adventures, of which Miguel had had many, having traveled budget-style around Bolivia, Chile, Colombia, Ecuador, Peru, and Argentina. When I finally hit the sack, I was tired but happy after a top-notch day.

I was beginning to see what the lifestyle on Margarita was all about when the following morning we did much the same as the day before–hung out at the beach. This time on Margarita itself. Miguel, Luis, and I traveled by bus to a tourist beach that couldn't have been more different to the tranquil ambience on Cubagua Island. It was teaming with vacationers. Here people reclined topping up their tans, nursed cocktails at numerous beachfront bars, cooled off in the glistening tropical waters, and strutted their stuff to impress members of the opposite sex.

We met up with a middle-aged friend of Miguel and Luis, who owned a bar that backed onto the sand, and with their friend, Santos. Santos spoke good English and was quite a character. He had an ultragroomed "metrosexual" look with not a hair out of place on his head or goatee beard and not a hair in sight on his waxed body, which was tanned all over and greased up to encourage more of the same. He wore a silver and black crucifix around his neck and the self-assured grin of a man who rates himself with the ladies. To me he brought to mind someone parodying a Latino Casanova type, but Santos wasn't acting.

"Jamie, let me tella you," he said, rolling his words together in a strong Latino twang. "In Venezuela, there's a lotta poosy. A lotta possy!" He grasped his thumb and fingers together in an upwards gesture, which he bobbed slightly up and down while nodding in satisfied agreement with himself.

"You come visit me in Barquisimeto. We go party, I show you around, let people know you're with me, you'll get plenty poosy too. Venezuelan girls love Europeans!"

I laughed.

Barquisimeto is in the west of the country in the general direction I planned to travel later. I told him I'd consider it.

"We stay in touch on the CouchSurfing. I make the plan, yeah?" He grinned and nodded to himself again in the same self-satisfied manner as before.

Despite Santos being a complete and utter numpty, I kind of liked the guy.

Being on Margarita Island, I felt it appropriate to indulge in a margarita cocktail and, before heading to the bar, offered to buy Santos a drink. He politely declined with an explanation only he could come up with.

"I'm in training for Mr. Fitness competition," he stated, before quickly pointing out, as if to put my mind at rest, "I'm naturally well proportioned, but need to be careful before an event."

I'd never heard of such a thing so inquired what a Mr. Fitness competition was. It sounded a rather confusing practice mixing modeling, dancing, and bodybuilding for those who weren't quite bodybuilder stature but had an ego more than sufficient to make up for it.

On my return from the bar Santos and I sauntered up the beach, and as we walked, Santos told me his life's dream.

"I wanna open Ibiza-style bar in Venezuela, with wet T-shirt competitions and chill-out music."

When I asked if he had any experience in the hospitality industry, he listed for me, in all sincerity, what he saw as his qualifications for the job.

"I like partying, women, chill-out music, and the beach. So I think I'd be good at it."

I didn't doubt he'd enjoy hanging out at a beachfront watering hole with a bevy of beauties, but wasn't quite sure this counted as an adequate qualification for the rigors of inventories, dealing with suppliers, managing staff, organizing the payroll or filing business taxes, etc.

We continued on up the beach, with Santos scanning for scantily clad young ladies as we went, until we reached a large flashy-looking bar filled with partiers. Flying on a flagpole high above the establishment was a skull and crossbones, under which was written, in English, Surrender Your Booty!

"What does 'surrender your booty' mean?" Santos asked inquisitively.

I laughed.

"That all depends on your interpretation of the word *booty*."

After explaining the two differing connotations, Santos came up with an idea for his future bar.

"I could have 'surrender your booty' written on the wall, and on one side have a picture of a treasure chest and on the other side have a nice tight ass!" He mimed grasping the aforementioned posterior. Maybe he was cut out to run a bar after all.

As much as I could have happily spent all my remaining time on Margarita relaxing at the beach, there were, unfortunately, a few more mundane things I had to organize before heading off tomorrow to my next destination, Ciudad Bolívar–namely, getting hold of some antimalarial drugs. Ciudad Bolívar was mainly used by travelers as a stop-off point en route to Angel Falls, somewhere I planned to go and had read beforehand that you needed antimalarial medication, as well as a yellow fever vaccination, to visit.

I had acquired the vaccination back in the U.K. but had failed to get the antimalarials before departure. Miguel gave me the necessary bus information to get to Porlamar, and after arranging to meet the guys this evening, I headed on over.

At the various drugstores in Porlamar they didn't have the required medication and all of them recommended I go to the hospital to get a vaccine instead. I'd never heard of a jab for malaria before, so when I was told this by an assistant at the first store, I assumed my query had got lost in translation. This seemed likely as after leaving my phrase book at Miguel's, I was restricted to inquisitively asking, "Malaria?" while miming popping pills. The assistant had spoken a tiny bit of English and responded with something that sounded like "amalaria" rather than "malaria" and then recommended I go to the hospital to get a jab. After several identical "amalaria" responses from different drugstores, and more or less identical recommendations to visit the hospital up the road, I concluded it must be me who was mistaken and that there was a jab for malaria after all.

The hospital was an interesting place with big long narrow corridors, sections of which were separated by barred metal doors manned by security guards, giving the place a sort of prisonlike feel despite it being a center for healing. After getting thoroughly confused and lost in the labyrinth of corridors, I finally managed to locate the tropical diseases department and went about my inquisitive "Malaria?" routine. A female nurse led me through to a side room and gestured for me to sit down. She spoke no English, so communication had to be through gesture and mime alone, and although it took a couple of minutes, I finally established that she needed to see my passport before the vaccination could be administered.

Shit.

Despite my run-in with the police in Caracas, and having subsequently made a photocopy of my passport, it dawned on me that I'd left the photocopy in the shorts I'd worn yesterday. I indicated this to the nurse, and she gave a reluctant shake of the head, as if to say, "Sorry. Then there's nothing I can do."

I really didn't want to traipse all the way back to Miguel's place so tried the sympathy vote and attempted pleading. She fetched one of her colleagues from the department's reception who spoke a smidgeon of English, and after a protracted effort in which both of us generally frustrated the other, I managed to decipher that I was being asked whether I had a national ID card instead.

I didn't, but thought "what the hell" and opened my wallet for something suitable to pass off as such. But what to use? I had an old train ticket, my U.K. ATM card, a *Nectar Points* shopping reward card, an outdated annual membership card for a skydive club, a London subway pass, an outdated horticultural college ID, and a small prayer card with a picture of the Virgin Mary on it–something my mother had insisted I carry before going traveling. My mum's sweet like that but my beloved late granny took the protective powers of religious paraphernalia to a different level, insisting that it was unnecessary for her to wear a seat belt in her car since she regularly sprinkled the vehicle with holy water.

I decided that whatever I presented as an ID card had to be one with a picture on it. This narrowed it down to the college ID and the Virgin Mary prayer card. Since I looked nothing like the angelic image on the latter, I handed over the college card. I didn't hold out much hope that they'd buy it, but after a quick cursory glance the nurse began scribbling down the reference number and gestured for me to recline in readiness for my jab. Moments later she had rolled up my sleeve and was ready to puncture my arm. Before she did, I thought it prudent to check a final time that I was being administered the correct vaccine and asked again "Malaria?" receiving, as before, although this time in reassuring tones, "Amalaria, amalaria." That was good enough for me. I nodded my consent and in went the needle. A second later I was signing a small booklet, which the nurse then stamped and handed back to me to keep, presumably detailing the procedure.

When I brought out my wallet to pay for the medication, the nurse waved me off. I was aware that Venezuela had free universal health care but had assumed as a foreigner I'd have to pay. On my way out I double-checked at the department's reception.

"No charge," the receptionist announced proudly.

Porlamar was crazy busy with a vast shopping district packed with Venezuelans taking advantage of its duty-free status. It was far from attractive; in fact it was a scruffy and rather run-down urban sprawl, and as it was a blisteringly hot day, I decided to lose the crowds and head to the seafront, in the hope of finding a cooling breeze and somewhere to grab a cold drink. The part of the coast I stumbled upon didn't have much in the way of either. What I found instead was a large crowd of red-shirted Chavistas congregated outside a municipal building. They stood listening to a speech from an animated woman in her late thirties who was dressed in similar garb. I went over to see what was going on.

The speech meant nothing to me, but every so often it received a rapturous applause from those in attendance. After roughly ten minutes the woman concluded her talk at which point the crowd began chanting together in solidarity.

The gathering disbanded soon after, but many remained in the vicinity socializing. I must have stuck out in my white polo shirt and fisherman's hat, as within seconds I was approached by a tall muscular man of about my age wearing a T-shirt emblazoned with an image of Chávez, triumphantly raising his fist in the air. I didn't have a clue what he said but it was clear from his mannerisms and welcoming smile that he was extremely friendly. He brought to mind a gentle giant. I asked if he spoke English.

"Si, señor," he said, so I decided to stick around for a chat.

It soon became apparent that he spoke very little English, as evident from the responses he gave to many of my questions: "Yes, sir."

When I told him I liked his T-shirt, he managed, "We have given our lives to Chávez." I'd heard of people giving their lives to God but never to a politician, and wondered if this rather fanatical reply was the result of his limited English or a genuine sentiment.

It didn't take long before it was clear we'd reached the limit of our dialogue, so I bade him farewell and headed off in search of transport back to Miguel's place. It took some protracted wandering before I determined the correct bus, and by the time I arrived in the main square of Miguel's town, it was beginning to get dark.

As I approached the gates of Miguel's house, the dogs began barking, alerting everyone inside to my presence.

"Did you get your pills?" asked Miguel, as he strode towards me to unlock the gates.

"I got a jab instead."

"You got a *jab* for malaria?"

As he undid the padlock, I handed him the card I'd been given at the hospital. When inside the light of the kitchen, he had a look at it.

"They've given you a yellow fever vaccination, not a malaria one," he stated emphatically.

I couldn't believe it. Miguel was adamant this was what the card said. It was then that I noticed that the card was almost identical to the one I'd received when getting my original yellow fever jab in English, being printed on a similar yellow background.

What a complete and utter fuckup. I wondered if there were any side effects to getting two yellow fever jabs in such close proximity. After all, I'd now received 100 percent more than the recommended dose, so perhaps that was a problem.

"Why didn't you check with the hospital staff?" Miguel asked.

I explained that I had indeed done this and that they'd responded to my inquisitive "malaria?" with a confirmatory "amalaria."

Miguel enlightened me to the problem.

"In Spanish yellow fever is *fiebre amarilla.* They weren't saying *amalaria,* but *amarilla.*"

I was not best pleased. However, there was little point worrying about it now as I could hardly undo the vaccination process. I was leaving Margarita early tomorrow morning, so I wouldn't be able to reenquire at the hospital about tablets either, and knowing my luck, if I did, it would probably get lost in translation and I'd end up on the operating table.

Miguel lightened my mood soon after by rustling up a delicious farewell meal of squid and pasta. The rest of the household joined us and we ate around the kitchen table before adjourning to the cooler veranda with a couple of ice-cold beers. It was the perfect way to end a wonderful stay with a generous and welcoming host. When it was time to hit the sack, Miguel got me to sign his Couch-Surfing guest book, which was packed with grateful messages from previous appreciative guests, understandably singing his praises. I exchanged fond farewells with Miguel and the rest of the household and thanked everyone for their generosity over what had been a couple of really enjoyable days. I hoped the next few weeks would prove just as enjoyable, and malaria free.

CHAPTER 7

Jungle Fever

A gentle breeze dancing off an iridescent Caribbean cooled me at the quayside of Punta de Piedras, where I sat eating a hearty breakfast of fresh empanadas, purchased from a street vendor nearby. I had arrived here early in the hope of reaching the mainland by midmorning, but had received bad news from a stern-looking woman in the ferry terminal's ticket office that the next available ferry wouldn't depart for three hours.

After finishing up my breakfast at the quayside, I decided to head back to the terminal, where I was greeted by the biggest cavalcade of motorbikes I had ever seen. There were a good couple of hundred vehicles, making their way onto an awaiting ferry, revving their engines as they went, causing an ear-splitting roar and a choking cloud of exhaust. The riders were all in police fatigues and rode standard-issue bikes, having presumably finished their detail after the culmination of the Africa–South America Summit, from which Chávez and the other world leaders had now departed. Accompanying the bikers were hundreds of foot soldiers who double-timed it up the gangway and onto the ferry.

Security must have been incredibly tight for the conference. I wondered how much this had been for the foreign leaders and how much for Chávez's own safety. Following the failed coup of 2002, Chávez references his safety frequently, often accusing the United States of plotting to assassinate him. And he's got genuine cause for concern. Three and a half years after the coup, Chávez and his Bolivarian Revolution were hysterically labeled by U.S. Army publication *Doctrine for Asymmetric War against Venezuela* as the "largest threat since the Soviet Union and Communism."[28]

Militarily, Chávez poses no threat to the might of the United States, so what crime has he committed to warrant such continued wrath from his foes from the North? There is much Chávez has done to antagonize the United States–branding the invasion and occupation of Afghanistan as "fighting terrorism with terrorism," holding up pictures of slaughtered Afghani children on national TV, selling discounted oil to Cuba, denying U.S. counter-drug flights access to Venezuelan airspace, asking the U.S. military mission in Caracas to vacate its headquarters, and refusing to cooperate in the U.S. war against Colombian guerrillas. But to understand the biggest long-term threat posed by Chávez to the United States, it is first necessary to understand the true nature of two pillars of economic power and control in Washington that Chávez has openly challenged and disrupted–the International Monetary Fund (IMF) and the World Bank.

The IMF and the World Bank were conceived towards the end of World War II at a conference held at Bretton Woods, New Hampshire, in order to fund the reconstruction of a devastated Europe. The IMF was created to provide the winners of the war with somewhere they could borrow hard currency to meet their short-term trading interests. The World Bank was created to provide capital for reconstruction and development projects in Europe. Later on the IMF and World Bank began to loan money to poor countries.

Today both institutions–which are best understood as different sides of the same coin–have transmuted into something very different from their original remit. Despite claiming to help the poor, they are, in reality, an instrument of power for the nations controlling the institution's greatest voting rights–the principal one being the United States.

Both the World Bank and IMF are based in Washington and were set up primarily by the United States and Britain. The head of the World Bank is nearly always American and is chosen by the U.S. president. The U.S. Treasury owns 51 percent of the bank, and the United States is the only nation that possesses a permanent veto on World Bank policies. The United States controls the largest quota at the IMF and is the only nation that can veto major policy decisions by itself. Chávez has described the IMF and World Bank as "tools of the empire" which only serve "the interests of the North." And he's right.

It was in the 1980s that the IMF and World Bank began their dramatic metamorphism into the tools of empire they are today. With Ronald Reagan in the White House and Margaret Thatcher in Downing Street, the banks began to push the president and prime minister's chosen ideology of "free-market neoliberalism." And they haven't stopped since.

Following huge fivefold increases in the price of oil and a similar increase in interest payments on the dollar, the early eighties saw many poor countries approach the IMF for emergency loans. What they got was loan sharking. In return for loans, debtor nations were forced to sign up to "Structural Adjustment Programs" demanding extreme restructuring of their national economies–something that proved catastrophic for the people of the countries but hugely profitable for U.S. and European corporations.

Such imposed restructuring, which continues to be forced on nations today, generally follows the same pattern: minimize the role of the state in just about everything; slash budgets and government departments; privatize state-owned assets such as water and electricity, and then let the market dictate the price of these essential utilities for consumers; sell national banks and deregulate the currency; permit currency speculation and allow capital to move unhindered over borders; remove all trade barriers; allow foreign corporations unlimited access to your markets; get rid of subsidies but permit heavily subsidized foreign products to flood your country; cut social spending on everything from welfare to pensions, from health care to education; pass "flexible" labor laws that destroy workers' rights and wages but increase hours. In general, deregulate everything and put corporations before people.

In countries where such IMF "Structural Adjustment Programs" have been implemented, the effects on the poor have been disastrous. Take, for example, the forced wholesale privatization of state-owned assets such as water systems. Such utilities were often invested in over decades through pubic taxes but sold for a fraction of their true market value to multinational corporations who predictably put shareholder profit above the needs of the populace. In country after country where this happened, water prices and service costs soared, often by inhuman amounts–in Argentina charges rose by as much as 400 percent, and in Bolivia[29] the cost of getting connected to the system equated, for many, to a year's salary.

Under these conditions your options are simple: pay up or get your water from a puddle or natural catch–often contaminated with viruses and bacteria, many of which cause diarrhea. With diarrhea being the single biggest killer of children under five in poor countries (3,900 children–about twenty jumbo jets full–die daily for lack of clean water[30]), such "conditionalities" from the IMF and World Bank are virtual death sentences.

But don't take my word for it. Former chief economist at the World Bank Joseph Stiglitz, who was fired for speaking out against the bank, admitted that "the whole system was rigged against the poor countries, rigged for the advanced industrial countries." Stiglitz, who won the Nobel Prize in Economics, charges that the bank's policies "condemned people to death" and that they "don't care if people live or die."

Award-winning investigative journalist Greg Palast, who has written extensively about the IMF and World Bank in his books *The Best Democracy Money Can Buy* and *Armed Madhouse*, obtained numerous secret internal documents from within the World Bank and IMF which lay bare the organizations' true agendas. Despite the confidential papers having fluffy titles like "Poverty Reduction Strategy" and "Country Assistance Strategy," they detail, point by point, how the IMF and World Bank implement what amount to financial coups d'état–turning nations' presidents or prime ministers into powerless figureheads subservient to corporate demands, where a virtual government of lenders, investors, and bankers set the county's policies.

The documents obtained by Palast are economic prescriptions for individual nations, all of which follow the same four-step plan: *privatization, capital market liberalization, market-based pricing*, and *free trade.*

Privatization. This stage Stiglitz described to Palast as "briberization"–a reference to the practice of government officials receiving tantalizing commissions for selling off their nation's assets at bargain basement prices. "You could see their eyes widen" at the prospect, says Stiglitz.

To give you an idea of how rampant such corruption is, a World Bank internal report on Indonesia makes clear that somewhere in the region of 30 percent of all loans made by the bank to the Suharto regime were either lost or stolen. "At least 20–30% of government of Indonesia development budget funds are diverted through informal payments to government staff & politicians," states the document.[31] When Suharto's genocidal dictatorship (which killed up to a million people[32] and was supported by the United States, Britain, and Australia) came to an end, he personally took with him an estimated fifteen billion dollars,[33] roughly 13 percent of the nation's entire foreign debt, a large proportion of which is owed to the World Bank. Regardless of where it went, the Indonesian people still have to pay it back, at crippling interest, of course

Capital market liberalization. This is technical jargon for saying ridding a nation of all controls regulating the movement of money in and out of the country. The claimed logic behind this is that it smoothes the way for investment capital to flow between countries. However, all too often it just smoothes the way for speculative money to flow out of a poor nation, which drains at the first sign of trouble as investors panic sell their assets, sending the money abroad. The country's economy is then left in tatters with its reserves bled dry, something that can occur in a matter of days, or even hours. In the case of Argentina, at least $189 billion in savings departed this way.[34]

The ever-caring IMF now moves in with demands that the country jack up interest rates–sometimes by as much as 80 percent[35]–in order to entice speculative money back. Local industry then becomes paralyzed and property prices plummet–providing a prime opportunity for foreign vultures to swoop on some greatly reduced bargains.

Market-based pricing. This helpful measure is the elimination of subsidies on products such as food and fuel, causing prices to hit the roof and sparking riots of desperation from the hopeless population. This, however, comes as no surprise to the heartless World Bank, who even predicts riots as a consequence of their plans. In a confidential document obtained by Palast on Ecuador, the bank states clearly that its program of raising domestic gas prices would likely cause "social unrest." According to Stiglitz, such predictable unrest was referred to at the bank as an "IMF riot."

But it's not all bad news, for a country on its knees provides another bonanza for foreign corporations to acquire the nation's remaining assets for pennies on the dollar. The greater the chaos, the greater and easier the consolidation. And if the government of the nation in flames fails to meet its original debt repayment conditions–which are intentionally set to be unreachable–then the country has to renegotiate a new IMF loan with tighter and tighter "conditionalities." And so the cycle continues.

Free trade. This sort of trade is, of course, anything but "free," and is something Stiglitz compares to the Opium Wars, where the British Empire forced Chinese markets open at gunpoint. It sees the IMF forcing nations to open their markets to foreign trade, often heavily subsidized in its country of origin. The market is then flooded with cheap foreign goods against which local producers cannot compete.

In desperation, poor countries often attempt to compete against each other as the cheapest source of similar "cash crops." With many poor nations in the same predicament, large-scale price wars ensue, making resources even cheaper for the lucky Western consumer.

In Jamaica, the imposing of "free" trade saw the decimation of the country's farming and dairy industries as it became swamped with cheap subsidized produce and powdered milk from North America. Mass unemployment resulted, and it is now nearly impossible to get fresh milk in Jamaica.[36] Such cheap foreign products result in increased imports, which in turn cause the nation's debt to rise further.

So why do countries agree to such devastating plans? If you ignore "briberization," then it's really no different to why someone accepts extortionate interest rates from a loan shark. If you're desperate enough for money and the private banks won't lend to you, then you're left with little choice. You either agree to the terms or starve. Since the World Bank controls a country's access to credit, they can, just like a loan shark, impose any conditions they want. And once you've signed on the dotted line, they've got you.

The danger that Chávez poses to this system of economic imperialism is the ever-dangerous "threat of a good example." Chávez stands in stark defiance of the IMF and World Bank's "free"-market madness–the imposition of which set the streets of Venezuela ablaze in 1989–and rejects their advice out of hand. In so doing he provides a viable alternative development model, distinct from Washington and the agenda of rapacious corporate power.

It is an alternative model that puts people ahead of profits, and one that has much support in Latin America. Since Chávez first came to power in 1998, the continent has seen a surge of left-leaning presidents elected to office. Many of whom have strongly allied themselves with him.

When the economies of Ecuador and Argentina were left in ruins by World Bank and IMF policies, it was Chávez who came to the rescue. In Ecuador, the banks demanded successive corporate-friendly prescriptions, insisting on greater and greater "free"-market policies with every preceding plan's failure–wreaking havoc with the country in the process. The details of these "remedies" are set out in a number of confidential documents obtained by Palast, under such headings as "Ecuador Interim Country Assistance Strategy." One "strategy" ordered the government to increase the cost of cooking gas by 80 percent. Another to cut twenty-six thousand jobs and slash by 50 percent the wages of those lucky enough to have avoided the initial cull. Other helpful remedies included forcing Ecuador to sell off its largest water system. No prizes for guessing what happened to the bills. Additional plans called for jumps in the cost of electricity and food and the sacking of 120,000 workers.

It was following the World Bank and IMF's demands that Ecuador change its currency to the U.S. dollar that the country's banks collapsed. After adopting the U.S. currency, money bled from the country as the rich spirited away their greenbacks to U.S. banks. (Ecuador now has to borrow, at interest, the very currency used on its streets.) The IMF then added a massive additional debt on the country by forcing it to rescue the private stockholders of the failed banks.

In desperation Ecuador's president pleaded with the World Bank and IMF to let him use a little of the country's vast oil wealth for essential social spending such as health care and education, as opposed to paying off the speculators who owned the country's bonds, most of whom were pocketing a 500 percent profit on their initial outlay. Another confidential document surreptitiously acquired by Palast from the World Bank makes clear that this was not an option. In it the bank lays out how the county's oil wealth from a new pipeline would be divvied up:

> *Ten percent to social spending; 20 percent for contingencies . . . ; and 70 percent to debt buybacks, not for regularly scheduled budget amortizations.*

Since the "contingencies" bit was to pay for an "oil stabilization fund" (an insurance policy for the bondholders), the government would receive just 10 percent for crucial social obligations–the 70 percent debt buyback is for the speculators holding the bonds. For merely having the temerity to suggest that a larger proportion of Ecuador's petrodollars could be diverted to help the country's poor, the World Bank and IMF cut Ecuador off. In order to save the country from credit oblivion, Chávez came to the rescue with $200 million to purchase Ecuador's debt and restore confidence in its bond market.[37] His generosity didn't end there. Chávez also provided some two million barrels of oil, naphtha, and diesel to the stricken country. This played a crucial role in keeping Ecuador functioning during a period when the country's oil production facilities were occupied by disgruntled protesters.[38]

When Argentina's banks suffered a similar fate–after years of following IMF and World Bank prescriptions–Chávez provided $500 million to buy up the country's bonds.[39] It was for this that *The Wall Street Journal* dubbed Chávez "a tropical version of the International Monetary Fund."

Interestingly, after the coup d'état of 2002 to remove Chávez, the IMF rubber-stamped the short-lived illegal dictatorship by declaring, "We stand ready to assist the new administration in whatever manner they find suitable."[40] In so doing, they effectively revealed that the U.S. government also approved the dictatorship since the IMF would never make such an announcement without prior U.S. governmental approval.

When not helping distraught nations get out from under the jackboot of institutionalized loan sharks, Chávez finds plenty of other ways to ruffle the feathers of the elite. On his return to office following his temporary incarceration during the 2002 coup, Chávez's economic reforms and social programs gathered pace. He raised the minimum wage by 20 percent and threw out privatization of the country's water system. He withdrew a cool $20 billion from the U.S. Federal Reserve, which was placed in the Bank for International Settlements for investment in Latin America, and entered into lucrative deals with state-run oil companies from India, China, and Brazil. Other laws abhorrent to the neoliberal free marketers have been the requirement of the country's private banks to set aside 20 percent of their loans for "microcredit"–loans to small businesses and the poor–and the repealing of the World Bank and IMF's beloved "capital market liberalization," that is, a restriction on the movement of capital across Venezuela's borders.

Contrary to their ruinous expectations, *The Wall Street Journal* reported that the controls

> *trapped liquidity within the country, which in part led to reduced interest rates and helped boost economic activity.*

Since Venezuela is currently, like most of the world, suffering the effects of the global downturn, such achievements have been conveniently swept under the carpet by those that oppose Chávez. With such a president in control of a country which at times has been the largest exporter of oil to the United States, it is not hard to see why those in Washington's corridors of power want to see Chávez and his "Bolivarian Revolution" fail. A brightly burning example of freedom and opportunity distinct from foreign domination and the economic order imposed by Washington is too powerful an influence to be left unchecked.

* * *

By the time the ferry docked in Margarita, it was already past midday, making my likely arrival on the mainland midafternoon, and in Ciudad Bolívar sometime after midnight. I got myself a window seat and relaxed as we cruised back to Puerto La Cruz. En route an enthused commotion broke out on the opposite side of the ferry with a group of passengers pointing excitedly into the water. I headed over to investigate. In the water below, slicing through the glassy sea like erratic miniature torpedoes was a shimmering pod of dolphins. Every so often one would break the surface with an explosive arching leap, emerging from the turquoise depths into the brilliant sun like a glistening and hallowed apparition. With every skyward bound the spectators gasped and whooped in delight. I wondered whether our mammal brothers in the water somehow sensed the pleasure they were eliciting on board. The dolphins' constant enigmatic smiles made me hope that they did. When they finally darted off, disappearing into the eternity of ocean, I retook my seat with a satisfied smile of my own.

It was something of a relief when the ferry finally reached the mainland and docked in Puerto la Cruz. I was significantly behind schedule and wanted to get on the road, so after a quick consultation with my guidebook's map, I started the long, hard hike to the coach station. The weight of my pack and the relentless sun soon had me sweating profusely. By the time I reached the station, I was feeling quite light-headed and surprisingly fatigued. I began to wonder whether I was coming down with something.

The station was a dirty, grimy hive of activity located in a rather run-down and uninspiring end of town. Its interior left me bewildered. A sea of people flowed between scores of dingy little offices, each of which housed a different bus company. The offices serviced different destinations, although some of these overlapped, with certain operators offering cheaper or better quality rides along a given route. I couldn't see any that advertized Ciudad Bolívar so popped into a random office and asked.

"No," was the contemptuous reply I received from a craggy-faced individual whose cowboy-booted feet rested on the office desk. He chewed away with a swaggering motion at a piece of gum, causing the muscles of his upper jaw to bulge unnaturally with every exaggerated chew.

With my best "lost tourist" face, I gestured inquisitively to the other offices in the hope of getting pointed in the right direction. He dismissed me with an almost imperceptible shrug of the shoulders. Thanks, mate. It required a further three attempts at different offices before I found someone willing and able to assist.

The recommended company was all locked up, but luckily for me a neighboring company's employee got me to wait while he went to fetch the necessary individual. The man in question, who looked Arabic in origin, approached eating a phonebook-thick sandwich.

All business was conducted outside the office, and although he didn't speak English, it was clear where I wanted to go from my unambiguous assertions of "Ciudad Bolívar." In order to free up his hands to fill out a ticket for me from a booklet in his pocket, the man stuffed the sandwich in his mouth, clamping it tight in the process. As he passed me the ticket, an unlikely bit of luck occurred. A guy in his early twenties selling chips and other snacks a couple of feet away leaned in and casually stated in good English, "Don't pay more than forty-five bolivars," before leaning out again.

Whether he did this to help me or to annoy the guy with the sandwich stuffed in his mouth, I don't know, but he achieved both. The ticket stated seventy bolivars, so I immediately protested the figure. I was kind of expecting a bit of animated resistance from the seller, but he quickly conceded without a fight–throwing the snack vendor a scowl as he changed the ticket to the correct amount.

When the bus arrived an hour later, I started to take a turn for the worse. I was beginning to feel feverish–something hardly helped by the roasting temperature. Soon after taking a seat, the guy in front of me, whom I had spoken to briefly when the bus arrived in order to confirm I had the right one, turned around and in broken English asked me where I was from. As the bus departed the station, the two of us went through the usual pleasantries before he warned me to be extremely careful in Ciudad Bolívar at night. It was, apparently, essential that I take an official cab from the bus station. We would be arriving after midnight, so I intended to heed this warning and decided to check up on my guidebook for a suitable place to stay. I circled a budget option in the historic part of the city and asked my fellow passenger how much a cab would cost to get there. Instead of just telling me the price–no more than fifteen bolivars–he wrote down on a scrap of paper the exact phrase I should say to the driver in order to make it appear that I spoke fluent Spanish and was therefore familiar with the correct price.

Written down was "Puedas tocarme al posada Don Carlos."

He practiced this with me several times, correcting my pronunciation in the process, until satisfied I could pull it off. I thanked him and then tried to get my head down for some sleep. As the journey continued and dusk passed into night, I began to feel progressively worse. I curled up as best I could but my swooning head made sleep impossible. After what felt like an eternity, I received a rousing shake from the guy in front of me. He was getting off at the next stop but informed me he had instructed one of the coach staff sitting at the front of the bus to find a taxi for me at Ciudad Bolívar. He wished me well, and I him, before departing. What a nice guy.

I retrieved his scribbled phrase and repeated it over and over in the hope of sounding convincing when dealing with the cabby. Maybe it was the mantralike repetition, maybe fatigue, but soon after I fell asleep.

The coach's bright internal lights shone in my face, startling me to disoriented consciousness as a stampede of passengers noisily made for the vehicle's exits. We'd arrived in downtown Ciudad Bolívar at just after half past midnight. I felt awful. My head throbbed, I was extremely feverish and on the cusp of vomiting. As I stood upright, the world seemed to spin and pulsate in a sickening rhythm around and through me. I grabbed the nearest headrest to steady myself and remained stationary in the aisle as I tried desperately not to be sick. A prod in the back from the passenger behind cut this short and got me shuffling towards the exit steps. I departed the bus in a state of significant confusion into the chaos of the terminal where passengers were crowded around collecting bags, meeting friends, and making connections. Before I could get my head together, the coach assistant grabbed me and thrust me towards a waiting cabby.

Shit. What was the phrase again?

I stared forlornly at the cabby for a second as I tried to remember. My mind went blank. I retrieved the paper from my pocket and handed it to him in defeat. So much for sounding like I spoke Spanish.

After picking up my pack, which seemed to have grown in weight several times over, the cabby walked me through the terminal. All I could think about was bed and not being sick before I got there. We passed a row of shiny official taxis making our way to a secluded section of the terminal where several battered-looking unofficial cabs were parked. One of these was his. I didn't know what to do. I hardly had the energy to walk back through the station and go through the rigmarole of finding and negotiating with another cabby, and so, in what was a rash and potentially stupid decision, I decided, against my better judgment, to get it.

He gestured me to sit up front in the passenger seat next to him. I declined and decided to sit directly behind him, just in case he tried anything. The car stank of gasoline. We pulled off into the streets, many of which were unlit and nearly all of which were completely deserted, giving the place an eerie atmosphere. I wondered if I'd just made a very foolish decision but I was feeling too sick to care. After all, I'd been warned not to get an unofficial cab by a local, and here I was doing the exact opposite. I didn't have a clue where we were, so if the driver did have ill intent, then it would hardly be difficult for him to pull out a gun and rob me before dumping me in the middle of some equally dangerous area. And in my current state I would hardly be in a position to do much about it.

I had other more immediate priorities though. The main one, not being sick. Every corner or rock of the cab nearly sent me over the edge, and I found myself willing the driver to arrive at our destination, wherever that might be, in order to end the nauseating motion of the car. After fifteen minutes we approached what looked like the historic part of town. We pulled up by what I assumed was my hotel–or "posada" as they're known in Venezuela–opposite a square containing a large church and several colonial buildings. As the car came to a standstill, it almost made me feel worse. It was as if the world was now stationary but somehow the external rocking motion of the journey was continuing and being amplified inside of me. I knew I wasn't going to be able to hold on much longer.

I was about to get out of the car but the cabby motioned for me to stay put. Getting out himself, he rang the bell of the posada, which, like the other buildings along the street, backed right onto the sidewalk. Thanks to a plaque on the wall I now noticed that this was not the posada I had asked for. I was just about to vocalize this for him but before I got the chance, a man opened the shutters of the posada's upper windows. Within seconds the man at the window was shouting venomously at the cabby. And with good reason. He'd been woken up at nearly one in the morning simply to be asked for directions to his competitor's posada. He was none too happy and, after a minute of infuriated yelling, slammed the shutters again.

It was a shame as I'd have happily stayed here instead; in fact I would have stayed anywhere as all I really wanted to do was lie down, but ringing the bell again to enquire about rooms didn't seem the wisest of options. The driver looked completely lost and in the end I was the one who worked out where to go. My guidebook contained a small map of the town which had both this posada and the one we were trying to find marked on it. I got the driver to get back in and, after a little map reading, had located the place and was standing face-to-face with the establishment's night porter.

The driver ended up charging me twenty-five bolivars, but by this stage I didn't care and just wanted to be horizontal without throwing up. I staggered inside and was directed to a guest book to sign and give my details. Everything was a bit of a haze but within minutes the porter was unlocking the door to a basic room containing two single beds, a large fan, and a shower room and toilet.

I turned on the fan to try and get some air circulating in the furnacelike, hot, and humid interior. The temperature was no surprise given Ciudad Bolívar's reputation as one of the hottest places in Venezuela. I stripped off naked in an attempt to cool down. I lay on the bed, my temples and forehead throbbing as if rocks protruded from under them, building like an internal force in my skull until it felt ready to explode. The world began to spin again, but I knew this time I was going to be sick. I struggled to my feet. Crashing through the bathroom door, I stumbled to the sink, grasping hard onto its unyielding china surface in readiness for the discomfort to come.

I retched violently, my head pounding with each convulsing heave, every one of which was accompanied by a strange and disturbing internal flash of light akin to the "stars" you see after banging your head, only far brighter. I vomited repeatedly and uncontrollably. By the time I'd finished, I was drenched in sweat and gasping for a drink. My only option was the tap, but I knew the water was unsafe to drink. Reluctantly, I fetched my mini water purifier pump, mug, and water bottle from my bag. Using the pump under normal circumstances was relatively easy, involving little more than a couple of minutes of concerted pumping. But in my present condition it was a task I far from relished.

I filled the mug with water and placed one of the filter's two rubber tubes in it before dropping the other in the bottle. As I began pumping, it sucked the water from the mug, processing it through the filter and infusing it with iodine before ejecting it into the bottle. From out of nowhere the lights cut out, plunging me into pitch-darkness. The fan slowly ground to a halt, letting out a final teasing wisp of air with its concluding oscillation. Within minutes the room became stifling. I continued to pump in the dark and when finished took my first sip of iodine-flavored water. No sooner had I swallowed it than another wave of nausea engulfed me. I desperately needed the liquid inside me so held on for as long as I could. It was an unwinnable battle. Moments later I was searching like the blind man that I currently was for the bathroom sink. Another bright internal flash exploded in my head followed immediately by a bout of grueling vomiting until I was retching bile from my contorted stomach. I lost far more liquid than I'd ingested. Slumped here bent over in the absolute darkness plagued with fatigue, I felt truly pathetic.

My breathing was weak and shallow as I gasped at the moist humid air that only intensified the repugnant acidic taste of bile in my mouth. I stumbled to the shower. As the cool water rained down on my body, I felt completely detached from the process, as if looking down on myself from above. I stumbled back to the bed and collapsed, exhausted. As I closed my eyes, the room seemed to pulsate with an all-embracing evil vibration, bestowing upon me one of the most tormented nights of my life.

CHAPTER 8

Touched by an Angel

"It's fucking hot!" said a brash Austrian woman in her thirties as she walked past the posada's English-speaking owner, who sat with me at a table in the establishment's courtyard.

"Did you hear the entertainment last night?" he asked me when the woman had disappeared out of earshot into her room. I told him I hadn't.

"She was up fucking all night. In the bathroom, in the bedroom, in the window, she doesn't give a fuck!"

Charming.

In my state the night before, I was unlikely to have heard anything other than my own rather less pleasurable groaning.

I had been up since early afternoon, having roused myself in search of food to assist in my convalescing. I'd purchased some soup from a store around the corner from the posada, which the posada's owner had kindly got one of his staff to cook for me. It went down well, having a soothing effect on my raw lining-stripped stomach. I was still feeling significantly under the weather and weak, although not nearly as bad as the night before and I had not been sick since then.

When he first heard that I was ill, the posada's owner had been genuinely concerned and quizzed me as to where I'd been before Ciudad Bolívar–checking whether I'd visited a malaria or yellow fever area in order to discount these illnesses. There was no cause for concern on this front, but he kindly offered to call a free doctor for me just in case. I politely declined as I was pretty sure it was just a rather nasty bit of food poisoning, most likely picked up from one of the many street stalls I had been eating from on Margarita. It crossed my mind that it could have been a bad reaction to the yellow fever jab, or possibly a combination of both. Either way, I figured my best strategy was to flush it out with plenty of water and to take it easy for the next couple of days. I'd inadvertently picked a good location for this as the posada was charming–an old converted colonial mansion with high ceilings, an airy open courtyard, and tasteful period features including an antique bar.

The proprietor and I sat discussing Angel Falls and the different types of tours that went there–this was the only way you could visit them due to their completely isolated location in the middle of a trackless jungle within the country's second largest national park. The tours cost around 1,800 bolivars (about U.S.$830 at the official rate of the time) and all departed by light aircraft from Ciudad Bolívar, where they flew for seventy minutes to a remote airstrip in the rain forest next to a scenic village of thatched huts, inhabited by the local Pemon indigenous tribe. The first day, I was delighted to learn, was spent relaxing around the village, which had proper amenities and was located next to a scenic lagoon fed by several smaller waterfalls. This sounded just what I needed to nurse myself back to health. The second day you headed out by motorized canoe along twisting forest tributaries to a base camp deep into the jungle–a journey that took about four hours. From here you hiked through the rain forest to the foot of Angel Falls itself. You then slept out overnight in hammocks at the base camp with its spectacular backdrop of the world's highest waterfall, before returning to the village by canoe and flying back to Ciudad Bolívar the next day.

I surmised that if the tour's easygoing first day was combined with today and tonight's rest, then it should be sufficient to get my strength up enough for the canoe trip and rain forest hike to the falls. I decided to search out a reasonably priced tour operator and book a trip for tomorrow. My only concern was my lack of malaria tablets, as the last thing I wanted in my condition was to contract a nasty tropical disease as well.

"Don't worry about the tablets," said the posada's owner. "They don't prevent malaria, they only slow it down and if anything make it harder to detect the disease."

He said that some people believed it was better to catch the disease without having first taken any medication so that you came down with clear identifiable symptoms that could be treated promptly, as opposed to taking tablets that reduced the symptoms, which might cause the disease to go undetected until later, and so prolong a person's exposure to it.

"If you catch malaria, the doctor will just administer some injections, you'll be horribly ill in bed for a week and then it's over."

I had no idea if this advice was correct or not but there were, apparently, no places in town where I could get the tablets anyway, so I put it out of my mind and concentrated on more pressing issues–sleep. I headed back to my room and crashed out for a couple of hours.

Despite the earlier soup having a rejuvenating effect on me, by midafternoon I was in dire need of something more substantial, and so headed outside in search of suitable sustenance that I could hold down. I was worried though that I might eat something as equally suspect as whatever it was that had made me ill, and so start the whole disgusting cycle again. With this in mind, I decided to stay well clear of any street stalls or local cafés with their tasty delicacies. When around the corner in the town's historic main square, I spotted a local family eating something that under normal circumstances I wouldn't dream of buying but which I concluded would be safe enough to eat from a hygiene point of view–my only consideration at the moment.

"McDonald's por favor," I said reluctantly to the bemused taxi driver I flagged down. I had no idea where the international king of bland and uninspiring takeaway cuisine was located, but felt too weak to stroll around aimlessly in search of it. Getting a cab proved the right decision as it was a good couple of miles away. I got the driver to wait while I went inside and grabbed some burgers, fries, and an iced tea, then got him to drop me off back in the historic section of town. I felt a pang of shame as I sat tucking into such multinational junk in so exotic a location.

It was now that I got my first real look at the colonial part of Ciudad Bolívar. It was located on a hill, perched above the mighty Orinoco River, which formed the town's natural boundary below. Most of the city's trophy buildings were located around the historic main square, in the center of which was a statue of Simón Bolívar surrounded by trees and manicured greenery. The buildings were delightfully preserved and painted in a spectrum of vibrant colors–orange and green houses, a red museum, a pink city hall–giving the place a gleeful welcoming appearance. Towering above them all was a huge yellow cathedral, its features highlighted in a contrasting brilliant white. Accentuating this artist's palette of colors was a blue Venezuelan sky, broken only by the occasional distant cumulous cloud mutating in the searing tropical heat.

Just up from the cathedral was the posada where my taxi driver from the night before had initially stopped. As I walked past, the owner nodded a "hello" to me. I stopped to apologize for his early wake-up call. He spoke good English and explained that it was not me he held responsible but the cabby, who had apparently done exactly the same thing the week before. After a brief chat, the owner told me about the tours he offered to Angel Falls. These cost slightly under the going rate, being 1,700 bolivars, so I booked a tour and made arrangements to be outside his building early in the morning.

By first light the next day I was standing on the green outside Ciudad Bolívar airport looking at the recovered and restored Flamingo single-engine propeller plane *El Rio Caroni* that U.S. aviator Jimmie Angel famously crash-landed near the summit of the waterfall that now bears his name. The tour representative, who had picked me up outside the posada thirty minutes earlier, led me inside the small local airport building over to the luggage scanner where the X-ray operator promptly detected my bushcraft knife and a pair of scissors in my backpack. On a normal commercial flight I would have checked these into the main hold, but as I was about to board a tiny Cessna, all bags, be they check-in size or not, qualified as carry-on luggage.

The rep and the machine operator discussed the situation.

"You have to hand me the knife and scissors. I'll give them to the pilot, who will give them back to you on landing," said the rep in an official-sounding voice.

Not a dozen steps later when we had exited the building and were standing next to the runway breathing in the unmistakable smell of aviation fuel, he handed them back to me.

"It's just security bullshit. Don't worry about the pilot, he doesn't care."

Up taxied a small Cessna, which by the looks of it had just been filled with essential items to take back to the village. These included a mountain of toilet paper and several crates of soft drinks. Reclining in the back using the paper for a pillow was an indigenous Pemon man taking it easy with his eyes closed, having presumably filled the plane up moments earlier.

The tour rep opened the front door of the single-propeller plane, introduced me to the pilot, then bade me farewell. Moments later we were accelerating along the runway then climbing steadily into the air. I had been in light aircraft many times before but had never sat up front with the pilot or indeed ever landed in one, having previously always jumped out–something I even did on my first plane ride ever. Despite having no parachute on me this time, I couldn't help but gaze down below and imagine leaping.

It wasn't long before we were bobbing up and down like a dinghy on a choppy windblown lake, as our airplane rode a bumpy band of turbulence, its engine wailing like a mosquito, varying in pitch as it rose and fell with the ever-changing tropical air pressure. It had been a surprisingly misty morning preventing much in the way of a view for the first twenty minutes of flight before suddenly the clouds cleared, the turbulence ceased, and we flew into a different world. Below us, stretching out to the horizon was an unbroken sunlit vista of pristine Venezuelan rain forest, which due to our elevation appeared more like a carpet of moss. With our gradual descent the distant canopy became sprouting florets of broccoli until finally the trees themselves came into view. Breaking up the expanse of green was the occasional colossal silvery skeleton of a deceased but still-standing former magnificent grandfather tree–ghostly wooden towers that would have been as much a source of life in death, for bugs, insects, birds, etc., as they were when alive.

From out of nowhere the plane's final destination, the indigenous village of Canaima, came into view. Located in the middle of the jungle amid flat-topped anvil-shaped tepui mountains was an immense lagoon fed by seven thundering waterfalls, bordered by pink sandy beaches and noble-looking upright palms. It was the perfect spot for a circular scenic flyby, but before I knew it, we were heading for terra firma and the plane's tires were squealing on the hot tarmac of the runway.

As I stepped out of the plane, there was a marked peaceful stillness that stood in blunt contrast to my excited anticipation at having arrived in such a location. And so for a few seconds I stood still and got in rhythm with my surroundings, listening to the low background symphony of chirping birds and humming insects. Flanking the runway was an exposed red gravel surface hewn out from the earth. Beyond stood a large open-fronted thatched hut–the "airport terminal"–and beyond this was greenery. Everywhere. In every shade imaginable. The pilot gestured for me to head over to the hut and take a seat. Inside were several travelers lounging about in the hut's shady confines. Some had just arrived on different planes, others were soon to depart. I struck up a conversation with a fellow Brit and Londoner, Paul, who would soon be leaving.

Paul hadn't experienced the best of starts to his Venezuela vacation and recounted for me his tale of woe. After flying into Caracas, he'd wisely insisted on catching an official taxi from the airport, but despite following all the advice he'd received on doing so, the driver, who was carrying a knife, promptly robbed him. The cabby got away with about $250 in cash and Paul's camera, which, if he wanted to claim back on his insurance, he would need a police report for. Acquiring this was easier said than done, as despite trying repeatedly to get hold of said report at a Caracas police station, the cops hadn't been in the slightest bit interested and refused to help. I thought back to my encounter with Señor Orta and his colleagues and was hardly surprised. Trying to get any of them to assist if the victim of a crime was not something I would like to attempt.

In desperation Paul had gone to the British embassy to see if they could give him some assistance in acquiring the report. What they gave him–I'm sad to say–was condescension bordering on ridicule. After explaining what happened to a British embassy staffer in dire need of a personality transplant, the official had responded, "Well that was a bit stupid, wasn't it?"

This understandably riled Paul, who explained to the patronizing prick that he was a lawyer in London, not some naive eighteen-year-old backpacker, and so would appreciate being spoken to as an adult. When he then asked if they could help obtain the police report, the pencil-pushing bureaucrat replied dismissively, "Maybe your hotel can help you."

"They were useless," stated Paul. "They would better serve the British public by picking up litter on Wimbledon Common rather than running an embassy here."

After wasting several fruitless days in Caracas, Paul had given up and flown to Canaima determined to enjoy the rest of his trip.

"The first day of my holiday began here," he said, before telling me how spectacular his last few days had been. Not only did he sing the praises of Angel Falls itself but also the boat ride there and the smaller falls that fed into the nearby lagoon which you could walk behind. Here you were enclosed by a thundering curtain of tea-colored water–an effect produced by tannins running off rain forest vegetation. He showed me a photo of himself behind this on his new camera. I couldn't wait to go there. Paul left a minute later, continuing his journey on to the Orinoco Delta.

A tour guide approached me now with news that, at first, I wasn't overly pleased to hear. In order to make up the numbers on a different group, I would be joining a couple of Spanish girls on their trip to Angel Falls, which left immediately. There would be no relaxing around the village today–I was off on the four-hour canoe ride now. Essentially, my tour was being run backwards, with the rest and relaxation at the end.

A short bumpy ride along a red dirt road in the back of a four-wheel-drive pickup truck took me and the Spanish girls–who were both in their late twenties and neither of whom spoke any English–through the jungle village and lush greenery to the river where our canoe awaited. It was a long rustic wooden vessel of about thirty feet painted in red and black, moored slightly upstream from one of the waterfalls feeding the lagoon below. Several local children played by the bank flashing big beaming grins our way. Our indigenous guides numbered four–three men and a woman–making them the majority on the canoe. No wonder they wanted me to make up the numbers. The woman handed out plastic bags to put our cameras in. It was clear from her hand motions there'd be some splashes in the rapids along the way. She gestured for us to step onto the canoe, which wobbled and rocked underfoot. The motion alone heightened my excitement as to the journey ahead. I took a wooden slatted seat up front. The only person ahead of me was a diminutive male guide wearing a baseball cap back to front–decorated with the yellow, blue, and red stripes of the Venezuelan flag–who had perched himself on the pointed bow with his bare feet dangling over either side. With a swift push from some helpers on the bank, we glided out onto the millpond-looking water. The outboard engine struck up, and off we sliced in a big arcing curve through the virgin water to the center of the river. Here we straightened onto a true course and began the long journey upstream through the arteries of the forest to the highest waterfall on the planet.

I dipped my hand overboard into the delightfully cool tea-colored river, my fingers acquiescing to the water's drag like reeds in the wind. I dug deeper, the resistance massaging my palm and throwing off a V-shaped spray akin to a plow through a snowdrift. A minutiae of gemlike droplets danced off the surface, erupting into an explosion of sparkling light and color, reminding me of a Native American saying, "To truly appreciate the grand vistas of nature, you must first know her smaller works." Looking up from the spray of water, I gazed out at the enormity of the panorama that stretched beyond. When viewed in its entirety, the water no longer appeared as if tea but transformed into a glassy silver-tinged azure. As with the water, the thick green forest foliage of the now-distant banks took on a new hue when discerned collectively with the expanse of undulating jungle rising up to the foot of tepui mountains beyond. A strange hazy blue blanketed the trees and mountains. I had seen a similar phenomenon in Australia where the aptly named "blue mountains" were likewise imbued–something attributed to the area's high density of eucalyptus trees that release oil into the atmosphere, which, along with airborne dust and water vapor, absorbs the long-wavelength red end of the light spectrum, leaving the remaining light with a blue tinge. I wondered if a similar substance was being released here.

The river twisted this way and that, sections of which narrowed dramatically, revealing new wondrous sights with every meandering turn: islands, secluded beaches, unknown exotic birds, alien-like trees, thatched huts with obligatory bowing hammocks. But most dramatic of all were the tepuis. We passed close by several of these enigmatic sandstone and quartzite mountains, jutting vertically from the jungle, towering ominously overhead in colors of rusty red and black. They were awe-inspiring. Their mist-shrouded peaks bringing to mind mythical temples of the gods. All around was some of the greatest scenery I had ever seen.

I felt a deep sense of reverence for the area–geologically one of the oldest places on earth–and immensely privileged to be exactly where I was, so very far away from the normal doldrums of everyday life and routine. It was a hot and sticky day but I felt extremely relaxed in the humidity and almost seemed to blend with the forest until there was no separation between my surroundings and me. I felt at peace and yet so very much alive. This was what traveling was all about.

From out of nowhere the weather turned. Clouds opened up overhead, releasing a torrential downpour that drenched us throughout–reminding me where the rain forest gets its name. In an instant the world was transformed; the water's surface, once glassy and reflective, warped into a kaleidoscope of merging and overlapping rings diffusing the clarity of the surface like an impressionist's painting. Bankside plants took on new forms, bowing down gracefully as their leaves shed ribbons of water like funnels. I had plenty of dry clothes in my backpack, sealed inside a waterproof inner lining, so I gave in to the cloudburst above. Lifting my face to the heavens, I closed my eyes with a smile, relishing the unique sensation of freedom that being exposed in such a torrent brings. As the cool water streamed down my face, it seemed to wash away all the discomfort from my previous illness, rejuvenating me in both body and spirit.

As quickly as the rain began, it ceased, and once again we were bathed in glorious sunshine. On our way we passed two canoes heading in the opposite direction that were far fuller than our own, packed with satisfied smiling occupants whom we exchanged obligatory waves with.

It was interesting to see our guides navigate through the rockier sections of the river. The guy perched on the bow did the reconnaissance, looking out for boulders and other obstacles, which he would relay back to the man standing a long way behind, steering the outboard motor. If we got too close to a boulder, out came a wooden ore to push us clear.

Up ahead in a narrow section of the river were several giant boulders that had once fallen from the tepui above. Several of them had split on impact. Soon after navigating our way through these, the guide at the front of the canoe turned around and pointed to a distant towering tepui with a river of water cascading down from atop. He didn't need to tell me what it was.

The closer we got to Angel Falls, the more magnificent it became. It was insanely high, measuring 3,211 feet in total with a continuous drop of 2,647 feet–sixteen times higher than Niagara Falls–making it by far and away the highest waterfall on earth. We moored up opposite the base camp where several open-fronted huts were located. The waterfall was still some hike away, although the camp had a clear panoramic view of it in the distance. One of the guides accompanied us, while the others went over to the camp. He led us off into the dense jungle along a thin twisting path. I was immediately struck by how much quieter it was in amongst the trees, such was their sound barrier effect against the rushing waters of the river. It was also much darker. As little as 2 percent of the light that reaches the upper canopy of a rain forest filters down to the lower levels, making the plants that survive there specially adapted to shady conditions. Those that aren't are in a battle for the light and often lie dormant for years as seeds on the forest floor, waiting for a tree to fall and create a doorway to the sunshine. At this point they spring into life, putting all their energy into upwards growth, only spreading out to form a canopy when the requisite height, and their access to the light, is achieved.

After about forty minutes of hiking through the forest, stopping off occasionally en route when the guide pointed out a plant, vine, or spider of interest, accompanied with an explanation in Spanish, we arrived at Angel Falls. Stretching up nearly a kilometre into the air was the table-topped mountain, Auyán-tepuí, from which a hydrant of tumbling water spouted from a central cleft, dropping all the way down to the ground through an arching rainbow. Its height almost defied belief. Under it you could fit two and a half Empire State Buildings, with room to spare. Everything about it and the surrounding area was scenic perfection–a little slice of heaven hidden away in a trackless jungle. It was so majestic it seemed the sort of thing that someone might only conceive of in an outlandish fantasy book. Only Angel Falls was real and in front of me.

The rocks, forming the backdrop behind the falling ever-changing water, were an artist's palette of colors: pink, red, orange, gray, black, and brown–and a myriad of shades in between. Framing the picture above was a deep blue sky mottled with fluffy white clouds, and below me spread the vibrant green of the forest floor. When the clouds permitted and sunshine ruled the sky, the rainbow would appear–as if a final finishing flourish on a masterpiece of artwork. It was truly a natural wonder of the world. And I stood transfixed, in awe and humbled.

Just downstream from the fall's main drop was a smaller waterfall flowing into a natural pool. The two Spanish girls and I stripped down to our bathing suits and waded in, gazing up at the cathedral-resembling tepui above, with its ladder of water stretching to the summit. I turned and looked back into the canyon from which we'd come. In the distance, amid a world of greenery, was another completely different waterfall cascading from another tepui. Had it been located anywhere other than across from Angel Falls, it would have been considered mammoth. I turned to face the star attraction again and lay on my back floating, wondering what Jimmie Angel must have thought and felt when he first set eyes upon it. Up until that point only the isolated Pemon people knew of its existence.

Unsubstantiated legends abound as to the exploits of Jimmie Angel: At the age of fourteen he taught himself to fly; he was a fighter pilot ace in World War I; he formed an air force in the Gobi Desert for a Chinese warlord; Lawrence of Arabia used him as a flying scout. Unfortunately, Angel was fond of telling tall tales, and much of his legendary exploits are most likely to be just that. This propensity for fibs is a likely reason why initially no one believed his claim of having discovered the gargantuan waterfall.

The story goes that sometime in the 1920s Angel visited Venezuela with an American geologist called McCracken, whom he had previously met in a Panamanian bar. McCracken paid Angel a whopping $5,000 to fly him to a secret location in the southeast of the country where they landed on top of a tepui and removed a huge amount of gold from a far bigger cache located in a riverbed. After McCracken's death, Angel became obsessed with finding the mountain again. It was in his search for the remaining gold that in 1933 he discovered the waterfall, which would later bear his name. When he returned to tell the world of his find, no one took him seriously. Determined to prove them wrong, in 1937 he set off to land atop the mysterious tepui with its humungous waterfall, accompanied by his wife Marie, the Spanish botanist Captain Felix Cardona Puig, Angel's friend and expert outdoorsman Gustavo Heny, and Heny's gardener Miguel Angel Delgado–presumably, in case they encountered some herbaceous borders that needed tending.

At first the landing on top the tepui seemed to go according to plan, but before the airplane had stopped, its wheels broke through the surface sod, miring the vehicle in the marshy landscape and propelling the craft's nose into the ground–breaking its fuel line in the process. There would be no return flight home for the explorers. To get back to civilization, they would have to do so on foot. What followed was an epic eleven-day trek led by Heny against the odds with limited food and supplies through uncharted territory to an indigenous village on the southerly side of the giant tepui.

It was in 1949, twelve years after Angel's ill-fated flight, that his discovery was finally externally verified when American photojournalist Ruth Robertson led an expedition to the base of the falls. Details of her expedition were published the same year by *National Geographic* in an article titled "Jungle Journey to the World's Highest Waterfall."

I may not have been the first to see it, but the euphoric feeling of gazing upon Angel Falls with my own eyes for the first time was uplifting in the extreme. When we finally headed back along the jungle trail to base camp, it was with a deep sense of satisfaction and happiness. A feeling that stayed with me long into the night.

CHAPTER 9

Paradise Found

I awoke the next morning in the cocoon of a mosquito-netted hammock to the majestic sight of Angel Falls filtering down from atop Auyán-tepuí, which was blanketed by clouds at its upper reaches, making the falls appear to be coming from the heavens themselves. It seemed an apt metaphor; although not intentionally named after an ethereal being, Angel Falls appeared every bit of one to me.

Over flickering candlelight at camp the night before I had looked at maps of the area and was amazed to discover that the majority of what I had assumed were different individual tepuis were, in fact, different arms of the same colossal formation of Auyán-tepuí, which encompassed both sides of the canyon and was a gigantic 348 square miles in size–bigger than the land mass of New York City.

Auyán-tepuí, like the other tepuis, is an eroded remnant of a vast two-billion-year-old layer of Precambrian sediment laid down when South America and Africa were connected. Consisting of sandstone and quartzite strata, the tepuis were formed as a result of movements in the earth's crust, creating areas of weakness that then eroded away over millions of years, leaving the more resistant rocks jutting out of the forest, which today form the evocative archipelago of isolated jungle plateaus. The tepuis are so old that there are no fossils within their rocks; their origins stretch back before life existed on earth. When plant and animal life first emerged from the oceans to live on land, the tepuis were already 1.4 billion years old.

Like the Galápagos Islands, the isolated nature of the tepuis' summits has, with the passing of millions of years, allowed flora and fauna to evolve independently there. Many of the species found on top of the tepuis are no longer present on the eroded forest floor below, and hundreds are unique to *individual* tepuis, retaining features of long-extinct remote ancestors. It is estimated that about two thousand plant species exist on the tepuis' summits, 50 percent of which grow nowhere else on earth. Such concentrations of "endemic" flora make the tepuis a fascinating treasure trove of rare, bizarre, and beautiful plants.

We said farewell to Auyán-tepuí and Angel falls by midmorning, setting off on the journey back to Canaima, where we arrived at around lunchtime. After a bit of administrative reshuffling by the tour company, I was tagged onto another far bigger group that had just arrived. The Spanish girls flew back to Ciudad Bolívar. The new group and I were taken by an indigenous guide through the village, which I got a proper look at now, en route to our accommodation. It was a delightfully sleepy hamlet with traditional thatched huts alongside more permanent tin-roofed buildings and even a stone church complete with big arching doorways. There were palms; vibrant flowers of pinks, reds, and oranges; mango trees; and countless other tropical arborists' delights that I hadn't a chance of identifying. Indigenous children played gleefully on the beach and in the water, while mothers went about their daily chores, a couple of whom scrubbed away at clothing in the lagoon.

Since Chávez's election to office, Venezuela's indigenous population have finally seen their rights enshrined in the country's constitution. When representatives of the constitutional assembly were being elected, Chávez made sure that the rules of the assembly guaranteed at least three indigenous representatives within the group. And when the assembly began drawing up the rights of this population of some five hundred thousand Venezuelans, they turned to these representatives to devise the legislation.

Amazingly, up until this point there had been no official recognition in the country's constitution of the indigenous population's right to exist, to its territories, culture, or languages–things that are now cemented in Venezuela's Magna Carta. Through its commitment to promote indigenous languages and culture, the state must now provide funding for projects such as bilingual education. Other state guarantees now see that the indigenous population have representation in the national assembly, that any use of natural resources on their lands does not impact on them negatively, and that their indigenous intellectual property rights are protected.

Our guide dropped us at our individual chalets and told us to meet in an hour at a big communal dining room for lunch. After a shower and a good session with my diary, I headed off for food. Sitting at a long dining table, I got chatting to a young British couple, Katie and Graeme, who had recently started a backpacking tour around South America.

"I don't mind what the food is so long as it's not fish," said Graeme, a minute before a plate of sautéed fish arrived. It tasted delicious to me. So far I had been surprisingly pleased with how good the tour's grub had been. The night before we had been treated to succulent chicken roasted over a campfire, and this morning's base-camp breakfast was fried eggs, tomatoes, and superstrong and aromatic sweet black coffee.

I asked Katie and Graeme how long they'd been together.

They looked to each other as if a tricky question had just been posed.

"Ah, well, we're not really going out yet, are we?" said Katie, inadvertently flashing a tongue piercing.

"We've been friends for a long time at work and recently got together. So we're seeing how things work out," said Graeme.

They were spending the next seven months traveling spontaneously around the continent, so by the end of that they'd well and truly know one way or the other whether they wanted to be an item. My money was on that they would. After lunch we took in the lagoon's main waterfall, which was three stories high and twice as wide. It was difficult to imagine that we would soon be enveloped by this giant liquid curtain. Excited internal butterflies erupted in me as I edged my way along the rocky track that approached the entrance to the falls, the water's roar intensifying with every step, and our route soon becoming shrouded in the nebulous blowback from nearby watery explosions. From out of nowhere a black tourist helicopter swooped in from above, descending rapidly in a steep arching maneuver, to hover in front of the falls–the sound of its rotors drowned out by the roaring wall of water.

Everyone stripped down to shorts and bikinis at the entrance. I opted for shorts. We shuffled inside, hugging the rocky wall as a shower of pinkish brown tannin-rich water soaked us through, eliciting whoops and hollers of excitement from us all. Within a few steps we were completely enclosed by the tsunami of water, like a surfer in a giant barreling wave. Only feet away thousands of gallons raged, warping into otherworldly shapes with a violent intensity. Despite the noise and the overwhelming power, there was a strange paradoxical peacefulness inside here, almost a sense of security. We were in the eye of the storm, enclosed in a bubble, safe from the chaos all around us. The helicopter passed by outside, prowling back and forth along the drape of water as if a giant predator hunting in vain for its prey hidden safely inside. In what seemed like a frustrated defeat, it darted off, abandoning the search to hunt elsewhere.

I wondered what it would be like to be here alone–enclosed from the world, meditating on the place's powerful and cryptic atmosphere. I could have stayed for hours. Our guide, however, had a different time frame in mind, and after encouraging the photo opportunity for those who were brave enough to take their cameras, we made our way back outside. Faces glowed with rapturous satisfaction. Everyone was on a high.

We headed back to the village now, by which time the light was fading. After dinner the sun had gone, replaced by a full orange-tinged moon and a cloud-dappled sky, creating a halo around the moon. I headed to the lagoon's beach, where I lay in the sand gazing out at the water sparkling in the moonlight, listening to the soothing rumble of the multiple waterfalls, amplified by the thin night air. On the horizon a distant thunderstorm lit up the sky with its silent flashes, illuminating the surrounding clouds in pastel shades of yellow and brown. Canaima was a very special place, indeed.

By lunchtime the next day I was boarding a Cessna flight back to Ciudad Bolívar with a different couple of Spanish girls. They spoke more English than the first two and suggested to me that we share a taxi from the airport back to the historic part of town where they were both staying. After a brief walk around with them, I bailed out to go into some tour agencies to see what they had to offer.

I normally avoid organized tours with a passion, much preferring to make my own way to places of interest and to interact with locals as opposed to fellow travelers, but in Venezuela several of the country's attractions are all but impossible to visit unless booked on to a tour. Angel Falls being a case in point, another being the country's most famous tepui, Roraima.

Located at the borders with Brazil and Guyana, Roraima was the iconic mountain from *National Geographic* which had inspired this journey so many years before, instilling in me a desire close to obsession to one day reach its flat summit–something the National Park Authority only allows you to do if accompanied by an indigenous Pemon guide. To the Pemon, Roraima is known as the "Mother of All Waters," due to it being the source for rivers feeding the great basins of the Orinoco, Essequibo, and the mighty Amazon.

Several of the agencies in town offered to make the necessary arrangements for me, but the lone agency that had a tour ready to go immediately was just waiting for their group to arrive from Canaima in a couple of hours. As soon it did, I could join them on an overnight bus to the nearest town to Roraima, Santa Elena, and then set off from there on the trek.

The tour lasted six days. It would begin in an indigenous village where Roraima could be seen looming on the horizon. This would be followed by two days of solid hiking to reach the base of Roraima and the best part of the next day to scale the 9,216-foot monolith, after which we would spend the following two nights on top, exploring the summit's valleys, rivers, and caves and then two days hiking back. There was no accommodation—all nights were spent camping out. It sounded fantastic.

I reserved a place on the 1,700-bolivar tour (about 790 dollars at the official rate of the time) and headed up to the posada I had booked my Angel Falls tour through to pick up some of my gear that they had let me leave behind until my return. Lounging about inside the posada's courtyard, I met a weathered-looking middle-aged Brit called Brian and a thirty-something French guy, Sebastian. We got talking, as travelers inevitably do, about each others' trips. Brian was traveling around South America with his girlfriend and so far had not had the best of times of it. He described their experiences in Peru—something which had made the local newspaper, a clipping of which he handed to me.

He and his girlfriend had booked onto a boat tour that spent several days cruising along a river. On the very first day after returning to the boat following a quick sightseeing stop, they found their hammock cut and possessions strewn about, many of which were missing. They asked a woman nearby if she had seen anything. She told them she'd witnessed the crew doing it. Brian went off to tell the captain, in no uncertain terms, that they were leaving the boat and wanted their money back, along with what had been stolen. The captain and the crew's response was to beat the shit out of him and his girlfriend–she received a nasty black eye–and to throw them off the boat and have them arrested. A nasty stint in the cells followed in which they were blamed for the melee. The report in the local paper followed this line, painting Brian as a mad British drunk who had gone crazy without provocation. It contained a photo of him looking decidedly beat-up and traumatized.

"They even got my age wrong in the article," he protested. "They said I was fifty not forty-five!"

After grabbing my gear, I bade them both farewell and headed down to the tour agency. The woman working there was the bearer of bad news.

"The group has been rained in at Canaima. We'll have to postpone your tour until their return."

Shit.

The group was now due tomorrow, which would mean spending tonight and tomorrow in Ciudad Bolivar and then getting the bus to Santa Elena the following night. In a gesture of goodwill, the woman offered to let me crash for free at the agency in one of a couple of windowless spare rooms. She lived here with other members of her family. I decided to go for it and, after dumping my bags, headed out to see if Brian or Sebastian fancied a cold one. It was dark by now and both were keen for a beer–but finding an open bar was no mean feat.

Despite being Saturday night, the place was a ghost town. The streets were silent and deserted, almost as if a curfew were enforced. All that was missing was some tumbleweed blowing across the abandoned road and a lone church bell tolling in the background. Despite the absence of life, Brian was confident, and after plenty of wandering, we came across what we were looking for–a liquor store whose long shop counter backed straight onto the street. This meant that all business could be done without the need to enter the shop. You simply gave your order to the staff member working behind the thick metal security bars, which separated the counter from the street, and then he fetched your booze.

It was open for business, although by the looks of it was not doing much. Propped up against the wall outside was a drunk finishing off his purchase of a bottle of rum while cursing the world and all who came near him in the process. We kept our distance. Handing our money though the gates to the assistant, we received a fistful of super chilled *Polar Ice* bottled beers. We drained these together back at the posada after which I crashed out in the tour agency where I positioned three separate fans to point directly at me in a futile attempt at getting a good night's sleep in the baking-hot and musty room.

"I'm afraid your group has disappeared," said the woman at the tour agency in the morning.

"Disappeared?"

"They have left Canaima but not flown back to Ciudad Bolívar. You will have to wait here until other people turn up."

I wondered if there'd been a group in Canaima at all. Was she just keeping me here until other travelers popped in with similar enquiries, at which point we'd all be bundled together and off we'd trot? With so few travelers in town, this could take forever, leaving me in a bit of a quandary. I desperately wanted to see the mighty Roraima but sure as hell didn't want to sit around in limbo.

I cancelled my booking, grabbed my gear, and headed outside for a walk to ponder my options. I spotted a sandwich-board street sign propped up outside a tour agency I hadn't noticed before. I immediately went inside.

"Habla inglés?"

"Yes," the proprietor replied, in a manner that also implied "of course!"

"I don't suppose you've got any tours leaving for Roraima soon?"

"Tonight, would you like to join it?"

I could have tongue-kissed the old bugger. After checking that it was indeed leaving tonight and that other people had genuinely booked onto it, I did likewise–handing over 1,650 bolivars for the privilege.

By the following morning I had arrived, by way of overnight coach, in the border town of Santa Elena situated on the frontier with Brazil. It was located in Venezuela's Great Savannah region, known locally as the Gran Sabana. The landscape was an endless savannah of swaying grasses and distant tepuis. It looked like a scene from *Jurassic Park*. And it was. Steven Spielberg filmed scenes for the movie here in what is the sixth largest nature reserve in the world.

I had been met here by the local tour organizer, Rafael, who introduced me to the rest of the group at a café in the center of town. There were four other travelers present who would be accompanying me up Roraima: a Polish woman in her thirties, Edyta; a German guy also in his thirties, Marian (the two of whom were a couple); a quiet, middle-aged spectacled Japanese man and his twenty-year-old son. An Australian guy and a French woman would apparently be meeting us in a couple of hours.

Rafael informed us of a slight change of plan caused by the two Japanese men. After climbing Roraima, they intended to cross the border into Brazil and needed help acquiring visas. Because of this, the hike was going to be cut short by a day while Rafael got their visas in town. We would now have the morning off relaxing in town, and then if there was time, Rafael promised to take us on a local canyon trip this afternoon. Our first day's hike of the Roraima trip would now have to cover twice the ground as before, with us cramming two days' distance into one. Our new friends weren't exactly flavor of the month for that one.

So instead of adventure, I got a mundane couple of hours milling around the uninspiring center of a quiet border town waiting for Rafael to return.

Santa Elena is something of a hub for smugglers and black marketeers–many of whom brazenly operate in the open in this border town. Walking down the high street, I was approached by several money changers keen to exchange currency. I checked out the going rate but was unimpressed, having got a far better deal from Austin's contact in Caracas. But the real money to be made was exploiting the difference between the price of gasoline here compared to that across the border. In Brazil (at the time of writing), a gallon costs six dollars and seventy-one cents whereas in Venezuela, it costs six cents.

With gasoline being over a hundred times more expensive, there are huge profits to be made here. Brazilians used to line up in huge convoys stretching a mile across the border to take advantage of the dramatically cheaper prices, but in 2006, the military began guarding Santa Elena's gas stations to prevent day-tripping Brazilians from stocking up. The locals are also gas rationed to prevent wildly profitable sojourns across the border. As a result of a flourishing black market, gas trade takes place from private residences with the sellers known by the tongue-in-cheek sobriquet of "Talibanes." With as much as a thousand dollars to be made on an outlay of around ten bucks, the authority's measures are insufficient to curb the black market. In an effort to lessen its effects, a gas station has now been opened just inside Venezuela, charging intermediate prices, which the Brazilians are permitted to use.

By the time Rafael made it back to our designated rendezvous spot–a posada that offered his tours–he had picked up the Australian guy and French woman but was two Japanese lighter.

"Those fucking Japanese have pulled out!" he told us with utter disdain.

He was not a happy camper.

"I got taxis for them, arranged appointments with my contacts for them, postponed your trip by a day for them, and bought them food for their hike, which will have to be thrown out."

He gestured to the food spread out on the posada's reception counter, which also served as a bar–it was nearly all tinned or dried. But I got the sentiment. For the inconvenience of having knocked a day off our tour, he promised to take us not only on the canyon hike this afternoon but also a day-long savannah tour on our return from Roraima.

The two new additions to our group were Josephine, a small but plump Frenchwoman who spoke barely a word of English or Spanish, leaving her mute most of the time, except when conversing with the new Australian arrival, Farrin–who, luckily for her, spoke rudimentary schoolboy French.

Farrin and I immediately hit it off. He was easygoing with an extremely sharp intellect balanced by a dry acerbic Aussie sense of humor. He'd taken a year off from his job as a geotechnical engineer working on the construction of a new mine and had been traveling for the last six months through South Korea, Japan, Mongolia, China, Kyrgyzstan, Uzbekistan, Europe, and Cuba. He was in Venezuela primarily to meet up with a lady friend who lived in Caracas but, while in the country, was also taking in the sights.

Sitting nearby was our short but powerful indigenous Pemon guide, Alex, who Rafael introduced to the group. He would be leading us up the mountain accompanied by a Pemon porter who was joining us at the start of the trail in the morning.

One of the functions of meeting in the posada was to leave behind in a storeroom all the nonessential items we didn't need to carry up the mountain. As we started stripping down our kit, Rafael hovered nearby, pointing out items to discard that were already provided on the trip. I had a chunky and weighty first aid kit, which I pulled out.

"I take it you've already got one of these," I said.

"The porters don't always bring one. They're bad like that," he said as if he bore no responsibility for his employees' actions.

I couldn't believe it! A six-day hike in the middle of nowhere up a nine-thousand-foot mountain was madness without a first aid kit. I wondered just how Mickey Mouse this tour was going to be and stuffed it firmly into my pack.

When we'd stripped our packs down to a fraction of their former weight, and borrowed the necessary items–which in my case was a flashlight after discovering mine had broken–we headed off on our promised afternoon canyon hike. After an hour of driving and hiking in blistering heat, we reached a narrow and shady canyon, at the head of which was a small waterfall (small by Angel Falls standards that is, as it was still seventy to eighty feet high). The canyon was mercifully cool inside, thanks to a breeze brushing furtively over a small stream and the occasional isolated pool of clear ankle-deep water. From the precipitous canyon sides grew trees fighting a war on two fronts: for scant light above and against gravity, such was the sheer position dealt to them by the random landing of a seed. From the towering sides, the occasional corpse of a fallen tree created picture-postcard walkways across the water. Dangling from above were liana vines–jungle rope, coiled around the upper canopy for support. I was familiar with these from books but had not encountered them in the wild before, so took a hold of a thin specimen in order to test how ropelike they really were. With a bit of dexterous fiddling, I succeeded in tying a looping "alpine butterfly" knot, which I left in place for posterity.

We sat beneath the invigorating falls on slick slabs of orange-and-red jasper while Rafael told us of Roraima and the trek to come.

"Nature will accommodate your shit on the way there. But Roraima will not," he said, explaining that everything that went up to Roraima's fragile and unique ecosystem had to come down again–including human waste.

"You shit into a bag, tie it up, and give it to the porters. They'll put it in a sealed tube, which comes down with you off the mountain."

Fires were also forbidden as was removing anything from the top, be it plants, quartz crystals–of which there was an abundance–and even soil.

"The park authorities will search you on the way out. So don't do it."

The authorities, Rafael told us, were considering closing Roraima for a few years in order to protect the ecosystem and encourage regeneration.

"Please treat Roraima with respect. The Pemon say that if you tell Roraima you come in peace, she will look after you and give you better weather."

We made our way out of the canyon and back up a steep hill to where the four-wheel-drive was parked. Before getting in, Rafael pointed out the flat-table-topped form of Roraima beckoning on the horizon. It was a long way off across a span of green savannah, capped at its summit by a tablecloth of clouds, as if the mountain were laid for a dinner service. Standing nearby to its western flank, and nearly as tall, was its sister mountain, Cuquenan.

Chugging down an insanely bumpy dirt track, the vehicle lurched violently from side to side, bounding up and down with sudden jolts, throwing those sitting in the rear on the communal bench seats high into the air.

The suspension groaned as we hit a particularly deep crevice, catapulting everyone upwards, arms flailing about in the process. A subsequent pothole followed a split second later, ricocheting my head off the roof as I went fully airborne, falling in an ungainly heap with my head on Farrin's lap.

"Don't worry, mate, we're all friends here!" he said, looking down at me with a wink.

Thankfully, a flat stretch of road followed, on which we had to stop for a quick cursory vehicle check by AK-47-toting officials at the start of the national park. Their eyes lit up as they spotted an unopened bottle of rum that Rafael had brought along for us to take up Roraima as something of a sweetener following this morning's debacle. Farrin's face dropped as the officials took a hold of it.

"Oh, take it easy, fellas," he muttered under his breath.

Carcas street murals

How the have-nots live in Venezuela—a Caracas barrio

Photo courtesy of Paul Rideough

Crystal clear waters of the Venezuelan Caribbean

Photo courtesy of Sabrina Durling-Jones

Chavistas

Photo courtesy of Charles Brewer-Carias

Canaima National Park. Look closely and you can spot three helicopters.

Photo courtesy of Paul Rideough

Canoe journey to Angel Falls

Photo courtesy of Paul Rideough

Angel Falls, the world's highest waterfall at nearly a kilometer tall

Photo courtesy of Charles Brewer-Carias

Angel Falls in full flood

Photo courtesy of Charles Brewer-Carias

Carnivorous pitcher plants, Mt. Roraima

Phtoto courtesy of Charles Brewer-Cari

The magnificent Mt. Roraima

Photo courtesy of Paul Rideough

Waterfall, Canaima National Park

Cave on the summit of Mt. Roraima

Photo courtesy of Farrin De Fredrick

Looking down from atop Mt. Roraima

Photo courtesy of Farrin De Fredrick

Farrin, Nuhella, me, Camilo, Virginia, and Juan playing dominos at the underground bar, Merida

Photo courtesy of Farrin De Fredrick

Farrin and me on Lake Maracaibo

Photo courtesy of Alan Highto
The famed Catatumbo lightning in all its glory

Anselmo and a typical Venezuelan taxi

Communist bar decor, Maracaibo

Photo courtesy of Sabrina Durling-Jone.

Traditional Cabinas house

Photo courtesy of Sabrina Durl

Maracaibo street scene

Photo courtesy of Sabrina Durling-Jones

Street stall, Maracaibo

The church of Iglesia de Santa Barbara, Maracaibo

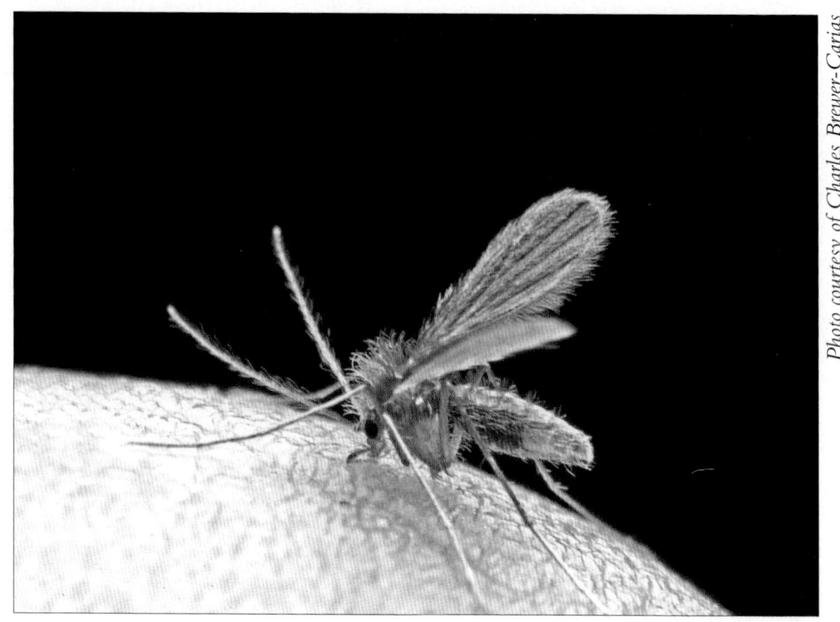

Photo courtesy of Charles Brewer-Carias

My least favorite of Venezuela's creatures. A minute sand fly sucking Charles's blood.

Practicing fire by friction with Venezuela's greatest explorer, Charles Brewer-Carias

The summit could be very cold and wet, particularly at night, so in the absence of a fire, a blood-warming shot or two of rum would go down a treat. After laying on a bit of charm, Rafael thankfully managed to sweet-talk the guards–who he seemed to be familiar with–into handing it back again. He passed the bottle to Farrin for safekeeping.

"This is for the group. Do not give it to the porter, there's nothing worse than a drunk Indian."

He turned to Alex, our indigenous Pemon guide.

"And don't pay him until the hike is over."

Soon we were on our way to the small indigenous village of Paraitepui–the beginning of the hiking trail for Roraima.

"See the fire in the distance?" Rafael said, pointing out several smoldering patches of savannah.

"The Indians walk around with lighters, randomly setting fire to stuff. It used to be a traditional hunting method to flush out the game, but now they just do it for the hell of it. They nearly set the whole mountain on fire a few years back."

"What do the park authorities make of it?" I asked Rafael.

"There was nearly a war between the Indians and the park rangers!" said Alex with a disparaging shake of his head, which I took, despite him being an indigenous Pemon himself, as an indication that he disapproved of the practice and came down on the side of the rangers–as well as that the term "Indian" wasn't deemed derogatory here.

The fires had changed the immediate landscape around Roraima dramatically, which was once forested to a degree inconceivable today. A legendary fire that is still recalled by village elders raged out of control in 1925, devastating much of the jungle that the early explorers would have had to negotiate to reach the mountain.

"What do think of Chávez?" Farrin asked Rafael out of the blue. Like me, Farrin had met both lovers and despisers of the president, but not much in between.

"I like him. He's done a lot of good for the poor people, particularly free health care and giving the poor things, like free glasses."

By the time we arrived in Paraitepui, the sun was setting. We pulled up outside a closed national park office where the trail leading to Roraima began and where we'd be spending the night in tents. It looked one hell of a long walk to Roraima, which loomed large on the horizon. I hoped I was up to it after my bout of illness from which I realized I had lost a surprising amount of weight. Rafael would be heading off soon, leaving us with Alex for the duration of the trip. Before departing, he added a taste of mystery to the journey we were about to take, embellishing it with tales of frequent UFO sightings and energy portals on the mountain.

"If you trace the lines of all the world's major energy portals, they all meet at Roraima."

Sure.

In the tropics, nighttime comes like the flick of a switch. One moment there's light. The next it's dark. With its sudden arrival, Rafael said good-bye, and Alex began organizing food for dinner–reconstituted ham sandwiches and a watery hot chocolate. It filled a hole but not much else. I hoped there'd be something a little more sustaining and tasty for the next few days' punishing hike.

Having only brought a jungle hammock and a tarp with me to Venezuela for portable accommodation, the savannah surroundings–having nowhere to suspend the hammock's two ends from–dictated that I borrow a tent. My heart sank when it dawned on me that the accommodation provided wasn't individual tents as I'd naively assumed but a three-person dome that I'd have to share, sardine fashion, up close and personal with German Marian and his polish other half, Edyta. The Australian and French element of the team, Farrin and Josephine, were both traveling with their own tents.

I just hoped my roommates didn't snore.

They did. Loudly.

CHAPTER 10

The Real Lost World

Roraima was first documented by English explorer Sir Walter Raleigh in 1595, who described the mountain and one of its many towering waterfalls in *The Discovery of Guiana*:

> *We saw it afar off; and it appeared like a white church-tower of an exceeding height. There falleth over it a mighty river which toucheth no part of the side of the mountain, but rusheth over the top of it, and falleth to the ground with so terrible a noise and clamour, as if a thousand great bells were knocked one against another. I think there is not in the world so strange an overfall, nor so wonderful to behold.*

It wasn't until 1838 that a European reached the foot of the mountain when German explorer Robert Schomburgk battled his way through the surrounding jungle to reach it. Schomburgk made no attempt to scale Roraima, considering its sheer walls unclimbable. Numerous subsequent expeditions followed, all failing to ascend the mountain, which remained unclimbed by explorers and the indigenous population alike–who were afraid of its mystical power–until 1884 when British botanists Everald Thum and Harry

Perkins finally discovered a route to the top, on an expedition that lasted two months. What they discovered on the summit was an island of prehistoric plant and animal castaways, marooned and evolving in isolation from the other tepuis and the outside world at large. Species that exist on Roraima alone are legion–totaling about a third of all life atop the mountain–including aquatic crickets, bright red pitcher-shaped carnivorous plants full of rainwater, and curious black frogs that crawl instead of jump. The summit's weather is frequently wet and cold and its upper landscape–which is five miles across–a bizarre mix of bare black rock sculpted by the elements into twisting towers and cavernous sinkholes. It is dotted with pink sandy marshes, quartz crystal valleys and caves–Roraima possesses the largest cave in silicic rocks in the world–and rivers that plunge vertically off the sheer sides.

On returning to Britain after their expedition, Thum and Perkins gave a lecture detailing their incredible discoveries at the Royal Geographic Society in London, attended by Sir Author Conan Doyle–author of the Sherlock Holmes novels. Hearing of Thum and Perkins's adventurous exploits and the unique flora, fauna, and landscape they'd discovered at the summit inspired Conan Doyle's classic 1912 adventure book, *The Lost World,* which tells of dinosaurs existing atop a secluded Amazon plateau. The book went on to inspire such works as *King Kong* and *Jurassic Park.*

As light started to illuminate the plastic condensation-dripping shell that would be my home for the next few nights, an agitated anticipation washed over me as I contemplated what the following days held. I could no longer remain inside, cloistered from the landscape that I knew lay beyond the thin veil of nylon. Unzipping the tent and leaving my snoring roommates behind, I stepped outside to be greeted by a fiery pink-and-orange sky, illuminated by a predawn sun that was soon to herald the arrival of the morn. Through blinking eyes, the enigmatic Roraima came into focus, standing proud and evocative on the distant horizon–almost beckoning me to it. Nobody else had risen yet, but I was itching to get started and hit the trail. The sun broke the horizon, its blissful orange hue creeping across the undulating savannah, filling me with a deep warmth and optimism. I felt a tremendous sense of privilege mixed with excitement to be setting off on a journey that, until Thum and Perkins, had flummoxed so many expeditions.

"Do you realize you got up at five am?" said a tired-looking Marian when the others finally roused themselves around seven o'clock–the implication being that I'd woken him.

"Do you realize you snored all night?" I countered.

He hadn't.

Breakfast was dumplings filled with melted cheese and ham, cooked over a small gas burner, as well as instant coffee or hot chocolate served in bright plastic picnic ware with teeth marks around the rim. Farrin took a sip of his morning coffee then peered into his cup with a mixture of curiosity and caution, as if half expecting to find a dead rat afloat inside.

"For the price we paid, you'd think they could have got some decent coffee."

By seven thirty, we were ready but our porter, who was supposed to be carrying additional food supplies, was nowhere to be seen.

"He'll have to catch up later on," said Alex.

Alex had warned us there'd be a couple of river crossings today, so I intentionally wore my jungle boots, designed with lightweight fabric around the ankles to shed water quickly and dry out fast–the outdoorsman's equivalent of catwalk chic–so I was keen to try them out for real, having previously only worn them around the wilds of London's Hampstead Heath to soften them up in readiness for Venezuela.

"I'm going to stay with the slowest person. So you can go at your own speed," he told us as we set off.

I threw on my backpack, and it wasn't long before I was powering ahead out in front–I wanted to work some of my enthusiasm out on the track. In no time, I was sweating buckets, and my chest was heaving like a bellows as I marched across the blazing shadeless landscape. There was a definite satisfaction in the exertion, which, coupled with the wide-open savannah and solitude from being alone, produced a meditation of sorts.

Lizards scurried over the stony track that snaked its way across the immediate terrain of gently undulating grassland, providing slight peaks and troughs along which to power up or coast down. The blue sky with a hint of purple was marked occasionally by a multicolored bird or vulture circling overhead, and always, the mighty Roraima in the distance. To the Pemon, all tepuis held special spiritual significance–being known as "houses of the spirit"–but Roraima, which is the tallest of them all, was especially venerated. Their creation stories speak of Roraima being the remaining stump of a mighty magical tree of life that once bore all the known fruits of the world. When one of their ancestors Ma'nápe, felled the tree against the wishes of his brothers, it crashed to the ground, creating the rivers with its branches and the jungle with its leaves. From the center of its stump then gushed a catastrophic flood–reflected in the literal translation of the word *Roraima*, which is "great flood."

I dropped my pack at a stream lined with trees following the curving route of moisture across the landscape. The water was apparently safe to drink, so I submerged my water bottles in the cool trickling brook. Staggered gasps of silvery bubbles scrambled from the flasks, racing for the surface as water quickly replaced air. I dunked my head in the stream and almost felt myself "hiss" with relief, like a doused overheating engine. The rhythms of my chest began to decrease in speed and amplitude as I sat in the shade, savoring the cool liquid from my canteen. When tired, hot, and seriously thirsty, water is without doubt the greatest of all drinks.

After what seemed an unfairly short while given the distance between us, the others arrived.

We continued hiking until we reached a thigh-high river crossing. Snapping loose the waist strap of my backpack, I shifted the pack onto one shoulder, poised to bounce it off if necessary when crossing. If you fall into a river with a backpack securely attached to your person, then the pack will float upright and you'll be suspended facedown underwater. To protect against this, you want to carry your pack in such a way that should you need to, you can get it off quickly and then clamber on top of it–using the pack as a float.

Safely on the other side we stopped for "lunch." Despite this morning's assurance that the porter carrying the food would be joining us, he had yet to materialize. In his absence, Alex handed out crackers and cookies.

With such meager rations, there was no need for us to worry about the perils of eating before swimming, so Farrin and I headed into the boulder-strewn river for an invigorating dip amongst the gushing waters. Moments later Josephine floated down to join us. When it was time to get out, she struggled against the current, finally hoisting herself in an ungainly manner onto a rock where she squatted momentarily on all fours, revealing now for the first time her bathing attire which had gone unnoticed in the water. About a foot from Farrin's face was Josephine's king-size ass split down the middle by a minuscule G-string, drawing your attention to areas you wished it didn't.

Farrin looked over with a smile when Josephine had moved out of earshot.

"The jungle she's got there could rival the Amazon."

We headed back on the trail now, the incline of the hike becoming more severe as did the sun, which tore through my sunblock and existing tan. Farrin and I walked out front together, leaving the group a long way behind.

Put an Aussie and a Brit together, especially somewhere the Brit can't escape, and in my experience, it's only a matter of time before the Australian steers the subject towards sports–with him rambling on about how much better at it his nation is than the British, or the "poms" as they like to call us. Farrin instigated some good-natured persiflage regarding rugby, cricket, and the Olympics.

"Listen, pal," I countered. "You may be better at sport than us, but at least when we host the Olympics, we'll have a better cultural icon to proudly display to the rest of the world than your beloved rotary washing line."

"Whoa there, British!" said Farrin. "The Hills Hoist is a hallowed and much-revered Australian invention, and I won't–repeat, won't–hear it spoken about disparagingly."

For those of you unaware of the significance to Australians of the Hills Hoist or rotary washing line–something I was ribbing Farrin about for it featuring prominently in the 2000 Sydney Olympics' closing ceremony, when stilt walkers minced about with replicas of it on their heads–then I'll enlighten you. It's a washing line. It rotates. And an Aussie invented it. End of story.

Now it's not that it's a bad invention, but if a washing line is held up with such admiration and affection as to be a central feature of a host nation's closing Olympic ceremony, then I think that speaks volumes about the rest of the country's contributions to world technological advances.

"So let me see," I said. "A Brit invented television, the steam engine, radar, coke smelting, the tin can, the jump jet, and the World Wide Web, amongst many other things, whereas you've got . . . a washing line."

"Not just *any* washing line. Its efficient rack-and-pinion winding mechanism allows for the raising or lowering of the line."

"It doesn't exactly rival the invention of the wheel now, does it?"

"Ah, but the critical floor in your argument, British, is that you're not taking the long-term view. Yes, over the stretch of human evolution *so far*, the wheel would probably come out on top. But who knows what joys and treasures the Hills Hoist will bring to humanity given the same stretch of time in the future?"

After seven hours of hard slog, some of the group were beginning to flag. Farrin and I had maintained our position out front and waited now on a rocky outcrop high above the surrounding plains for the others to appear below.

Josephine was first on the scene, followed a good half an hour later by Alex, Marian, and Edyta. As they approached in the distance, it was clear that Edyta was struggling, with Marian carrying both his pack and hers. Arriving with us, Edyta had lost her characteristic smile and near collapsed onto Marian, lying now with her head on his thighs and her eyes closed. Within seconds, she seemed to be asleep. She looked completely and utterly exhausted. If we could have camped here, then I'm sure we would have done so, but it was no spot to throw down a tent.

"How long have we got to the camp?" asked Farrin.

"About two hours," replied Alex.

Edyta didn't react. She was out cold, and it was probably just as well she didn't know how much farther remained, at least until she'd got some of her strength back up. Marian, who had been hauling twice the amount of kit as everyone else, was looking tired too. I wondered if going at a slower fragmented pace to help Edyta had also worn him out. For me, it seemed far easier to maintain a constant steady rhythm than constantly stopping and starting.

"Would you like me to take your pack for the final stretch?" I asked.

"I'll be OK. Thank you, though."

Earlier on when taking a water break, Farrin and I had briefly picked up each other's packs to check out the relative differences in weight. With a tent and other camping gear in his, Farrin's was significantly heavier. I was curious as to whether I could keep pace with his heavier pack and offered to exchange for a while. He'd declined but said he might take me up on the offer later.

Forty minutes of uphill struggle after leaving the group, and Farrin and I were parallel with Roraima's sister tepui, Cuquenan, from which a waterfall dropped roughly two thousand feet before hitting a section of steep rocks and cascading into the mountain's forested lower reaches. This was Cuquenan Falls, often described in Venezuela as the second highest waterfall in the world, although there is some dispute over this arising from whether or not the lower portion of the falls that hits the rocks should be included in the official measurement.

The savannah had begun to recede, replaced by scrub vegetation, much of which was burnt. Roraima loomed much closer now, jutting out from the surroundings like a giant impassable, wedge-shaped barricade. I could well imagine how past expeditions considered the mountain unclimbable and wondered how on earth we'd get to the top. Around its base, rising up a sloping section to the mountain's two thousand feet vertical main wall, was thick jungle. And from the wall itself, several tumbling ribbons of water cascaded into the forest. The rock face was a crusty mixture of soft pinks and oranges, charcoal grays and browns. It was damned impressive.

I was getting pretty tired myself now, and Farrin and I began fantasizing about having a cold beer on our arrival at the camp site. I could almost feel the glass of the bottle pressing gently against my parched lips and the distinctive symphony of bubbles on my tongue.

Suddenly, out of the blue, we stumbled into camp.

"That wasn't two hours!" exclaimed Farrin, surprised to have arrived in about half that time. Alex had been very conservative with his ETA.

The camp's main feature was a small traditional hut thatched with palm leaves. Nearby were some clear patches of sandy ground to pitch tents, one of which was already here, flapping about in a rather sorry state of repair, clearly abandoned. It had tear marks down its front, through which could be seen a bagful of trash.

It wasn't long before the group made it to camp. Amazingly, Edyta looked a new person. She was cheery faced and bright eyed. I couldn't believe my eyes.

"You look so much better!" I exclaimed.

"I took some aspirin and electrolytes."

They'd certainly done the job. Thankfully, the porter had now caught up with Alex and was carrying ample supplies lashed together inside a strange homemade external-framed open backpack. It wasn't long before we had set up camp and were settling down to a hot meal of spaghetti Bolognese cooked over the stove and were knocking back a couple of neat shots of rum served in plastic cups. As night arrived, we sat around in the hut, illuminated by flickering candlelight. Through its open-fronted side, we watched a distant thunderstorm which, along with the iridescent fireflies drifting across the landscape, provided the perfect prebedtime entertainment.

We started early, heading steeply uphill one minute, abruptly down the next, but always through the dense jungle towards Roraima's towering rock wall.

Earlier on over breakfast, Alex had pointed out today's initial target. Riding up the vertical rock face was a foliage-covered diagonal ramp of a path ascending at roughly thirty degrees all the way to the summit. From a distance it looked just about wide enough to walk on, that is until I spotted the tiny figures of a group descending. It was huge, putting the mountain, and the daunting climb ahead, into perspective.

Thanks to blisters I suffered yesterday I swapped my boots for some lighter weight worn-in sneakers, and in no time, Farrin and I had left the group long behind. After about an hour, we passed the descending group–the last member of whom looked exhausted and had got the porter to carry his backpack–and made it to the start of the ramp.

"I'll take you up on that offer of swapping packs now if you like," said Farrin, jokingly, as we stared up at the challenge ahead.

Oh what the hell, I thought. Why not?

"All right then."

Farrin promptly swapped backpacks with me. The tent, gas burner, and camping supplies in his made one hell of a difference even before I'd taken my first step while Farrin powered off with my lighter pack bounding up the ramp like a mountain goat. For a while, I managed to keep up, but soon he was a good distance ahead of me. The higher up we went, the more impressive the view below across the sprawling savannah became. Up ahead, a waterfall showered the ramp, making slippery and slick the mosses underfoot. I stood beneath it and cooled off. Brightly colored orchids decorated the route, and little birds darted about nearby. The ramp was supposed to take four hours to ascend, but in the end I managed it in three–Farrin slightly less than that.

"Wow!" I announced in a state of euphoria as I suddenly stepped onto the summit of the mountain that I had dreamt about and gazed at pictures of for years. I couldn't quite believe I was finally here. In a state of light-headed rapture, I bounded across the rugged rocky landscape to join Farrin perched by the edge, gazing across the plains. The view was staggering. Stretching as far as the eye could see was an ocean of green–yesterday's challenging hills looking now like mere insignificant ripples. Rivers appeared as thin lines of thread, burning swathes of savannah as tiny camp fires, trees as broccoli, distant forests as moss, those climbing below as ants. It was a strange grounding feeling standing here, as if at the axis around which the world and creation revolved. Somewhere, that time stood still, and I could remain forever. I felt at the center of my own universe and wouldn't have wanted to be anywhere else than exactly where I was at this moment–maybe Rafael was onto something after all with his tales of energy channels meeting here.

Farrin and I sat for a long while, taking in the grandeur as our sweat- and waterfall-saturated clothing dried out in the wind and sun. From his pack, Farrin retrieved and shared some candy, nuts, and raisins that he'd bought in Kyrgyzstan. They were a damn fine accompaniment to the view and the perfect way to replenish our energy after the punishing climb.

"Coooeee!" Farrin yelled out, Australian Aboriginal–style across the landscape, echoing repeatedly in the distance.

The surface of Roraima was more like a different planet than the summit of a mountain. Black rocks contorted to form towers and troughs, arches and gullies, caves and canyons. Pools of water and strange unearthly flowers and plants dotted the eerily quiet landscape, around which snaked paths of fine pink sand, while overhead flew green and yellow parrotlets.

"Up there is the seven-star hotel," said Alex, pointing to a tower of rock containing a cave beneath an overhang. As we got closer to it, we spotted tents inside from another climbing group.

We detoured to an overhang of rock up a little gully. We dropped our packs there and settled down for a lunch of ham and cheese sandwiches. Alex got the gas burner going and cooked up the saltiest soup I've ever had in my life. It was like trying to drink seawater.

"Alex, old chap, why in heaven's name have you put so much salt in it?" I asked, struggling to swallow the vile liquid.

"Because you can't get salt up here."

Mmm.

After a few subsequent attempted mouthfuls, I could take no more. It left me feeling decidedly queasy. And I wasn't the only one.

"Don't leave your passports or money in camp," warned Alex ominously before we set off to explore the summit.

After a couple of days' hard slog strapped to a backpack, the walk was wonderful. I felt light on my feet and soon was hopping over rocks on the way to our first destination–the Jacuzzis.

En route, Alex pointed out an edible plant (*Stegolepis guianensis*). If you pulled out a leaf from the stalk, it made a squeaking sound as it released a succulent white heart from its inner sheaflike casing. Alex passed several around, which–it's got to be said–were a damn sight better than his salt soup.

The thing about walking atop Roraima is that you can soon forget you're on the summit of a flat nine-thousand-foot mountain. By now, the edge was a long way out of sight and the landscape full of the sort of canyons and bare rock formations you'd expect in a desert environment–albeit a rather wet one. In fact, the summit is often referred to as a "rain desert," derived from the high frequency of rains which occur nearly every day, sometimes for several days on end, which wash away everything in their path and strip the surface of nutrients, leaving predominantly exposed rock with only scattered patches of sediment. This means that the plants of Roraima have been forced to develop curious ways of surviving, with many of them supplementing their food by becoming carnivorous.

As we walked, Alex was keen to point out rock formations that had been named for their apparent likeness to objects, people, and people. I stress the word "apparent" as some required a rather generous impressionistic license. They included "Fidel," a "camel," and a "donkey's rear end taking a shit."

The Jacuzzis were a collection of naturally formed depressions in the rock filled with yellow-tinged water. Some were hot tub sized, others the shape and dimensions of a coffin. Despite their appealing-sounding name, the water was bloody cold. Given the temperature, it was a brief although refreshing dip, in a freeze-your-balls-off kind of way. While getting changed, we noticed something seemingly innocuous and insignificant that would later be the source of all manner of trouble for our guide Alex–a towel hanging from a nearby rock left, presumably, by an absentminded member of the other group.

Our next stop was a scenic viewpoint on the edge of the mountain that overlooked Cuquenan. We shuffled along on our stomachs to peer over the edge, revealing a sheer vertigo-inducing drop of a couple of thousand feet into dense jungle. Nearby a pointed rock ledge stuck out from the surrounding cliff, forming the perfect vantage point on which to sit and take in the view. Farrin and I headed over to pose for the obligatory shots of us standing perilously close to the edge. As I looked back away from the drop towards Farrin, behind me with the camera, I tried to look unfazed by the stomach-churning precipice I knew was just a foot or so behind me. I could feel myself leaning involuntarily towards him to prejudice the direction I should go were I to slip. The wind struck up, releasing a drop of adrenaline in the pit of my stomach that persuaded me to step onto terra firma proper and call it a day.

It all kicked off on the way back to camp when Alex took a call on his radio from the porter who had stayed behind, getting things set up. He signed off looking upset.

"The other guides on the mountain are accusing me of stealing a passport and a wallet with six hundred dollars from a Frenchman at the Jacuzzi."

What the fuck?

After a bit of digging, Alex explained that the Frenchman had apparently absentmindedly left his belongings there and that his group had returned to pick them up but found nothing except the towel we'd seen earlier. Since our group had been the last to pass through, they were accusing Alex.

"They want me to sign a confession and return the passport or I'll be banned from being a tour guide."

They surmised that as this was the first tour Alex had led up Roraima, and since all the members of his group were foreigners, and therefore didn't need the money, it must have been him.

They didn't have much of a case, and I was sure it would all be sorted out once we told them Alex had nothing to do with it. He insisted it would be the end of his career as a tour guide.

"This is my first day ever leading a group on top of Roraima. No one will believe me. They will never let me work or come up the mountain again," he insisted.

By dusk, we had arrived in camp. Alex and the porter went off to talk with the other guides at the "seven-star hotel," leaving us alone to discuss the situation.

"Of all the things to happen on your first day at a new job, getting accused of stealing has to rank pretty damn high up there as the worst," said Farrin.

I agreed, although if sheer embarrassment to the extent of being immortalized in company folk-law was the barometer by which a bad first day was measured, then I knew of worse.

I had once briefly worked for an investment bank in London's financial district where I was told a wonderful story about an unfortunate young trainee's first day on the job that I was assured was true.

At lunchtime on his first day at the bank, the spotty school-leaver had been given a seemingly straightforward errand.

"We're having a working lunch today," said the section's boss to the witless new guy. "So I'm going to get you to pop down the shops to grab lunch for us. Daniel would like a BLT, Kieran wants a tuna and sweet corn, and I'll have a cheese and tomato." He handed the new boy a crisp fifty-pound note, adding, "And get something for yourself with the change."

He did. Returning fifteen minutes later with a thirty-five-pound anorak.

When Alex and the porter returned, they seemed more convinced than ever that Alex was screwed.

"They are going to search all of us at the Inparques office when we get back. If I do not sign the confession, they will ban me."

"And if you do sign it, they'll ban you anyway," said Marian.

Searching everyone would be a complete waste of time. If someone had taken the wallet and passport–as opposed to the French guy losing them–then they would have ditched the items already and kept the six hundred dollars.

Soon after daybreak the next morning, we headed off to the so-called triple point, where Brazil, Venezuela, and Guyana meet–although a lot of Venezuelans would dispute that point, as Venezuela claims Guyana's land west of the Essequibo River as theirs, with the region labeled on maps as *Zona en Reclamación.*

En route, we stopped at a valley covered in magnificent sparkling quartz. This was something Venezuela's greatest explorer, Charles Brewer-Carias, discovered in 1976 and appropriately named, Valle de los Cristales–"valley of the crystals." All around were thousands of these beautiful white-and-pink crystals that you could pick up off the floor in huge handfuls. It was, however, highly prohibited to keep any as souvenirs, and the park rangers looked for them when conducting their routine searches.

To get to the triple point took several hours of hiking through an impossibly difficult landscape to navigate, comprising of countless similar-looking gullies and rock formations. By the time we arrived at the "triple point," it was something of a disappointment. There was a modest white triangular monument in the middle of a landscape that looked much the same as what we'd walked through to get there. The monument contained a sign for Venezuela on one side, a sign for Brazil on the other, and nothing on the third side.

"When Chávez came here, he removed the sign for Guyana," said Alex with a cheeky grin, having perked up considerably since the night before.

More interesting was our next stop–a hidden underground grotto with a little beach that led to a natural open-air sinkhole, large enough to swim in. From this were several partially eroded walls forming natural columns, which gave the place the feeling of a Roman bath. We relaxed here and ate a sandwich before starting the long twisting trek back. On the way, Alex pointed out the tiny black Roraima frogs that crawled instead of jumped and rolled into a little ball if threatened. They existed nowhere else in the world, with their nearest relative being a frog from West Africa–both of which share a common ancestor from when the continents of South America and Africa were joined. Other curiosities included a beautiful orange-breasted falcon and white-collared swifts with distinctive rings around their necks as well as several brightly colored carnivorous plants, including insect-eating sundews and bladderworts, which like much of the strange life up here, occurs nowhere else but in these plateaus.

When walking past a particularly high black rock tower, I spotted a dog-sized black-and-white creature that resembled a raccoon, scurrying off into a crevice.

"A coati," said Alex.

These were the largest mammals on the summit and apparently quite a rare thing to spot.

Another odd creature that lived up here was the oilbird. This bizarre orangey brown nocturnal bird is about a foot and a half in length, has tiny practically useless feet, is nearly blind, and lives in caves–where it navigates by following the echo of its own distinctive clicks. The oilbird's name is derived from the tendency of its young to become extremely fat before developing flying feathers, which led to them once being hunted and rendered for oil. It is found elsewhere in South America, but like most things on Roraima, up here it goes a little mental. On Roraima, the colony of about five hundred birds, which live deep within a slot canyon, nest not in caves but in the full glare of sunlight.

It started to rain, hard, lashing us with an icy downpour combined with a chilling wind that funneled through the canyons, inducing involuntary shivers. We were a long way off, and the walk seemed to drag on forever–at one point I was convinced we'd walked in a circle. As we trudged on, Farrin and I again began to fantasize aloud–cold beers were far from our minds now with our thoughts now turned to a full roast. We chose a king prawn and scallop starter, medium-rare roast silverside beef served with all the trimmings for main, and finished up with a steam pudding drenched in hot custard. For wine we selected a full-bodied Shiraz and a sweet pudding wine with dessert–followed by brandy and biscuits, of course. It was pointless torment really but passed the time on the cold and arduous trek back to camp. Needless to say, we were thoroughly disappointed with the reality of dinner when some pasta and limp beans materialized. To make up for it, I promised Farrin that when he visited England, which he was planning to do in the next few months, I'd cook him our meal. About two months later, I did.

There wasn't really much to do after dark on Roraima, and with campfires prohibited, there was no illuminating and warming focal point around which to sit and let the conversation flow, so soon after dark, we hit the sack. Our tent was pitched on an incline, I discovered, and right in the middle of my bedroll protruded an annoying rib-digging bump. I shifted onto my back. I hated sleeping on my back. I moved onto my left side then tried my right. It was no better. In desperation, I tried shifting past the bump so that I was squashed right in the corner of the tent. It didn't work. Returning to my original front position, I discovered that things had gone from bad to worse. An opportunistic German landgrab had occurred while I was crammed in the corner. Marian had swooped, blitzkrieg-style, to occupy the tent equivalent of Poland–his knobbly elbow now protruding far beyond his original recognized border.

This was no time for appeasement. Britain was about to declare war. I launched a counterattack; faking a stretch that raised my arm high into the tent, I brought it down with a thump on top of Marian's elbow. With a jolt, he pretended to awaken, as if having been unaware of his encroachment.

Yeah, right.

He moved onto his side, facing me now. The inevitable retaliation occurred just minutes later when he was genuinely asleep and brought out the big artillery–his snoring. It was several decibels higher than the previous night's groaning and pointed straight at me–his mouth flapping about, releasing a stream of rhythmic hot air into the back of my head. It drove me insane. Every staggered grunt felt like the ultimate slap in the face, as if announcing through a bullhorn, "I'm in a state of total relaxation. You're not! And I'm preventing you from being so. Sleep well, my English friend!"

God, I hate sharing tents.

Farrin and I greeted the dawn gazing for a final time across the incredible views of the savannah, wrinkled with shadows from the low morning sun. A cool breeze blew our way and served as a rousing kick in place of a morning shower. We would be descending Roraima after breakfast. As we sat and talked of our journeys to come, the outside world with its chaotic repetitious rushings and commitments seemed so very far away–insignificant and trivial compared to the stark and beautiful reality of the present. The awe-inspiring view from Roraima had that effect on me, stripping away the unnecessary baggage of the mind, bringing the truly important into clarity.

With a distant shout, Alex called us back to camp for breakfast. Over a meal of dumplings and bad coffee, Marian turned to Edyta and briefly asked her something in his native German.

"How come you never speak to Edyta in Polish but she always speaks to you in German?" Farrin asked.

"Yes, Marian," Edyta responded, her face souring. "Why don't you make the effort to speak to me in Polish?"

Marian groaned reluctantly. A touchy subject had been exposed.

A devious idea flashed across my mind.

Before Marian had a chance to answer, I chipped in, like a complete and utter bastard. "Is it, like you told me last night, because it's such an unattractive language to listen to?"

Edyta whipped to face Marian, mouth agape in shock.

"No, I didn't say that!" he protested, holding up his hands submissively.

I let it hang in the air for a second or two, watching him squirm before finally saving his bacon by admitting I was kidding.

By noon we had descended the ramp and were sitting around at our first night's camping spot, looking up at the giant vertical wall that we had scaled just days before. There was a palpable sense of achievement in the air and a satisfaction unique to approaching the end of a long demanding journey. We were tired but happy. And it was all downhill from now.

I spent most of the day walking alone, pushing myself along the trail, reveling in the intensity of the heat and exertion. I felt so very alive, and my spirit soared to the sky. By midafternoon, I waited on the open planes and rejoined the group, who had somehow lost Alex and the porter. After waiting a good half an hour for them, we began to get concerned. Just when we were discussing whether it was worth going back to see they were okay, their sluggish-looking figures appeared on the horizon of a nearby rocky slope. A couple more hours and we made it to our camp for the night. Situated next to the Cuquenan River were several Pemon houses made in the traditional manner with materials from the two surrounding environments. The structural frames and roof were made of wood from the jungle; the solid walls of sun-baked mud from the savannah. Thatching the roofs were thick palm leaves, said to be harvested when the moon wasn't full–so that its gravitational influence didn't pull excessive moisture into the leaves, causing them to rot quicker.

"Fancy a fire tonight?" asked Farrin, who was keen to try his hand at something I had mentioned to him on the summit–hand-drill friction fire lighting. This was something of a specialty of mine, the necessary components for which I had in my backpack.

We collected some wood near the river where the greatest stash was located high above the water on the upper banks, deposited there by the river during last year's rainy season. In the process, we were descended upon by a rapacious squadron of tiny but aggressive sand flies, feasting on our skin, causing instantaneous and severe itching.

During our search for wood, it became apparent how tourism had decimated the vicinity. Strewn amongst the savannah's swaying grassland were piles of old cans and plastic bottles. Dotted around the bushes near the river were piles of decaying faecal matter and toilet paper left close enough to the water as to contaminate it come the first sign of rain. With no taps or wells nearby, this was the water the locals drank from. Why the park authorities hadn't erected a permanent drop toilet in the village for those not intelligent enough to work out where to go, I don't know.

We collected a fine hoard of firewood but held off lighting up until nightfall when we planned to while away the night with the bottle of rum, which had been two-thirds full the night before. Farrin went to collect it and came back, carrying a practically empty bottle.

"What happened, mate?"

"Alex and the porter polished it off last night!"

No wonder they'd been lagging behind.

By dusk, another group who were on their first day of hiking arrived. Amongst their group was the Frenchman, Sebastian, whom I had met at the posada in Ciudad Bolivar. As we were chatting, we suddenly spotted a rattlesnake next to one of the huts. It was a magnificent-looking creature with defiant eyes and skin that blended in superbly with the track. I had only seen a rattlesnake once before when I nearly stepped on one just off a trail in Arizona. It had been very agitated, shaking its characteristic rattle alarm. Sadly, the one in camp seemed equally distressed, and it had good reason. The locals were adamant that, in the interests of safety around camp, it had to be dispatched. I left them to get on with the sorry task.

Sebastian was also keen to learn fire by friction, so when night-time fell, he and Farrin joined me at the village fire pit. Just as I started rotating the drill between my palms, in order for it to rub against a small wooden board below, an old, weathered-looking Pemon woman came over and looked at me as if a fool. She held out her cigarette lighter. Farrin and Sebastian were in fits of laughter. I politely declined. She shook her head dismissively and went off to sit, not ten feet away, where she began laying her own fire. After a minute of drilling, I'd produced a smoldering ember, which I dropped into a bundle of dry grass to ignite, and soon had a proper fire going. Nearby, the Pemon woman dowsed her wood with a small bottle of kerosene and sparked it up.

"That's priceless," said Farrin. "The Pemon native's got a bottle of kero on the go, but the Brit from London's using a couple of bloody sticks!"

CHAPTER 11

Rough Justice

"What's the word for *stupid* in Spanish?" I asked Alex in the crowded confines of the small Inparques office at the start of the trail in Paraitepui.

"Estúpido."

I flicked the handwritten piece of paper that the park officials were trying to get him to sign back in their direction, accompanied with my new learnt Spanish dictum. They'd been harassing Alex for over half an hour in an attempt to force him to sign a confession they'd written out for him, admitting that he'd stolen the passport and money. We told him to admit to and sign nothing.

"This cannot be. This cannot be," Marian kept repeating to himself incredulously, as if due process meant something here. None of the officials standing over a distressed-looking Alex spoke any English, and none of us Spanish, so we were simply lending moral support during the interrogation. Our group had already been searched with no results.

This wasn't the way I wanted to end such a wonderful journey, although even before Alex's ridiculous treatment, my final day had not really gotten off to the best of starts. I'd awoken in the wee hours of the morning to water dripping in my face and to the unfortunate realization that one of the tent's corners was flooded. Much of the gear piled there was saturated. My sleeping bag had become soaked on the outside, although thankfully had not seeped through. When heading to Roraima, we'd had dry nights and, on the mountain itself, had camped beneath an overhanging rock ledge, so last night's downpour was the tent's first proper test. It failed miserably.

Eventually, our ride back to Santa Elena rolled up, driven by a moody young guy in his twenties, wearing dark black shades and the permanent frown of a wannabe hard man. With his arrival, Alex left the office–thankfully without signing the officials' silly little confession.

The door of the four-wheel-drive emitted a satisfying and precise clunk as it enclosed us inside the distantly familiar but wholly welcome world of fresh-smelling air-conditioned civility. Discovering modernity and its conveniences again was like becoming reacquainted with an old and reliable friend. Taking the weight off my feet, I almost melted into the comfy and the generous rear seat. The wheels spun, and we set off. Careering along the dirt track, we threw up huge plumes of red dust in our wake as the grassy landscape flew by outside. I felt a whole new appreciation for the wonders of the internal combustion engine and its alchemy-like transformation of fuel into piston power, rotation and motion, manifested through the chunky tread of the vehicle's oversized tires that propelled us in minutes over distances that would have taken us hours on foot. It was bliss.

It was a fun journey back to town in which our tough-guy driver shattered his image by slipping on and singing with gusto to a Backstreet Boys album, tapping away on the gear stick to the beat as he belted out the effeminate lyrics. When we pulled into Santa Elena, it no longer seemed quite the sleepy backwater it once had been–more a dazzling metropolitan hive of commerce and activity. Such were the effects of a week of near isolation in the wild.

With the exception of Josephine, who had to leave on an early bus, we all booked in at the posada where we had left our excess kit and indulged in a leisurely session cleaning ourselves up. There is something deeply satisfying about taking a prolonged steaming shower, having a slow methodical shave, putting on some crisp clean clothes, and generally sprucing yourself up after several days of letting yourself go. By the time I finished, I felt like a new man.

Despite Rafael's promise of a relaxing day tour at the end of our hike to make up for us having lost our first day, none materialized. In fact, neither did he. In his absence, Farrin and I spent a lazy afternoon pottering around town. By the evening, Santa Elena had transformed into quite the nightspot, and although much smaller in size than Ciudad Bolivar, it was a hell of a lot more lively. The occupants of big gas-guzzling 1970s cars drove around town with their windows down and sound system blaring reggaeton beats, cruising past locals hanging out on the street, socializing and drinking, while others packed out the bars or danced the night away at "rumba parties"–something Alex had been looking forward to all week.

Farrin and I patronized a sports bar where we nursed several cold *Zulia* beers–or as Farrin described them in delightful Aussie parlance, "malt sandwiches"–and indulged our food fantasies, with me getting stuck into a succulent and sublime wedge of steak served with a creamy mushroom sauce and Farrin chowing down on some roast chicken.

Over our food, we discussed our journeys ahead. I was planning to venture next to the city of Mérida, located in the west of the country deep within the Andes. Farrin was undecided as to his next stop. After telling him of Mérida's many attractions, he agreed to come along. He'd done a bit of CouchSurfing himself outside of Venezuela so was equally keen to give this a try, and so before we headed back to crash out at our posada, we got down to an Internet café and messaged a load of CouchSurfers to try and secure a place to stay.

"Where's my flashlight?" demanded Rafael in an accusatory tone after popping into the posada in the morning–the implication in his voice being that I was trying to pull a fast one and make off with it.

Well, up yours, I thought. After all, it wasn't as if I could have handed it back to him yesterday since he didn't turn up to take us on our promised savannah tour, nor could I have taken it to him since I had no idea where his offices were or of his telephone number. I fetched his beloved flashlight then mentioned the leaking tents.

"That's the national park office's fault. We hire the tents from them."

Nothing, it seemed, was his responsibility, be it the guides not carrying first aid kits or the shoddy equipment supplied. I couldn't be bothered to make an issue of it as at the end of the day, I'd still had a great time, although this was thanks to Roraima, not him.

"I hear there was a problem with the guide," he said, referring to Alex.

In an attempt to help Alex out, Farrin and I explained the situation on the mountain and that there was no evidence whatsoever to implicate him in taking the Frenchman's things.

"Maybe I shouldn't say this," said Rafael, looking about furtively as if checking whether anyone nearby was listening. "But whenever there's a problem with a group, it's *always* the fucking French!"

We laughed.

"I had two of them arrested once after they cancelled their credit card payments and tried to slink off after a tour without paying."

I wondered if he'd have done the same for the flashlight.

An overnight coach ride saw Farrin and me arrive at the bus terminal in Ciudad Guayana en route to Mérida. Dumping our packs by a large communal bench, we sat down to discuss what to do until our connecting bus arrived. Moments later, we were approached by a group of odd-looking guys and girls in their early twenties. They were suspiciously friendly and spoke excellent

English, initiated by a charismatic, handsome and well-built alpha male type who did most of the talking.

"Hi there, where are you both from?"

We told him.

"Wow, that's really fantastic," he said, the group nodding agreement with strange insincere smiles.

"Where have you both been in Venezuela?"

After a cagey description of our destinations, he asked, "Is there anything we can help you with?"

We explained that we were fine, but I was curious as to how they spoke such good English, as generally in Venezuela, people don't.

"We are Jehovah's Witnesses and practice English to evangelize."

Oh great.

No sooner had he said this than they were giving us the good news, telling of the paramount importance of casting out devils from our lives and trying their damnedest to force booklets onto us and personal e-mail addresses and telephone numbers out of us. Farrin politely refused a chunky textbook-sized offering from an odd-looking guy, who began to get aggressive on failing to off-load his material.

"In Venezuela, it is rude not to accept something someone gives you as a gift!"

"In Australia, it's rude to keep pushing something onto someone who doesn't want it," replied Farrin.

The lead guy was all smiles and smoothed things over, gently reprimanding his colleague and apologizing for his wayward tone.

"You must excuse my friend, it's just, after seeing the transformation our message has made to his life, he is very passionate about spreading it to others."

He was a very slick operator indeed, and I could imagine his "sales" figures were far higher than the rest of the group. He turned to me and asked if he could take my e-mail address so he could send me some interesting literature. I was about to make up a fake e-mail on the spot but then had a better, if slightly mischievous, idea. Years earlier, I had been at a house party in New Zealand where some drunken kiwis had tried to stitch up one of their friends, whose place it was, by setting the homepage on his computer–which he shared with his girlfriend–to a hard-core S&M website. The name of the website–which had stuck in my head–had given no indication as to its nature, having a rather innocuous address that sounded rather like an extreme sports site.

"I run a website specializing in adventure sports," I said. "If you want to contact me, then the easiest way is through the website, which has an e-mail contact section. I'd be delighted to hear from you. And maybe you could have a look at the site and let me know what you think. It's something I'm very passionate about spreading to others too."

I told him the website's name.

"Please do contact me. I'd be genuinely interested to know more."

He jotted down the site's name, as did several of the group, then turned and addressed them, saying something in Spanish that I took to be along the lines of, "You see, you've just got to ask nicely."

I stifled a giggle.

When they departed, Farrin shook his head at me with a knowing smile.

"Just what the fuck is on that site, British?"

We caught an overnight bus to get to Barinas and then boarded a far smaller and seriously rickety bus to Mérida, the engine of which coughed and spluttered as we went–causing a similar reaction from all on board who ended up inhaling clouds of noxious fumes that drifted back our way from its stressed mechanical depths–and by lunchtime, we had arrived in the mountainous city of Mérida. The landscape here was dramatically different to anything we'd seen so far in Venezuela, with the snowcapped rugged mountains of the high Andes dominating the town on every side. We immediately put through a call to one of the CouchSurfers, Juan, who along with his friend, Camilo, had offered us accommodation–something we'd managed to check at an Internet café in Ciudad Guayana. Juan was currently preoccupied at university where he was studying graphic design but passed on instructions on how to meet up this evening. The recommended rendezvous was the city's main square.

When we arrived in the heart of Mérida's vibrant center, we discovered beautiful colonial buildings and crowded narrow streets, along which hordes of shoppers and animated young people thronged. Sandwiching the city on either side were the towering peaks of the longest continental chain of mountains in the world–the Andes–which rose majestically skyward to heights of over fifteen thousand feet.

With time on our hands before this evening's meeting, Farrin and I purchased a corn turnover from one of the numerous street stalls and sat amongst the greenery of the main square opposite the city's imposing old cathedral. Here we kicked back with our feet resting on our packs, reading up on the area and its attractions.

Mérida was home to around three hundred thousand people, of which nearly fifty thousand were university students studying at the prestigious *University of the Andes*. With such a demographic, it was a great spot for a night out, with plenty of nightclubs and watering holes. It was Venezuela's main hub for adventure sports including mountaineering, white-water rafting, paragliding, mountain biking, and bungee jumping, and possessed the world's highest and longest cable car system which rose from its beginnings in the center of town to the top of the mountain, Pico Espejo, 15,633 feet up. The cable car not only provided spectacular views across the Andes but could be used as a convenient method to begin a mountain hike, saving you the exertion of the gruelling uphill leg.

Mérida was founded in 1558 by a Captain Juan Rodriguez Suárez while leading an expedition to find gold. He named the city after his Spanish birthplace and very nearly paid with his life for doing so. For to take such action without a royal decree from

Spain–something he did not possess–was seen as an audacious affront to the crown. And so the unfortunate captain was charged with "usurpation of royal prerogative" and summarily found guilty. His punishment may seem a tad out of proportion to the offense committed. It entailed being tied to the tail of a horse and dragged to a bumpy death through the cobbled streets of Bogotá. When thoroughly dead, his lifeless carcass would then suffer a thorough defiling by being sliced into quarters and left in the city streets to decay and be feasted upon by scavengers. Not surprisingly, the prospect of such a demise concentrated the mind of the unfortunate captain, who managed to escape before the gruesome sentence could be enacted. He fled to Trujillo where he sought, and was granted, political asylum–making him the New World's first political refugee. Just two years after his illegitimate founding of Mérida, it was officially bestowed with the same name, making you wonder what all the fuss was about in the first place.

After a good deal of exploring the center of the city, by early evening we had made our way back to our agreed rendezvous spot to meet up with Juan and Camilo. Farrin was first to recognize our hosts as they ambled towards us through the square. Both were in their twenties. Camilo, having come from work, was wearing a shirt, tie, and dress pants whereas Juan sported those Venezuelan favorites of a striped polo shirt and jeans. Both had beaming smiles, Camilo's framed by a well-trimmed beard. After a brief introduction, it was decided that I would stay with Camilo and Farrin with Juan. We parted ways now but arranged to meet up at Camilo's house first thing in the morning.

A stroll through the city and a short walk uphill along one of the Mérida's main traffic-choked highways, and Camilo and I arrived at his humble ground-floor apartment, located just off the main road. Here we were greeted by his mother, who despite speaking no English, immediately conveyed a hospitable welcome through her motherly smile and warm friendly gestures. By now I was kind of getting used to rocking up at a stranger's home and being treated like one of the family. That's not to say that I was taking such fantastic generosity for granted–in fact quite the opposite–but it no longer seemed quite so alien a process after sending but the briefest of e-mails to a prospective host.

The apartment was clean and modern inside, set out with an open-plan living and kitchen area, off where a secluded television room and a couple of cozy-looking bedrooms were located. Camilo led me into a bedroom.

"This is your room. My home is your home."

I hadn't been expecting my own room but was delighted with the news. After two nights sleeping on buses, preceded by a six-day hike and mountain climb, I was good and ready to crash out on a nice comfy bed where there was no chance of getting drenched from above or kept awake by those snoring like a foghorn nearby.

"The superhero pictures are for my nephew when he comes to stay," explained Camilo, on seeing me inspecting the room's curious décor of Spider-Man, Superman, and Batman. Superman watched over me as I fell asleep.

CHAPTER 12

The Domino Effect

"Actually, I guess I do love Chávez!" exclaimed Camilo with a big toothy grin and a laugh of unexpected realization, for moments earlier he'd said he supported Chávez but did not "love him like the Chavistas." He'd quickly revised this position after explaining to me and Farrin how Chávez had stood up to Bush and Obama. The more he described his admiration for Chávez, the more he convinced himself that, actually, he did share the Chavistas' affection for the president after all.

Farrin and Juan had arrived earlier at Camilo's place for breakfast, which came in the form of fried eggs, strong black coffee, and thick corn bread, all cooked by Camilo's wonderful mother. While eating, we discussed our hosts' political persuasions and what they thought of the Bolivarian revolution. Of the two, Juan was far more neutral on Chávez than Camilo. Both, however, shared a general affinity for his defiant stance towards the United States. Camilo in particular had a disdain for Obama and the crushing disappointment of what he saw as his broken promises.

"Has Obama closed Guantánamo? No. Has Obama left Iraq? No. Chávez asked him, 'Mr. Obama, who are you!?'"

I got in on this one and chipped in that Obama had voted to reinstate the Orwellian-named Patriot Act;[41] excused torture;[42] opposed habeas corpus;[43] that despite his promises of ending the war in Iraq, there would be, in reality, no voluntary withdrawal, with some fifty thousand U.S. troops set to remain in ninety-four permanent military bases after any token departure (along with over one hundred thousand "military contractors");[44] and that he had expanded the war into Pakistan where his computer-game-style pilotless predator drone aircraft–which are largely controlled out of the United States by remote control–had killed over one thousand innocent Pakistani civilians.[45] Such is Obama's collateral damage. For me, former Democratic congresswoman and African American Cynthia McKinney said it best: "[The Democratic Party] would like to make a distinction that . . . there is a difference between a Bush drone that kills a family in Afghanistan and an Obama drone that kills a family in Afghanistan. I say, there is no difference."[46]

The general plan today was for Farrin and me to go and see a few sights with Juan, who had managed to wrangle a day off from his studies. Camilo, unfortunately, had to work today. He was employed with an orchestra foundation funded by the government, which was putting on a free concert for the town's residents this morning at a municipal building in town. He offered to take us to this before we set off exploring.

As we left his apartment, Juan pointed out two white-coated nurses going from door to door in the street. These, he explained, were offering free advice to residents on health matters and were checking if anyone needed assistance. We saw much the same in the city's main square where similarly dressed medical staff worked out of a small red marquee, offering free health and nutritional advice to passersby, and providing free consultations–one of which was in progress with a woman being weighed on a large set of scales labeled "health-o-meter." Across the side of the marquee were pictures of fresh fruit, grains, and vegetables, next to which was a cheesy picture of a grinning Chávez.

The concert was held in the spacious grand lobby of an old municipal colonial building. The orchestra filled much of this space so we positioned ourselves on a balcony overlooking it and watched from above. Soon after arriving, the glorious and uplifting music began. Don't ask me who the composer was, but the music was delightful.

Such free concerts are common in Venezuela and classical music extremely popular, with the country having produced some of the finest musicians on the planet. The Venezuelan Youth Orchestra in particular is globally renowned and has captured the imagination of millions, breathing new life into the often staid and formal world of classical music through its energetic and dynamic performances. Many of the country's top musicians come from extremely underprivileged barrio backgrounds and learnt their chosen instrument through a unique and wonderful music program known as El Sistema, or "the system." This, along with the Venezuelan Youth Orchestra which comprises part of it, is a source of extreme national pride.

El Sistema was developed in 1975 by amateur musician and economist José Antonio Abreu, who believed that if young people from poor backgrounds were given the opportunity to learn a classical instrument and experience the community of an orchestra, it would instill such a sense of self-esteem and confidence in them that it would help protect the child from the dangers of their environment–such as participation in crime and drug abuse. José Antonio Abreu describes El Sistema's mission as assisting in "the fight of a poor and abandoned child against everything that opposes his full realisation as a human being." The system's motto is "To play and to fight."

To date, eight hundred thousand children have been through the program, most of whom would, under normal circumstances, have had little chance of learning a classical instrument. The program is run nationwide and takes children from as young as two years old who are taught the language of music and the basics of rhythm. When they get to four, they begin to learn their first instrument and are encouraged to play in front of audiences. By six or seven years old, they are playing in proper orchestras. In Venezuela, the sound of children practising their instruments is commonplace. And "the system" doesn't just take on young children; many of their greatest success stories have come from juveniles who, before learning an instrument, were heavily involved in serious criminal activities but who, through El Sistema, have transformed their lives.

The main focus of the system is not to produce world-class musicians, although it does plenty of that, but as José Antonio Abreu explained in an interview with *60 Minutes*, "Music produces an irreversible transformation in a child. This doesn't mean he'll end up as a professional musician; he may become a doctor, study law, or teach literature. What music gives them remains indelibly part of who he is forever." In an interview with the BBC, Antonio Mayorca, who played first violin in the Simón Bolívar Youth Orchestra and taught music for El Sistema, described the transformation children go through. "I saw the whole evolution. [In the beginning] you saw a certain sadness in their faces. But when they started to play music, it was different. The light that they transmitted taught me a lot."

That "light" had a dramatic effect on renowned tenor Plácido Domingo. When he saw the Venezuela Youth Orchestra play, he wept, saying that during the concert, he had experienced the strongest emotion in his life. And on the strength of just one performance, the director of the Berlin Philharmonic Orchestra–generally considered the finest orchestra in the world–invited them to play in Germany. Such is their effect on people.

Most of their current budget comes from the Chávez government, although they have successfully functioned through eight different Venezuelan administrations both left and right wing. Despite receiving huge state assistance, this does not fully cover their huge overheads, which have to pay for incredible quantities of instruments, and so they are always looking for donations.

Although I couldn't know for sure, it seemed likely that the orchestra we listened to would have been made up, at least in part, of graduates from El Sistema; such is the system's size and scope.

After bidding Camilo farewell for the day, Juan took us to an art gallery located inside a large concrete building that brought to mind a multistorey 1960s car park. On the ground floor was a shop which, Juan explained, was run by the government to let artists and craftspeople exhibit and sell their work for a fraction of the fee privately run galleries charged. I thought it was a great idea and that some of the work inside was excellent.

Our next stop on Juan's tour of the city was a very interesting establishment indeed. At first glance, it appeared to be an extremely small and dusty secondhand record store, run by a kindly old gentleman who didn't seem to be doing much in the way of business. It was a mighty strange choice of location to have brought us, but since we were here, I decided to have a flick through the records. Just as I was about to do so, Juan and the old man shared a curious informed nod of the head. Without further ado and with no word spoken, the old guy lifted up the store's folding counter and escorted us through to a nearby door. On the other side was a different world.

Here out the back of the "shop" was a bar–which Juan confirmed for us was unlicensed–complete with domino tables, televisions showing sports, and an open courtyard beyond. It was decorated with pictures of what in Venezuela I would describe as a celebration of women–elsewhere, porn. Pictures of naked nymphs coming out of the water stood alongside topless women and a large psychedelic-colored close-up shot of a woman's face midorgasm. As we grabbed an ice-cold beer and took a seat, I queried Juan on this peculiar Venezuelan obsession with the female form and in particular, the popularity of beauty contests.

After chatting about this for a while, Juan mentioned that his brother, Eduard, had a good friend who has dated a former Miss Mérida, who went on to compete for the Miss Venezuela crown, and that if I wanted, Eduard could arrange for me to visit the headquarters of the Miss Venezuela beauty pageant school on my return to Caracas. This was where the most outstandingly beautiful women in the country went through something like a boot camp of beauty in their quest to be crowned the national champion. The thought of getting better acquainted with the cream of Venezuela's lovely ladies wasn't the sort of offer I needed to think twice about, and so I dutifully accepted. Caracas hadn't been my favorite of destinations so far in Venezuela, but the thought of returning there now seemed wholly appealing.

The Miss Venezuela school sounded a bizarre and intriguing place. Based in a sprawling pink mansion located at the foot of Caracas's highest peak, the school was run under the ever-watchful eye of a sixty-four-year-old former draughtsman and dressmaker, Osmel Sousa–known as the king of the beauty queens. Under Sousa's tenure, Venezuela has become the undisputed world champion of international beauty pageants. Venezuelan women have dazzled and strutted their way to nearly sixty international titles, including five Miss Worlds, five Miss Internationals and six Miss Universes, two of which were won back-to-back, a feat unparalleled by any other country.

Although viewed in many countries with derision as an outdated throwback to a more sexist time, beauty pageants are unfathomably popular in Venezuela, with the Miss Venezuela pageant being the most watched television program, eclipsing even major sporting events. This national obsession with beauty can be seen in many different walks of Venezuelan life; there are queens crowned in schools (both grade and high school), corporations, carnivals, even penitentiaries where female prisoners compete against each other.

Thousands of aspiring young women apply yearly to enter their regional beauty pageants, the sixty winners of whom get to attend the esteemed Miss Venezuela school in Caracas. These beauties are then whittled down to a final twenty-eight who compete for the national crown. Upon arrival at the school, the lucky few do not, as you might imagine, encounter an extensive pampering session in order to ready them for the contest, but receive a gruelling four-month training regime with working days that can last up to fourteen hours. The select few who progress to international competitions remain at the Caracas school for a whole year. The girls have to follow strict diets and exercise regimes and are repeatedly drilled in the finer points of makeup, bikini modeling, etiquette, walking in heels, and public speaking in the pursuit of their Barbie doll–like perfection.

For those aesthetic blemishes considered beyond the capabilities of mere makeup, and too time-consuming to warrant a labor-intensive prescription of vigorous exercise, there is always the surgical option. The school has its very own cosmetic surgeons and dentist, or "smile doctor," who carry out free operations for those at the school. With former Miss Venezuela competitors going on to have glittering careers as soap stars, TV reporters, even writers and politicians, it is perhaps unsurprising that so many girls go under the surgeon's knife.

The country's unrivalled success in international competitions is often put down to the exotic genetic mixing bowl of Spanish, African, and indigenous genes that makes up the county's demographic. However, the majority of contestants that make the national championships come not from the majority darker-skinned barrio backgrounds but affluent lighter-skinned areas, leading to accusations that the competition panders to a white concept of beauty that bears little resemblance to the majority of Venezuelan women. But whether light or dark, indigenous, African, European, or a combination thereof, Venezuela is certainly a country with a staggeringly high proportion of attractive women. I couldn't wait to visit the school and critique the young hopefuls.

A few rounds later and the bar was packed out, doing a thriving business. Camilo joined us after work, accompanied by his mother and two female friends, Nuhella and Virginia. Virginia was first up to introduce herself and did so struggling with the words.

"When I speak, I break the English," she apologized.

"And do you break the Englishmen as well?" asked Farrin with a smile and a suggestive glance my way. Everyone laughed.

For the next few hours, the beers flowed over multiple games of dominoes, and it wasn't long before I was suitably intoxicated. Arbitrarily, when the fancy took them, Camilo and Juan would jump up and dance salsa next to our table with one of the ladies. They were all very slick movers indeed.

Just like this morning, it wasn't long before the conversation turned to Chávez. Soon the Venezuelan president's many exploits were being contrasted against the U.S. president and announced by way of a toast with raised beer bottles.

"Was Obama a paratrooper?"

"No!"

Clink.

"Can Obama dance salsa?"

"No!"

Clink.

"Did Obama play professional baseball?"

"No!"

Clink.

"To Chávez!"

"Chávez!"

Clink.

It was a great laugh. God knows how many beers we had–which the women were putting away as easily as the guys–but it was a significant amount.

Playing on one of the television screens was a soccer match between Venezuela and the world supremos of the sport, Brazil. I hadn't been paying too much attention, and neither was the rest of the bar–not surprising given that baseball is far and away the most popular sport in Venezuela–but all of a sudden, the barman jumped up out of his seat as if someone had stuck a red-hot poker up his bum, yelling at the top of his voice "Venezuela!"

All eyes were immediately locked on the TV screen where the home team had just scored. Baseball fans or not, to score against Brazil is a big deal for any country, and the place erupted into raucous celebrations. The replay showed a spectacular strike, receiving more applause from the appreciative crowd. Oddly though, a moment later, a different goal against a completely different team was shown. Then after that another one. Followed by another. It didn't take long to figure out what had happened. There had been no goal against Brazil. It was a montage of previous Venezuelan goals shown during the half-time break, which the barman had glanced up at from his newspaper and assumed was live play. He looked an idiot now and was told so as much by several disgruntled punters. With an apologetic smile, he buried his head back in his newspaper.

A guy wearing the red jacket of a fervent Chavista entered the bar. He smiled at a few of us and had a presence about him, drawing many approving nods and warm handshakes from around the room. The guy was obviously an important individual.

"That's the mayor of a neighboring town. He's a big Chavista and friend," explained Juan.

I liked it very much that the mayor was hanging out in an unlicensed drinking establishment and wondered whether other local bigwigs frequented the place. We spent four or five hours socializing, drinking, and playing dominoes before heading on to a nightclub near Camilo's place. By this stage, his mother had left. To get into the club, you didn't queue up and buy a ticket at the door but did so from a posse of ultratrim high-heeled beauty queens hovering around outside in minute hot pants and tight T-shirts displaying the club's logo and their oversized fake assets. The establishment was much the same as other nightclubs the world over except for the higher proportion of beautiful women and competent dancers, who not only danced the more traditional styles such as salsa but, when the music was appropriate, indulged in the super suggestive reggaeton–grinding away in an imaginative array of positions as if trying to wear through the fabric of their partner's clothing to get to the prize inside. It was quite a sight.

I awoke feeling hungover and needing food, something Camilo's wonderful mother kindly provided in the form of tasty home-cooked arepas and strong black coffee. Farrin and Juan joined us for breakfast, over which my Aussie traveling companion and I said our good-byes to our fun-loving and generous Venezuelan hosts.

Today, Farrin and I were heading off towards Lake Maracaibo in search of the famed Catatumbo lightning–lightning that purportedly occurred in almost continuous succession throughout the night but with no accompanying claps of thunder. According to some of the promotional material I had seen in Mérida, a single bolt contained enough energy to illuminate all of South America's lightbulbs. The lightning was focused around the mouth of the Catatumbo River, which fed into the continent's largest lake, Lago de Maracaibo. It was situated on the other side of the Andes to our current position, where the phenomenon was known as the Maracaibo beacon.

I'd always loved electric storms, but despite how appealing the Catatumbo lightning sounded, Farrin and I were damned if we were going to do another tour and determined to go there independently. Surprisingly, our *Lonely Planet* guidebooks gave no advice on how to do this, simply stating, "Tours organized from Mérida . . . are the best way to see the Catatumbo lightning close-up." Juan and Camilo had likewise been in the dark on the matter, so under the guise of potentially booking a tour, Farrin and I popped into a couple of agencies to rustle out the necessary details. All the tours included some general local sightseeing before arriving in the village of Concha, which although some distance from Lake Maracaibo was located next to the beginnings of a marshy waterway that meandered through an expansive national park out onto the lake's 5,100-square-mile surface. Perched here above the water were several stilted buildings with prime unimpeded views of the surrounding area. These were used as viewing platforms to watch the lightning and as basic overnight accommodation.

As nice as this sounded, we couldn't help but wonder whether all this was unnecessary extravagance in order to justify the cost of the tour. On a good night, the lightning could apparently be seen from as far away as 250 miles, so we surmised that if we camped out at a suitable village on the lake's shore, then there'd be a pretty good chance of seeing it without shelling out for, or being constrained by, a tour. The only problem was there were no villages on the water's edge particularly close to the Catatumbo River mouth, with Concha itself being set well inland behind the national park. The nearest one indicated on our maps was San Antonio, some 30 miles (as the crow flies) away from the lightning's focal point. But whether San Antonio was a particularly good place to watch the lightning or had unimpeded views, we didn't know. There was only one way to find out, so we decided to head there. We agreed, though, that if the area turned out to be useless, then we'd make our way to Concha afterwards and attempt to source a boat-owning local willing to take us out to the stilted buildings–hopefully for significantly cheaper than booking a tour in Mérida.

With the towering Andes blocking the most direct route to our desired destination of San Antonio, we initially had to take a bus heading in the wrong direction until we passed through the twisting Andean valley in which Mérida sat. Our first stop was the town of El Vigia, where we changed buses entailing a tedious two-hour wait for an old battered 1970s minibus to fill up with the requisite number of passengers before it could set off. Whenever you take this type of transport in Venezuela, before you depart, a load of salesmen and women board the vehicle, taking turns to give an animated presentation of the product they're trying to sell–tea towels, candies, cookies, pens, pads of paper, trinkets, little plastic packets of water, fruit, that sort of thing. They nearly always start by handing out a sample of their wares to every person on board then walk up and down the aisle, giving their presentation before collecting up the products that haven't sold, or money for the ones that have, at the end.

The interesting thing about this whole process is that it doesn't matter how mundane and obvious the product is; those doing the selling will still give a dammed passionate, almost evangelical, sales pitch as if pointing out the supposed "features" their particular tea towel or trinket possesses. When a guy came on selling Oreo cookies, he waxed lyrical about the packet for a good five minutes straight. Holding it up like a game show hostess, he swished his hand beneath the cookies as if underlining and emphasizing the Oreos. He read out the writing on the back as if a piece of classical literature, gestured to the picture on the front as if a renaissance masterpiece, and with facial expressions that wouldn't have been out of place on the Broadway stage, described the sublime taste that those sensible enough to make a purchase could expect. This was no simple biscuit, ladies and gentlemen, this was a lifestyle choice. When he walked past me, I recognized the word "Premier" in his presentation.

"Premier?" I asked, as if for confirmation that this was indeed the finest cookie known to mankind.

"Premier!" he repeated emphatically.

I gave a little impressed nod of the head as if this crucial bit of information might just sway me into buying one. In the end, he did a pretty good trade, with about two thirds of the passengers buying his biscuits–I wasn't one of them.

When we got on the road, we headed in roughly the opposite direction to the one traveled in to get here but on the other side of the fortress of a mountain range–this time heading towards the town of Trujillo, which San Antonio was halfway towards. Our ride would not be going to San Antonio itself, which was located a few miles off the main road, so we planned to jump off at an appropriate spot and to hitchhike, or just plain hike, the final leg.

The landscape on the other side of the mountain range differed vastly from the valley in which Mérida sat, containing coffee, sugar, pineapple, and banana plantations, as well as huge ranches of swaying grasslands, punctuated by occasional grazing cows and the odd lonely tree.

Marking the side of the road were disturbingly frequent shrines constructed in honor of motorists who had died in a crash. Whereas grieving relatives might place a bunch of flowers, or possibly a small wooden cross at the site of a road accident in the U.K., here, proper permanent brick shrines had been erected, many of which were professionally constructed and in the shape of miniature churches or cathedrals. If our driver's ability on the road was anything to go by, then I could well understand why they were so plentiful. It was a long straight road we traveled on, which served to encourage insane overtaking along it. Drivers pulled out at the flimsiest of opportunities, causing Farrin and me near heart attacks as an uncompromising truck or coach hurtled towards our minibus on the wrong side of the road, struggling to gain the necessary forward thrust to pass the vehicle in front, and letting out a fleeting beastlike roar as it swerved back onto the side of safety with the narrowest of margins.

"If I die and you live, I'll be expecting you to erect one of those nice little shrines for me," said Farrin.

"Be a pleasure. I'll make you an Aussie-themed one if you like. Maybe a barbeque as a base with a Hills Hoist rotary washing line sticking out the top of it from which dangle cans of Fosters and little jars of Vegemite."

"I'd be honored, British."

We came to a stop by a section of road lined with a few random shops. Our driver turned around and indicated this was our spot. Jumping out, we surveyed the surroundings. A minor road led down to the lake and the village of San Antonio, both of which remained unseen several miles away through grassy ranchlands. The blazing tropical midday sun put paid to any notions of hiking out to the lake, and with no taxis or public transport heading our way, we stood by the side of the road in readiness to hitch. There were few vehicles going our way, but eventually, a modern black SUV with tinted windows approached. I hadn't hitched for several months but got the same characteristic buzz I always do when it graciously pulled over.

A smartly dressed middle-aged male welcomed us into a delightfully comfy, air-conditioned interior and set off at a gentle cruising pace ideal for taking in the scenery.

It soon became apparent to him that we spoke little in the way of Spanish, so Farrin asked if he spoke English.

"A litt . . . le," he responded, carefully pronouncing each individual syllable, emphasizing them in a deliberate considered manner.

In broken Spanish, Farrin managed to query what his occupation was.

"Err, veterinary *cirujano*, err, sur-geon," he answered.

"So is my father, err, *mi padre es* . . . veterinary *cirujano*," responded Farrin.

As we drove through the lush green landscape, we attempted to communicate further but struggled with each other's languages—especially Farrin with mine. It was a labored effort all-round, which had us speaking in super slow, broken, and horrendously mutated syntax, mostly in our native tongues, but without achieving much. I was more than familiar with this phenomenon, having ended up speaking this way for such a protracted period once when hitching, that when a car finally pulled over whose occupant asked me if I spoke English, I responded on autopilot like a complete idiot, "A lit . . . le." It made for an interesting explanation as to where I was from, to which I replied, "Australia."

After a few miles of leisurely driving through a lush green landscape, the village of San Antonio came into view. It was a tiny settlement comprising a few basic weathered dwellings, two or three small shops, and not much else. The road it sat on led directly to Lake Maracaibo which, if we hadn't known better, we would have concluded was the ocean, such was its size. We thanked our driver for the lift and went for a look around.

It was an extremely sleepy backwater, and on our way to the palm-fronted beach, we passed only one soul, an old woman who did something of a double take on seeing two gringo backpackers. The beach wasn't particularly long, being roughly the width of the village. Beyond this, a small vegetation-covered headland jutted out next to a trickle of a river, beyond which, just visible farther along the coast, was another larger headland. In the opposite direction the beach faded out, replaced by more vegetation and what looked like the backyards of a couple of fisherman's dwellings. Sheltering under the shade of several large palm trees was a group of guys in their early twenties, cutting up fishing bait with knives and attaching it to hooks on a large fishing line. Nearby, hammocks were strung between palms and a number of small vessels moored. Several young boys aged around eight or nine sat here, not so much playing or hanging out as holding council.

Today was incredibly hot and humid which, although good weather for lightning tonight, was not so good for being out in the glare of midday. On our way towards the shade of some palm trees, several looks were thrown towards us by the older fishermen, none of which I could really describe as being particularly friendly. There was a hint of curiosity at us being around but a far larger dose of animosity. We collapsed near the water's edge, resting our packs against palm trees to lean on. Cooling off with several chugs of water from our bottles, we were interrupted by the arrival of the young kids who came over en masse to check us out. One in particular was an arrogant little upstart who stood not two feet from us, staring our way, hands on hips, thumbs in the loops of his cutoff pants, jutting out his chin with a silly little pathetic snarl. He looked back towards the older fishermen to see if they approved, having obviously been sent over by them to gauge our response.

In the manner of a parent scolding a wayward child, he spoke at us in Spanish.

"Cocky little bugger, isn't he?" said an incredulous Farrin, shaking his head.

He certainly wasn't short of self-confidence. We ignored him for a while, but he was persistent and began speaking at us again, this time in an even more condescending manner. I decided to respond accordingly and so spoke back to him in a similar manner in rapid-fire English, rambling on about nothing in particular for the next fifteen seconds. It threw him off-kilter, and with a look of surprise, he stepped back to rejoin his little group, who were all looking our way but without his petulant attitude.

A couple of the older guys came over now and relieved him of his duties. They displayed none of the little man's overt animosity, at least to our faces, but were cagey and standoffish at best. A bit of very broken dialogue followed in which they essentially asked what we were doing here. When we mentioned the lighting or "Relámpago del Catatumbo" as the phenomenon is known in Spanish, they gestured farther down the coast.

Did this mean we couldn't see it from here?

Given their attitude, probing further seemed too taxing a notion, so we left it at that. They lost interest soon after, as did Farrin and I with their company, and so we moved away back into the village proper to discuss our options for tonight.

CHAPTER 13

Everlasting Brightness in the Sky

As I waded through the murky waist-deep waters around the headland on my way back to camp, a jolting pain shot through my foot as I stepped onto a sharp unseen object underneath–puncturing the sole of my bare left foot, nearly causing me to drop the precious armful of firewood I cradled above the surface of the lake. I'd spent the last twenty minutes clandestinely collecting this under the cover of darkness from the area I'd earlier seen the fishermen slicing up bait and was damned if I was going to lose such a handsome horde now.

Farrin and I were keen for our camping location and presence in the village to remain as incognito as possible, so had pitched up on a tiny secluded beach beyond the small headland, which lay just out of view from the main settlement. The only problem with our camp's situation was getting back there after forays nearer the village, several of which we had made for firewood and freshwater–the latter taken from a small stream running off a plantation. With the headland covered in thick thorny vegetation, the easiest route back to camp was wading around rather than walking across it, but as I took another tentative step, coming down on the outer edge of my foot to avoid applying pressure to the unseen laceration, I began to question the merit of this semi-submerged option.

After a minute of painful shuffling, I finally reached the beach, dropping the firewood onto the sand with a palpable sigh of relief. Grasping my foot, I hopped around to get my balance and surveyed the damage. Although difficult to see clearly in the near-absolute darkness, there was, almost smack in the center of my foot, a deep flap of skin accompanied by the beginnings of a fresh trickle of blood–the previous gushing having washed away in the lake. I pogo-sticked it over to camp–comprising a fire pit, a couple of logs large enough to sit on, and Farrin's expensive-looking tent, something we both planned to share tonight given there was nowhere suitable to sling my hammock.

I showed him my injury.

"Nice, mate. What d'you step on?"

"Don't know. My guess is a bit of broken glass."

I wished now I hadn't left my jungle boots back in Mérida, which would have saved me wading through the lake barefoot. Retrieving my first aid kit and water bottle from my pack, I set about patching myself up. With some iodine-infused water from my bottle, I opened up and rinsed out the flap of skin, clearing the grit and sand caught inside with the tip of my index finger. I dried it as best I could with my T-shirt then cleaned out the raw squelching lesion with several alcoholic swabs, causing an electric shock-like sting in the process. An application of five Band-Aids clamped it shut, over which I then put a sock and sneaker, and was now good and ready for a strong shot of rum in front of the fire.

It was a fantastic location to camp, under a brilliant star-blazing night sky, but so far there had been scarce lightning. A few spectacular isolated flashes had occurred on the distant horizon, but nothing in the way of the constant illuminations, billed by the tour agencies in Mérida as the "everlasting brightness in the sky," under which you could apparently read a book.

So reliable was the lightning normally that it had even been used as a navigational aid in the past. In 1598, the phenomenon was written about in an epic poem by one of Spain's greatest playwrights, Lope de Vega, who waxed lyrical about how it betrayed the presence of English ships attempting a stealthy attack on the Spanish garrison at the lakeside city of Maracaibo, forcing the British to abandon the assault. And in a reversal of fortunes, in 1823, independence fighters are said to have exploited its illuminating effect to locate the Spanish fleet.

There is no scientifically agreed reason for the occurrence of Catatumbo lighting. One theory holds that the area's unique topography of towering mountains next to marshes and a giant sea-level lake is responsible. The strong and cold Andean winds are believed to collide with methane gasses released from decomposing organic matter in the marshes, forcing the gasses higher than the heavier and colder incoming air. These gases then ionize as they rise into the cloud layer, generating an electrical charge, resulting in the frequent discharges. Some scientists believe Catatumbo lighting is the planet's largest individual generator of ozone molecules, and that the phenomenon helps to replenish the ozone layer of the upper stratosphere.

But for now, at least, there was nothing in the way of a spectacular light show. And we weren't particularly optimistic things would change for the better. It had been dark for several hours now, and the few flashes we'd witnessed had occurred in the wrong part of the sky. The Catatumbo lightning was supposed to originate at the mouth of the Catatumbo River, to the west, whereas the lightning we had seen was to the northeast, leading us to conclude that we'd most likely just witnessed a normal tropical storm. Our other concern was that our westerly view was partially obscured by another, far larger, headland. Was this, as well as the thirty miles we were from the mouth of the river, preventing us from seeing the lightning? It had always been something of a gamble for us to look at a standard tourist map and pick an unknown lakeside village without having first known the reality of the landscape on the ground. And so, if the lightning didn't improve tonight, we made up our minds to journey to the village of Concha at the start of Cienegas de Juan Manuel National Park and try our luck there.

With no light show in the sky, we settled down in front of the "bush TV" (fire) to a meal of pasta and tuna served with sliced capsicum pepper, tomato sauce, and a large, although unintentional, garnish of sand–cooked over Farrin's nifty little gasoline-powered camping stove. It was a delightful way to spend the night, and the soothing primeval crackle of the campfire encouraged us to chat. I was extremely interested to hear of Farrin's travels but also his occupation as an engineer. He'd done some really interesting work and been involved in many big projects, the most recent of which was the construction of a new mine. Of late, he'd been applying his engineering expertise to a subject that had fascinated me for years, the building collapses on 9/11. His research had convinced him to join a group called *Architects and Engineers for 911 Truth*,[47] which at the time of writing comprises 1,460 architects and engineering professionals who are putting their careers and reputations on the line by questioning the U.S. government's official version of events as to how the towers came down on 9/11.

This was something that Chávez had commented on during a 2006 speech, stating, "A building never collapses like that, unless it's with an implosion. The hypothesis that is gaining strength . . . is that it was the same U.S. imperial power that planned and carried out this terrible terrorist attack, or act, against its own people and against citizens from all over the world. Why? To justify the aggression that was immediately unleashed on Afghanistan, on Iraq, and the threats against all of us, against Venezuela too." In doing so, Chávez became one of the first heads of state to question the official account. Farrin, however, as an engineer, was reluctant to stray from a strictly scientific analysis of the collapse of the buildings and was quick to point out that *Architects and Engineers for 911 Truth* were not conspiracy theorists, but building and technical professionals examining the science-based forensic evidence of the three towers' collapses.

For those of you now convinced that my editor has missed a trick by not spotting that I wrote three towers instead of two or twin, let me enlighten you. At 5.20 pm on September the 11, 2001, a third tower, forty-seven-storey 7 World Trade Center (7 WTC), collapsed. No plane hit it. No building fell on top of it. No jet fuel was in it. It was a block away from the twin towers, yet nearly seven hours after the destruction of the north tower, this huge skyscraper–every floor of which was as big as a football field–collapsed in perfect symmetry, at free-fall speed, through the path of *most* resistance into its own "footprint," leaving a tidy pile of rubble within its former boundaries. Were it not located close to the twin towers, 7 WTC would have been considered giant. It stood nearly six hundred feet tall, contained two million square feet of office space, and would have been the tallest building in thirty-three U.S. states.[48]

It is without doubt the most inexplicable engineering failure in world history, yet even today, nine years after the event, many people have never heard of it. To fully grasp the oddity of its demise, it helps tremendously to watch some footage of the building's rapid and orderly descent, plenty of which can be found online. For Farrin, and many of the technical and building professionals calling for a new investigation into the events of 9/11, 7 WTC is a smoking gun, establishing–beyond doubt–that something is deeply amiss with the official version of events. [49]

We dismantled camp by midmorning, dousing the smoldering remnants of the fire and scattering them widely so to leave no scars or indication of our presence on the land.

Back in the village, edging its way along the only road leading into and out of San Antonio, was a very strange car indeed. It was, like many automobiles in Venezuela, a big, beat up to hell, gas-guzzling U.S. car from the seventies, although this one had a rather strange modification–a rock concert-sized rectangular speaker strapped to its roof. It was subwoofer heaven. Out of it played earth-shattering reggaeton beats loud enough to blow every eardrum in the vicinity, and certainly the driver's, who was most likely already tone deaf–and certainly dumb. Despite being mildly amusing, in a "point and laugh at the village idiot" kind of way, I was glad when it finally departed and civility was once more restored to the sleepy backwater.

In order to cook tonight, we needed to acquire some additional gasoline to top up the dwindling supplies of Farrin's gas stove. There was no gas station in San Antonio, but with the stuff costing a twentieth of the price of water, Farrin decided to simply ask a local for a handout. A laid-back portly man of African descent, who was lounging about on his veranda with his gut hanging over his shorts, seemed a suitable candidate. Farrin's Spanish was vastly superior to mine, but that was hardly difficult, and he soon accomplished the inquiry. With a quick "si" and a nod of the head, the man disappeared into his shed to fetch the requested substance, returning a moment later with a large clear plastic bottle filled with the yellowy liquid. We only needed a fraction of its contents, but he offered us the whole thing–for free. Although such a quantity would have cost several dollars back home, it was barely even a cent's worth here. And so despite Farrin trying to pay–first by way of money then cigarettes–the local graciously waved him off.

There were zero cars leaving the village, so we started walking down the road in the hope one would eventually materialize and take pity on us. About ten minutes later, a red farming pickup did. With a quick "gracias" to the burly cola-skinned driver, we jumped on the back, throwing our packs against the rear of the cab to use as backrests and stretching our legs out as if on a first-class flight. I loved lifts like this where you were exposed to the glorious elements and could feel the glare of the sun and the cooling rush of air all around you; so easily eclipsing the confined, sterile interior of the cab.

We hitched to the end of the road, getting off when we arrived at the T-junction our bus had dropped us off at the day before. No longer surrounded by the cooling rush of air on the back of the truck, the roasting weather soon had me gasping for a drink. I wasn't the only one.

"Jeez, mate, I'm as dry as a nun's nasty!" exclaimed Farrin in characteristic Aussie vernacular, rubbing his parched throat. We headed for a quick refueling stop at a nearby shop. Farrin sank some bright red Gatorade while I drank a bucket load of water.

It took us two buses and several hours driving through scenery of lush grassy ranchlands and sprawling plantations until we neared our destination. During the journey, the conversation shifted arbitrarily from one subject to another. At one point, we briefly discussed the global banking crisis during which Farrin treated me to another priceless Aussie turn of phrase.

"Those bloody bankers will bend you over and won't even pay you the courtesy of spreading your cheeks before ramming it in!"

Too true.

Concha was bigger than San Antonio with significantly more people around, although it was still a one-road village. The road stopped abruptly by a quay, where several small open-topped boats with outboard engines were moored. These sat gently rocking on the beginnings of a thin stretch of swampy estuarine wetland, flanked on either side by lush tropical forest. Encouragingly, on a nearby shop wall was a mural of a dramatic bolt of lightning crashing down at nighttime onto the surface of the lake, silhouetting a stilted building in the foreground. Next to the moored boats was a sort of open-fronted bar and barbeque area where a man was butchering a large mammal of unknown origins and hanging up the different joints of meat. Several locals relaxed here, chilling out in the shade.

"Relámpago de Catatumbo?" I asked one of them, gesturing optimistically to the boats.

They pointed to a man nearby in a red baseball cap conversing with the blood-covered butcher. I approached and repeated the query, receiving a slightly surprised, although affirmative reply. Our potential skipper spoke surprisingly good English and began to negotiate on price. We braced ourselves, expecting an extortionate initial figure from which to negotiate southwards. The tours from Mérida had cost around 700 bolivars each, but to our surprise he quoted 150 to take us to, and then tomorrow bring us back from, the lake's stilted houses. This would include our accommodation, and was for both of us. Cutting out the middleman certainly made a big difference. We cemented the deal with a manly, superstrong handshake and soon were clambering aboard his vessel.

The outboard motor spluttered into life, propelling us across the shimmering mirrored waters of the swampy marshlands dabbled with carpets of lilies floating on the surface in collective little islands, around which our helmsman graced. On either side of the waterway was the most vibrant explosion of life. Tropical forest towered high above in spectacular shapes, highlighted by a vivacious splattering of flowers. Multicolored parrots glided overhead, calling out with lonely piecing cries. Giant ancient trees warped into ghostly forms, atop of which eagles perched and red-furred howler monkeys roamed–prowling for fruit and nuts exposed in petal-like clusters on the branches, as if a gift held out in an open palm. Lurking elsewhere, unseen within the park, were other magnificent creatures: manatees, pumas, freshwater dolphins, anteaters, iguanas, tree boas, and jaguars.

The outboard's revolutions decreased to a near halt as we glided to a stop under a colossal tree. Pointing upwards, our driver gestured to a monkey, then another and another, until we counted six in the tree. By now, the sun was low in the sky, no longer possessing the oppressive sting of midday but casting a soothing and warming glow across the marshy channels. It was a surprisingly long ride through the twisting waterways until we reached the mouth of the mighty lake. Perched here above the water were numerous stilted houses, in greatly differing states of repair. The worst were in a very poor condition, with the wooden slats of their walls and precarious undulating flooring looking ready to disintegrate at the first sign of a strong breeze. The best on offer was a solid-looking concrete construction with a durable metal roof and a large open-fronted section.

"I hope that's our one," said Farrin, gazing hopefully in its direction.

It was.

We pulled up by a jetty protruding from the main structure, which was raised about four feet above the surface of the lake. The building served as the headquarters for officials of the national park, several of whom greeted us on arrival. All but one was uniformed; the exception being a robust individual wearing a red Chávez T-shirt. After some cursory negotiations, our skipper slipped the main-looking official a couple of banknotes then gave us the lowdown. He was leaving now but would be back at seven o'clock tomorrow morning. Although he had intended to let us have a lie-in until later, it was imperative that we leave before eight o'clock. The "captain" was turning up then, who under no circumstances should know we'd stayed the night. To prevent anyone in the other nearby stilted properties from discovering the same, we were to refrain from stringing up hammocks until after sundown. He bade us good night, powering off into the distance as we settled down to watch a spectacular orange sunset across the water.

None of the officials spoke any English or seemed particularly interested in us, so we kept ourselves to ourselves and turned our attention to supper, in the form of some tinned tuna and limp pasta. Sitting on the edge of the concrete platform with our feet dangling over the side, we gazed out across the waters and tucked into our meal as dusk slipped into night and the lightning began. What we saw was spectacular, lighting up the sky with a brilliant intensity of incandescent yellow, red, and white. And nearly all of it was indeed without accompanying thunder, said to be silent because the majority of the strikes–which can produce a current of up to 400,000 amps–occur between clouds at so great an elevation as to render them inaudible. Similar phenomena occur in Indonesia, Uganda, and Colombia although the duration of these electric storms is generally far shorter. Sadly though, tonight's discharges, despite being spectacular and a worthy spectacle, were few and far between, and nothing close to the constant repetitive lightning the area could produce, which can rain down as many as twenty thousand bolts in a single night and last for nine hours straight. At its best, Catatumbo lightning can illuminate the whole sky with such ferocity that it becomes a flashing beacon of white. And it has done so for thousands of years.

But perhaps Farrin and I should count ourselves lucky to have seen any Catatumbo lightning, for not long after we returned to our respective countries, word got out that the lightning had ceased altogether. (It has since returned after a prolonged absence of several months). The last time the lightning disappeared was in 1906, after a colossal earthquake off the coast of Ecuador and Colombia, setting off a devastating tsunami. Back then, the lightning returned to normal after just three weeks. This time, its lengthier disappearance has been attributed to the El Niño weather phenomenon, which affects weather patterns globally and, in Venezuela, has resulted in a severe drought. For the local indigenous population who live in stilted huts in the nearby community of Congo Mirador, the disappearance of the regular-as-clockwork lightning was a huge concern. Even before the onset of the El Niño effect and the drought linked to it, the lightning's regularity had waned significantly–thought to be the result of agriculture and general deforestation, clogging up surrounding rivers and lagoons with silt. In a bid to protect the decreasing phenomenon, authorities in Venezuela petitioned the United Nations to designate the area a world heritage site, something which to date has been unsuccessful.

And so, despite not seeing the area's lightning at its best, I still feel thankful to have at least witnessed some of the famed Catatumbo lightning at all.

CHAPTER 14

Sizzling in Oil Country

Standing naked covered from head to toe in foamy soapsuds, the shower came to a demoralizing dribbling halt. It was an eventuality I had been warned might occur by my new CouchSurfing host, Marcos.

"We get a lot of water and power cuts, so you might have to wash from the bucket," he had said before departing for work moments later, leaving me alone in his father's spacious home in a suburban district of the oil city of Maracaibo. I did as advised and rinsed off using pails of water drawn from a giant barrel nearby.

I'd arrived in the city alone twenty minutes earlier, after bidding Farrin a fond farewell the night before at the bus station in Mérida, accompanied with promises to stay in touch and host each other when we were next in each other's countries. He was sticking around in the Andes to do some mountain hiking before heading on to Caracas to meet his lady friend.

With Maracaibo being the last big city in the west of the country before the border with Colombia, it seemed as good a choice as anywhere for me to explore next, if an incredibly hot one. Despite it being little later than seven in the morning, it was roasting outside. This was one seriously hot location, considered the very hottest in the whole country.

Sadly, Marcos had to spend the day at work–having already lied to his boss about his father being ill so he could come and meet me–so I would have to go exploring by myself. We had planned to meet back here by early afternoon when he returned from his job of supervising nearly a hundred offshore oil wells for state oil company PDVSA, a senior position for a guy in his early thirties. Normally, he got up for this at the wholly unappealing hour of 4:30 am, and so was already significantly late.

Not only had Marcos skived off work to help me, but had presented me with some gifts, which he'd laid out especially on one of two beds in the room that I had all to myself. There was a tube of Pringles chips, a candy bar, a bottle of water, and a cell phone. The phone was on loan for the duration of my stay in town so I could get hold of him in case of emergencies. I was touched by his generosity and thanked him for his kindness. Marcos explained that he liked to make all his hosts feel at home, and that in the two years he'd been registered on the CouchSurfing website, he had hosted a total of thirty-five people from eighteen different countries.

It was without doubt the best room I'd had so far. Not that it was a particularly plush place, in fact it was rather humble. But it was extremely clean and delightfully air-conditioned, something which had transformed the interior into a cool oasis away from the stifling heat outside. The room contained a PC, television, desk, wardrobe, even an en suite shower room and toilet.

After getting dressed, I headed outside. The heat hit me immediately. After unlocking and then relocking the property's clanking padlocked main gate, which separated the front yard from the sidewalk, I set off up the street. It was staggeringly hot, and it wasn't long before I could feel myself becoming fatigued. I followed a rather basic map that Marcos had kindly drawn for me of the house's location in relation to the route that a local shared taxi, known as a carrito, drove. This could take me to, and get me back from, the center of the city. On the reverse of the map, Marcos had drawn the layout of the city, not marking out places of interest but public buildings that possessed air-conditioning or provided free water, where I could stop off for respite from the sun. I wondered how much hotter it could get outside. The answer to that, I would discover later, was a lot.

Although a relatively short distance to reach the spot where Marcos had indicated the carrito leaving from, by the time I arrived there, I was sweating buckets. It was situated next to a small triangular traffic island created by the meeting of two roads, in the middle of which several people congregated beneath the shade of a small tree. An old man sat selling cool drinks from an ice box, an overweight guy wearing oil-covered tatty clothing tinkered with a mechanical device of some sort, and a couple of women stood about chatting.

Out of the blue, the overweight guy paced towards me, approaching with unexpected venom in his eyes. He was about to enter my personal space and with malice, so I hastily checked his advances, blocking his forward motion with my left hand on his chest while subtly lining him up for a big right-hander–just in case. A jolt of adrenaline shot around my bloodstream. Staring me in the eye, he rubbed his thumb and forefinger together to indicate money then thrust out his palm, not asking but demanding. *No chance, fatso.* I shook my head at the grumpy prick. With a menacing snarl, he mouthed off at me in Spanish, getting angrier by the second. It was too hot for this sort of nonsense, and I was dammed if I was going to get into a row here, so with a shake of the head, I walked on to another shaded spot slightly farther up. Minutes later, the carrito arrived.

It was without doubt the most battered taxi I had seen yet in Venezuela–which was saying something–being a hunk of junk in a laughable state of disrepair. It had great big dents on every single panel, including the roof, and most of the entire front panel was missing, exposing a large coiled suspension spring behind the wheel. It had rust aplenty and a front bumper held in place with a bit of string. Two people were crammed into the spare front seat, so I squeezed into the back next to three existing passengers who were sitting on a very strange seat indeed. Fastened in place somehow was an old worn-out two-person sofa, complete with removable cushions that most likely once originated from the driver's sitting room. It made for quite a novel journey, although with so many people, not a particularly comfortable one. En route, I tried to make a mental note of the prominent landmarks we passed in order to know where to get off at on my way back. We stopped numerous times along the way, the space inside increasing or diminishing as passengers hopped on and off. At one stage, there were five of us in the back, with an elderly lady sitting on the lap of the woman next to me.

We reached the end of the line a short distance from the city's historic center, which was set around a long thin strip of parkland with a dramatic church at either end. The nearest of which, the Basilica de Chiquinquirá, I headed for now–as much to take refuge from the sun as to admire. The church stood proudly on the outer reaches of a pedestrian square, which separated it from the park's outer reaches. Its size and striking form dominated the surrounding area. The frontal approach consisted of two large towers standing boldly either side of a Greek templelike central entranceway, complete with a triangular pediment roof supported under four giant columns. Its exterior was painted in cheery yellow and white, softening the appearance of the otherwise dramatic and imposing structure.

The church's inner sanctum was an uplifting world of light, with much of its ornamental ceiling decorated in brilliant white with subtle embellishments of blue and gold. It was delightfully cool inside and a good enough spot to shelter from the glaring sun. But the church's real attraction was not its temperature but what lay beyond a glass screen in the high altar–something a surprising number of visitors were respectfully lined up to see. Residing here was a revered icon of the Virgin Mary painted onto the surface of a small wooden board. According to legend, in 1709, the board was found floating on the surface of Lake Maracaibo by an old peasant woman washing clothes near the lake's shore. She brought the curious board back to her home where it began to glow. After much astonishment from her neighbors who she gathered around to view the icon, it was taken to the local church, where soon after, miracles began to occur. As its renown grew, the authorities decided that the icon should reside in the capital. But while the image was being carried away from the city, it became increasingly heavy, to the point where it could no longer be lifted. This was seen as a sign that the Virgin had chosen to stay in Maracaibo. She was dutifully retuned and has remained since. The icon was known as the Virgin of Chiquinquirá, shortened to La Chinita, and attracted pilgrims throughout the year. In 1942, the Virgin became the patron saint of the state of Zulia–of which Maracaibo is the capital.

Stairs led up to the high altar from either side of the church where a procession of people filed, stopping momentarily by a glass security screen to offer a prayer or brief reflection in front of the icon before continuing down the other side. I joined the queue and approached. The icon consisted of a humble wooden plank with a faint impression of the Virgin holding the baby Jesus. On either side were figures said to be Saint Andrew and Saint Anthony. The icon's original simplicity was charming, but this had been altered–and to my mind spoilt–by a later embellishment, with the addition of two small golden crowns on the heads of the Virgin and child. Surrounding it was a grandiose sparkling golden frame. Next to this, looking completely out of place, were–amazingly–several CDs. It looked, to all intents and purposes, like the church was having some sort of promotion on a choral box set and hoped that a little of the icon's magic would wear off on the number they shifted. Considering the icon was venerated, it seemed a mighty strange thing for the church authorities to have propped up next to it. But there you go.

After a good look around, I headed outside in search of a cool drink and a shady spot in the park to sit down and read up on the place. From a nearby street vendor, I selected a green coconut floating in a tub of ice water. Holding the hulking great nut in one hand, the vendor struck it smartly with a deft blow from his machete, slicing its crown clean off, releasing a thin trail of inner liquid into the air. A straw was placed inside this natural vessel, and I was good to go. The liquid was beautifully chilled, having a subtle natural sweetness with just a suggestion of contrasting sour. It was so good that I considered having another but thought it best to ration myself–after all, coconut milk is an extremely strong laxative.

Once a sleepy indigenous village backwater, Maracaibo had been transformed by the discovery of oil and was today a sprawling city of some two million people. In 1499, Spanish sailors exploring Lake Maracaibo spotted the indigenous population's traditional stilted houses, known as *palafitos*, perched above the surface of the lake and, in a sarcastic reference to the opulent waterfront mansions of Venice, named the country Little Venice–Venezuela. The name appeared on the first map of the area a year later and has stuck ever since. Maracaibo was founded in 1574 as a trading post and remained a quiet and humble hamlet until 1914, when drillers first struck oil. In just six years, Venezuela became the world's largest exporter of oil, and Maracaibo the country's oil capital.

I continued strolling through the thin stretch of park, which up until 1973, had been the location of the vast majority of the city's old colonial buildings. These had been torn down in a controversial development scheme and the park established in their place. Although an attractive-enough feature today, with statues, fountains, and eye-catching trees and shrubbery, the park was mostly surrounded by gray and uninspiring concrete tat, making the majority of what I saw walking through the "historic district" anything but historic. Within the park, a lone building had survived the developers' bulldozers, a beautiful deep blue neogothic church, Iglesia de Santa Bárbara.

Outside the park at its far eastern end was another prominent church, Catedral de Maracaibo, inside which was the city's other acclaimed and revered religious relic, the Cristo Negro, or Black Christ. This was a wooden figure of Christ that had once been attached to a crucifix in a church in the town of Gibraltar on the southern shores of Lake Maracaibo. In 1600, the indigenous population set the church ablaze, destroying everything but the figure itself. Legend has it that despite the crucifix being consumed in the flames, the figure of Christ that was attached to it remained exactly where it was, floating unassisted in the air, unharmed by the fire. When the indigenous population saw this, they ran away in terror. The statue has been venerated since. To keep the statue safe while the church was reconstructed, it was sent to Maracaibo. However, when the church in Gibraltar had been rebuilt and the town's inhabitants asked for the smoke-blackened figure back (hence the name Black Christ), they were told by the authorities in Maracaibo that it was staying put. It developed so devoted a following there that they insisted they could not return it. To settle the dispute, opposing officials from either town took the issue to arbitration with the Spanish Empire's most important organ of administration, the Council of the Indies. The council concluded that the issue was beyond their mortal abilities and so decided that the figure should make up its own mind. To decipher the figure's decision, it would be placed in a boat in the center of Lake Maracaibo. If the boat turned in a southerly direction towards Gibraltar, then it would reside there; but if it turned to the north towards Maracaibo, then this would be its home. It chose the latter. Some historians have noted, however, that the idea of putting the statue in a boat on the lake may well have originated as a clever ruse of the crafty Maracaibo officials. Knowing the lake's predominant currents flowed towards their city, they stood an extremely good chance of winning.

There really wasn't much to look at in the city center, and any whims of strolling around aimlessly were put paid to by today's incredible temperatures, and so I decided to go in search of more liquid refreshment. I headed to a sprawling flea market located along the southern side of the park, in a quarter of town known as Las Pulgas. It was a hive of activity with theatrical salesmen and women hawking their wares of everything from bootleg DVDs and clothing to fried plantains and juicy doorstep-thick arepas. I spent a good while pottering around and ended up spending a fortune on multiple cold drinks before catching a carrito back to Marcos's place.

Marcos arrived shortly after I did, accompanied by another CouchSurfer who had just contacted him. It seemed he had something of a production line going with visiting foreigners and that I'd be sharing the lovely big bedroom after all. The new addition was an enthusiastic thirty-year-old Brazilian guy called Anselmo. We hit it off immediately.

"You're from London?" he stated rhetorically with wide-eyed enthusiasm. "Man, I love London. Do you know Camden Town?"

"I live there."

"Oh man, I love Camden Town! Do you go to the market a lot? I love the market."

I explained, tactfully, that actually I tended to stay clear of the market to avoid all the tourists, and that the parks nearby were more my cup of tea. This didn't dampen his enthusiasm.

"Yeah, London's got some great parks! I want to go back, but if you're Brazilian, getting a work visa is difficult."

He'd told me of his time working there illegally as a waiter and of his travels in the U.K. and around Europe.

While Anselmo showered–or more accurately bucketed–I helped Marcos cook up some burgers and prepare a salad for supper.

As we cooked, I queried Marcos as to what he thought of Chávez. "I am a supporter of Chávez but not fanatical," he said and explained that despite his pay from the state-run oil company having effectively been cut–in that it had apparently not risen with inflation–he continued to support Chávez because he believed in his social projects and considered them important for the country at large.

Over our meal, Marcos adumbrated tonight's plan for Anselmo and me. We were going for a drink with a group of local CouchSurfers whom Luis regularly met up with. It sounded like they had quite a community established and would help each other out should any of them receive a request from a visiting CouchSurfer whom, for whatever reason, they were unable to host. Not long after it got dark, we left in a classic white 1979 Malibu that Marcos had borrowed from his aunty, and drove to pick up one of the "surfers." Pulling up outside an apartment block in town, Marcos made a quick call on his cell. Moments later, a bubbly and pretty olive-skinned girl came out to meet us. She jumped on board and introduced herself. She was Maria, a twenty-two-year-old law student and fellow CouchSurfer. The bar wasn't far off, where outside waiting for us were two further CouchSurfers, Sabrina and Laura. Both came from the United States but currently lived in Maracaibo. Sabrina was an independent documentary filmmaker in her thirties who had married a Venezuelan–currently at home with the kids–Laura was twenty-one and in the country to complete her thesis on the oil industry.

We sat outside in the bar's patio area where Marcos ordered a round of beers that arrived in a big bucket of ice. I chatted to Sabrina for a while about her time in the country, who told me of a quirky and amusing practice she had observed here.

"Venezuelans love to queue. If there's a queue in the street, then it doesn't matter what it's for, people will join it as they figure there must be something worth having at the end. And once a Venezuelan has joined a queue at the supermarket, they won't leave it even if the checkout next to them becomes free. I want to start an arbitrary queue in the street one day with nothing at the end of it, to see how many people I can get to line up!"

We all shared a nice evening chatting and generally taking it easy before heading on to another bar, the front door of which was locked, requiring us to press a buzzer to get in. I nursed a super strong rum and coke and got chatting to Maria. Over some general chitchat, I asked her what her hobbies were.

"I love to dance."

I asked her what style and was expecting something traditional like the popular local dance, the gaita, but instead this sweet and innocent-looking girl answered, "reggaeton."

She asked me if I was familiar with it.

"Yes, it's quite, err . . . ," I struggled for the right word.

"Sexual?" she asked bluntly.

"Yes."

"It's very sexual," she laughed.

"What do your parents think of it?"

"They don't like the music's lyrics."

These, she explained, were equally explicit and gave me a couple of examples.

"I wanna bend you over and fuck you," she stated, unabashed in a matter-of-fact kind of way, before glancing upwards to one side as if working out the translation for another. "I wanna lick you."

Not the sort of music I should imagine your mother would like–although that does, I suppose, depend on your mother.

We left the bar soon after as Sabrina, Laura, and Maria had to head home. While standing around outside by our respective vehicles, Sabrina invited Anselmo and me to join her family for a meal tomorrow, and offered to take us on a bit of a tour to visit the nearby area of Cabimas. Some brightly colored traditional housing was located there as were many oil rigs that were stationed just off the shore of the lake. We accepted immediately and, before saying good night, arranged a time and place to meet.

The next of Maracaibo's bars to be graced by Marcos, Anselmo, and me was an interesting establishment described by Marcos as "a communist bar." The place was decorated with Cuban and Venezuelan flags, pictures of Che Guevara, anticapitalist artwork, and general leftist memorabilia. The interior was cooled by a huge industrial-sized metal fan painted a rusty orange hue and positioned high in the rafters to point down into the seating area below.

Other than a solitary barman, the place was deserted. And so after a quick drink and a good look at the pictures on display, we called it a night.

Marcos had to work ridiculously early and so was up way before Anselmo or me, leaving us, essentially, with the house to ourselves since his father remained in his room all morning. It was quite a remarkable thing about CouchSurfing in Venezuela, that despite the country having a notorious crime rate, a complete stranger would give you the keys to his home and leave you there effectively unaccompanied.

We caught a carrito to town together where, on seeing the striking exterior of the Basilica de Chiquinquirá, Anselmo suggested that we pop inside before making our way to Sabrina's apartment.

"In Brazil, we say that when you enter a new church for the first time, you can make a wish."

"I'm afraid I've already been in."

"Don't worry, you can have mine. What d'you want?"

I pondered this for a second then asked for the dates of my return flight to be confirmed–something I had tried to do over the phone to the airline when in Mérida but, despite several frustrated calls, had got nowhere.

As we stepped inside the church's cool interior, Anselmo reverently bowed his head and began whispering almost imperceptibly, as if directly interceding on my behalf with the Almighty. All of a sudden, he broke off the dialogue, looking my way as if conveying a message from on high.

"You want business class?"

I laughed and answered in the affirmative. I should be so lucky.

He passed my answer on and concluded the prayer.

"Everything's arranged. I got you a window seat too."

A couple of carritos later, followed by a bit of wandering around lost, and we managed to locate Sabrina's apartment block.

She introduced us to her ten-year-old son Joaquin, her adorable two-year-old daughter Olivia, and her husband Oleski, who was a professor of social sciences (sociology and anthropology). Also here, and accompanying us later, was Laura. Sabrina had laid on a wonderful spread of burritos, mince, tomatoes, guacamole, and cheese. It looked delicious, and tasted even better.

After lunch, Laura, Anselmo, and I set off with Sabrina and Olivia in the family car to see the oil rigs and traditional housing, and to check out some of the surrounding areas. We drove across a huge bridge measuring just shy of five and a half miles that spanned the mouth of the lake where it spilled out into the sea beyond. Although opening into the Gulf of Venezuela, Lake Maracaibo was not considered a bay as it was fed by substantial river systems and had been, in its geological past, separated from the Caribbean.

Anselmo and I sat either side of little Olivia, who was perched in her toddler seat between us in the back. At first she was a little difficult to coax a smile out of, but soon our peculiar and generally funny faces began to win her over. Our winning routine was the British and Brazilian monsters where we would do impressions of decidedly silly, although rather likeable, monsters with their own characteristic roaring sounds and facial expressions. It was great fun and quite the success, to the point where if we stopped for a brief moment to take in the view, Olivia would get upset. We maintained the routine until we arrived at her grandparents' house where Sabrina dropped Olivia off for an afternoon of fun with Grandma.

On the way to the oil fields, Sabrina told us about the alarming number of kidnappings that were sweeping the country like an unchecked cancer–one of which her friend had been a victim of.

One afternoon, when driving her son from school, Sabrina's friend, Jesmary, had been ambushed by a gang who carjacked her vehicle. The group interrogated her repeatedly, asking over and over again for details of how she acquired the expensive Toyota SUV and her husband's line of work. All of her answers were relayed via a cell phone back to an accomplice elsewhere. Convinced she was the victim of mistaken identity and that the gang had been after a wealthy family that drove the same vehicle, Jesmary attempted to persuade them that she wasn't worth the bother. She claimed to be an assistant at a law firm and that one of the lawyers had sold her the vehicle at a very reasonable price. She was in fact a lawyer herself and her husband a gringo working in the oil industry which, needless to say, she also did not admit. Her ruse paid off, and both Jesmary and her son were taken to the middle of nowhere and dumped without their truck. Roughly ten minutes later after the dust had settled, she dialled 0800-kidnapped–yes, that's right, abductions are so common in Venezuela there is a 0800 number for it (0800-sequestrado in Spanish)–to which she was informed by the police that they were already aware of her situation, had located her truck, and were now holding it for her. Her suspicions were immediately roused by the police's miraculous efficiency in knowing what had happened and in locating the vehicle, which had likewise been dumped in the back of beyond. The only logical conclusion being that the police themselves had somehow been involved. When she picked up the vehicle within the hour, all her multiple bags of groceries were missing. Since the kidnappers had been real pros, Jesmary was convinced they wouldn't have wasted time riffling through her groceries and that it was the local cops who had pilfered the goods.

Kidnapping first became a serious problem in Venezuela around the remoter border areas with Colombia when, about a decade ago, people began to be abducted in increasing numbers–a large proportion of whom were farmers. All sections of society are vulnerable to the crime today, including poorer families from the barrios who are as likely to become victims as the wealthy, with gangs just demanding smaller ransoms. Whereas a rich family might be forced to sell their home to pay for the release of a loved one, poorer families have to gather the money any way they can, often by selling their limited household possessions–as was the case of a woman from the barrios who in order to secure the release of her toddler daughter had to sell the family's most valuable asset: their fridge.

Conventional kidnappings as well as what Venezuelans refer to as "express kidnappings" and "virtual kidnappings" are common. Express kidnappings involve ambushing someone at gunpoint–often in broad daylight on the street–and holding the victim for a relatively short duration (a day or two) to try and extract a quick payment. This is frequently done by escorting the victim to an ATM just before and immediately after midnight in order to withdraw the maximum amount from their account. Other methods include draining credit cards, forcing victims to pawn goods, or demanding payment from the victim's family or friends but within an extremely short time frame–sometimes giving only hours to stump up a ransom to save the victim's life, thereby minimizing the kidnappers' risk of getting caught. One recent case saw a professional couple driven throughout the night from one friend's house to a succession of others, where donations towards their ransom were demanded. At every location where the kidnappers failed to obtain a payment, the couple were pistol whipped–quite the motivation for coming up with a better suggestion next time. Victims have been abducted in their cars at traffic lights, at shopping malls, in hotels, on college campuses, in parks, at the airport terminal, even standing at the bus stop–as what happened to a three-year-old girl who was snatched out of the hands of her mother by a gang of three in Barinas.

Thankfully, virtual kidnappings on the other hand are not actually real; being a ruse where fake surveys are conducted to gather personal information, which is then used to convince family members that their child or relative has been kidnapped. An immediate ransom is then demanded, and often paid, before the family can discover that, in reality, no abduction has occurred. Increasingly, kidnappers of both the express and virtual kind are using websites such as Facebook to glean personal information so as to build up a picture of their intended victim's assets and routines.

Pinning down an accurate figure for the number of kidnappings carried out annually in Venezuela is nigh on impossible, as it is thought the majority go unreported due to the widespread belief that many police are directly involved in the crime–a justifiable concern given that the Venezuelan version of the FBI, the CICPC, recently uncovered a gang of kidnappers made up of police officers. One recently busted gang, going by the moniker Los Invisibles (the Invisibles), would threaten their victim's relatives with swift retribution should they call the police, claiming they had agents within the force who would tip them off, resulting in the victim's death. Accusations have even been made of police stations being used as holding locations for victims and of officers identifying potential kidnapping targets. Official figures for people taken against their will hover around the five-hundred-a-year mark, but if the numbers quoted in *Time* magazine from the Venezuelan Observatory of Violence are to be believed, then the true figure is far greater: as high as nine thousand. Whatever the real number, kidnapping is a major problem in the country and one that is growing, with 2009 seeing an increase of 40 percent in the official number of reported cases compared to the year before.

While I was in the country, a particularly nasty kidnapping occurred where a team of twelve amateur soccer players were abducted from the pitch on which they played near the Colombian border. Two weeks later, all but one were found dead–killed execution-style, the sole survivor having miraculously survived being shot in the back of the neck.

We arrived in the La Rosa area of Cabinas, home to the brightly colored traditional houses and, just offshore, the towering oil rigs. Parking up, we got out to stretch our legs and have a good look around. Many of the houses were little more than wooden sheds made of haphazardly attached slats, often patching up previous holes or weak spots in the walling. Despite their ramshackle appearance, a loving application of colored paint was applied to their exterior. The tradition of painting the houses with colorful facades had, according to Sabrina, originated when leftover paint used to coat the overground oil pipelines was distributed to the villagers.

Being keen photographers, Sabrina and Laura were interested in not only showing the area to Anselmo and me, but also taking some pictures of the place. It was interesting to see them go about this as what I might have deemed worthy of a photo generally didn't pass muster with them–and vice versa. As we meandered through the village streets, Laura and Sabrina would spot the most arbitrary of objects to take a picture of: a discarded piece of corrugated iron roofing with an interesting coloration of rust, the crusty flaking paint of a house's wooden slat walling, the texture of some crumbling brickwork. The locals thought this most amusing and gave us no shortage of bemused looks as we went about the village. At one stage, a group of women spotted Laura taking a photo of a dilapidated alleyway. One of them called something out to her, eliciting laughs both from their group and ours. Sabrina translated, "You should send the picture to *Panorama* [newspaper] so the council will come and fix it up!"

We stopped nearby by a small beach covered with thick patches of oil and piles of plastic bottles where several towering rigs could be seen offshore. This, along with the other mighty oil fields in the east of the country, was where the country's wealth, influence, and power were derived.

Even before Columbus arrived on the shores of what would become Venezuela, the indigenous population knew of the land's abundant treasure of oil that bubbled up to the surface and was put to use in their traditional medicine. Oil has played such a fundamental role in the shaping of modern Venezuela that it is hard to imagine the country today without it. It has established the nation's strategic importance in the world and the influence it commands; it is the source of many of the country's future challenges and its likely salvation from countless others. Were it not for oil and the economic muscle it provides, it is unlikely Chávez would be able to transform his vision of building "21st-century socialism" in Venezuela into reality, or that he would suffer such hysterical attacks in the Western media for attempting to do so.

Ask most people which nation possesses the world's largest oil reserves and you are likely to receive the reply "Saudi Arabia." Actually, it's Venezuela that has the largest oil reserves on the planet. Venezuela possesses the biggest conventional oil reserves in the Western Hemisphere and the greatest reserves of extraheavy crude oil in the world, having an amazing 90 percent of the earth's entire heavy reserves. Combined, these eclipse the reserves of the Saudis by as much as five times.[50] As if that wasn't enough, Venezuela is also a huge player in the field of natural gas, having giant reserves that by some estimates are the largest in the Western Hemisphere and possibly the fourth greatest in the world. Such resources provide tremendous potential, through their staggering revenue-generating capacity, to transform the country through social spending–if left unhampered by undue external interference, that is. Until Chávez, this gargantuan national largesse had remained solely in the hands of the few, with the poor majority barely picking up the crumbs at the table of the oligarchy that controlled the oil flow. To reverse this state of affairs, early in Chávez's presidency, he instigated steps for the "renationalization" of the country's supposedly state-owned oil company, PDVSA–which was, in reality, subservient to foreign oil majors instead of the government–pledging to finally redistribute the nation's oil wealth to its people.

One of the first areas of conflict between Chávez and those running PDVSA–which led in part to Chávez's push for the company's "renationalization"–was its aversion to sticking to OPEC quotas. This was something that, prior to Chávez's election, many OPEC countries had become lax about, leading to an oversupply of oil, which in turn saw a lower price per barrel and a weakened cartel. Soon after becoming president, Chávez began actively rebuilding

OPEC's strength by petitioning other member countries to strictly adhere to their quotas, something he successfully achieved through sending his minister for Energy and Mines, Ali Rodriguez, to visit with leaders of OPEC countries to lobby them into adopting such a policy. The result was a complete success with prices rising almost immediately, more than doubling within a year of Chávez, taking office to over $20 a barrel. In 2000, Chávez himself began personal lobbying trips to press OPEC into adopting a price band system.

Maintaining a high oil price is crucial to Chávez's hopes of building "21st-century socialism" in Venezuela in ways beyond simply having increased revenues to fund social projects. For if the country's "extraheavy oil" reserves–which by some estimates total 1.36 *trillion* barrels worth[51]–are to be considered economically viable to extract and refine, then they require a stable long-term oil price of more than $28.[52] (At the time of writing, a barrel of oil costs over $70). If prices fall below $28, then such heavy reserves are considered obsolete; they are simply too costly to extract and process. But if prices remain high, then this has staggering ramifications, for it is the country that possesses the largest reserves who controls OPEC, and it is the country that controls OPEC who has the ability to set the price of that slimy black product which serves as the lifeblood of every industrial nation on the planet. At the moment, the controlling country is Saudi Arabia, but should prices maintain their lofty reaches for the foreseeable future, then the reserve king of the world will be the Bolivarian Republic of Venezuela.

Initially, Chávez's attempts to renationalize PDVSA, and gain control of this tremendous national resource for the good of the country, didn't go smoothly. Disputes arose with PDVSA over issues ranging from the government gaining access to accurate financial records for the company to Chávez appointing a new board of directors, from increasing PDVSA's transparency to reducing its costs. Such disputes led, in the run up to the botched coup, to the management staging an illegal lockout and the closing down of a crucial refinery. Immediately after the coup, Chávez acted with a marked degree of caution towards PDVSA, offering them an olive branch in the form of reinstating the company's old board of directors who had previously been replaced as one of the first steps towards renationalization. This conciliatory step, however, was taken as a sign of weakness by the opposition, who soon began renewed moves to force Chávez out, this time by attempting to bring the country to its knees with an indefinite out-and-out shutdown of the oil industry. Despite the opposition claiming the action was part of a wider national "general strike" and that the shutdown was legitimate, neither was true. For in general, it was only large U.S. fast-food chains and shopping malls in the more affluent districts of the country that joined the strike, with areas where the majority of the population lived functioning, more or less, as normal. As for the shutdown being legitimate, for it to be deemed so, it needed to be related to labor issues whereas in reality, the strike's true aim was forcing the resignation of the country's democratically elected leader. Rather tellingly, none of the three main labor unions of PDVSA supported the strike.

After lasting for two months, the shutdown was finally defeated, with the government turning to willing and able retired employees, military personnel, and contractors from abroad to keep the industry afloat. In response to the shutdown, roughly nineteen thousand of PDVSA's staff–about half of its workforce–were dismissed for abandoning their workplace, leading to the opposition suffering a further crushing defeat by losing another of their former power bases, their sole remaining now being the media. As a result, Chávez was able to properly implement the full renationalization of PDVSA–something which is enshrined in the new Venezuelan constitution–and finally start to "sow the oil" in the interests of the majority rather than the few. This has been successful in redirecting 80 percent more revenues to the state and has been crucial in the funding of the "mission" social programs.[53]

Some of Chávez's more significant actions that have ruffled the feathers of the world's oil kingpins are his signing off on deals that circumvent them and go instead to the state-run oil companies of China, India, and Brazil, doubling royalty taxes on foreign oil companies' new oil finds within Venezuela, and his refusal to continue with business as usual regarding a practice considered the modus operandi for most other oil-producing nations–"petrodollar recycling." This ingenious system is where OPEC countries such as Saudi Arabia and Kuwait "recycle" their billions of dollars in oil revenues straight back to the United States by purchasing titanic swathes of low-interest U.S. government debts, which the United States then cycles out to the world as high-interest loans. It's a remarkable deal for the United States and a shrewd move for a dictator of an oil-rich country. For the United States, it not only provides the difference between the interest paid out and the interest received, but also an endless line of credit to fund the national debt, allowing for vast amounts of red ink to pay for military and other expenditures, which are funded, in large part, by U.S. citizens' previous purchases of foreign oil at the pump, money which ends up cycling straight back into the country's coffers again. And for a Saudi or Kuwaiti dictator, the practice serves as an insurance policy, protection against a domestic uprising or foreign invasion, which the creditor can rely on his debtor ally to crush. And should such action be unsuccessful and the repressed masses force a hasty and prolonged holiday on an unfortunate dictator, then he can rest assured that his nation's money is stashed far from the populace's baying reach.

Chávez, however, has demonstrated his unwillingness to act as a servile puppet of this system and believes his country's petrodollars belong not in the United States but south of the border. As seen by his withdrawal of $20 billion from the U.S. Fed, which he deposited in the Bank for International Settlements for investment in Latin America. Such actions from the leader of a nation set to become the world's future oil supremo have made Chávez plenty of enemies in extremely high places. There is little doubt his foes will continue to seek ways of deposing, or indeed, disposing of him, lest he succeeds in achieving his vision of creating "21st-century socialism" in Venezuela and serves to inspire other countries seeking to develop independently of U.S. influence to follow. With such oil reserves at his disposal, he stands a far stronger chance than most of success.

CHAPTER 15

Missionary Position

I'd seen some fat chicks in my time, but the woman who clambered on board my bus to the coastal town of Coro took the biscuit, in fact, several packets and more besides, by the looks of her. She was giant, dripping in sweat and panting away in short rapid breaths characteristic of the morbidly obese. Despite feeling sorry for her, as she waddled down towards the only seats available–an aisle seat next to me and another one directly opposite–I found myself internally imploring her not to take the one by me, knowing full well that she would try and appropriate half the seat of whoever was lumbered with sitting next to her.

She paused by both seats.

Looking either way, she pondered which way to go. I was to her left.

Go to your right! Go to your right! I shouted at her in my head, as if possessing some telepathic power.

With a quick mop of her sweaty brow and a heaving pant, she turned to her left.

Shit. My heart sank.

Squeezing between the seat next to me and the one in front–no mean feat–she positioned herself in readiness for the descent. Not so much lowering herself as hitting the free-fall button and letting gravity take over. She flopped down into the seat like a big blacmange pudding, her ripples of flab reverberating in an obscene wave that engulfed my previously comfy position. Her elbows and sweaty pillowlike bare arms nudged mine clean off the armrest, digging at my ribs, and leaving a horrible trail of perspiration on mine. My lower half fared no better, with her Michelin Man legs effortlessly swatting mine aside, stealing the majority of my legroom. It was like being back in the tent with Marian, although this time I was in no mood for a fight. Instead, I rather indignantly clambered over her mountain of a form and took the seat opposite, throwing a look of disdain towards her five-chinned face. She was lucky I couldn't speak Spanish; if I had been able to, I would have aired my discontent, firing off some forked-tongued invective directed at her eating habits and need to see a reputable dietician.

I had caught the bus to Coro after bidding Anselmo farewell, who had taken a carrito to the nearby border with Colombia. Here he planned to stay with a couple of CouchSurfers he had previously hosted in Brazil. With Marcos getting up again at 4:30 am, to avoid a fatigued and sleepy-eyed good-bye, Anselmo and I had said our farewells and expressed our gratitude to him the night before, and so woke again to an empty house. In Coro, I had arranged to stay with a new CouchSurfer, Henry, who had agreed to meet me in the town's central bus station. The rendezvous part of the plan seemed unlikely now, as unfortunately, the bus had departed a good half an hour behind schedule, and due to severe traffic and the bus being pulled over en route for a police ID check, we arrived in Coro a full two and a half hours late. Having had no way of contacting Henry–other than the CouchSurfing website which I had zero access to–I no longer expected him to be waiting for me at the terminal. And so it was something of a shock when

I grabbed my backpack from the bus's rear luggage compartment and heard someone calling my name.

Standing there was a big dark-skinned grizzly bear of a man with a broad and welcoming smile.

"I'm Henry," he said, opening his arms wide in a welcoming first gesture–perhaps a tad over familiar for a repressed middle-class Englishman like myself, but what the hell, I went with it. "Welcome to Coro!" he exclaimed.

I apologized for being late.

"Don't worry, I wasn't going to leave you here alone," Henry replied, in good spirits.

He spoke excellent English, as was to be expected for a professional Spanish-to-English translator. We jumped in a cab and stopped off at Henry's family home in the dusty suburb of Pantano Abajo, on the other side of town. It was quite a basic house in which he lived with his parents, two brothers, sister, adorable grandmother, and cat Leono. I was received with a warm welcome from one and all and shown through to the room I'd be sharing with Henry's brothers, Henbert and Hebert, as well as fellow CouchSurfer, Jay.

Jay was from France and had been staying for the last couple of days. He was sticking around for tonight also before heading west across the border to Colombia. On a PC in the corner of the room, Jay was showing Hebert some photos of his travels around Venezuela. On screen was a picture of Jay in the middle of a white sandy beach with his arms around three drop-dead gorgeous girls in skimpy bikinis. His expression in the photo said it all. He had a cheeky sideways glance, a singular raised eyebrow, and a grin from ear to ear like a cat that got the cream.

"I have a little to do with the one on the left," he said in a deep French accent, punctuating it with an expression identical to the one in the photo.

"We call him Pepe Le Pew," said Henry, with a laugh and a dismissive shake of the head.

"Does he smell?" I asked facetiously.

"No," said Henry, missing the joke. "He likes the ladies. Don't you, Jay?"

Jay turned to me, puffing out his cheeks. "Venezuelan women, they drive you crazy!" he exclaimed, shaking his head as if it was all too much for a hot-blooded Frenchman to bear.

The computer died.

"Power cut," stated Henry, with a sigh of resignation.

Jay cursed in French with theatrical Gallic flare.

"They happen all the time," explained Henry who, to illustrate how regularly they occurred, told me of a funny postcard you could buy in Venezuela. Its title was something like, "Great cities of the world at night," and depicted the dramatic nocturnal skylines of London, Paris, New York, and Rome as well as the not-so-great Caracas. Under the name of each relevant city was a picture of their majestic nighttime skyline lit up with twinkling lights. Except, that is, for Caracas, which was simply depicted as black.

Henry explained what an excruciating hassle such power cuts could be and gave the example of trying to write a thesis or college project when they occurred. If it was due the next day, then you had no way of finishing or printing it. And if you hadn't been saving your work every few minutes, then you would end up losing big chunks and having to do it all over, often only to lose it once more when the computer cut out again.

Since much of Venezuela's electricity relies on hydropower, the drought the country was currently suffering was severely exacerbating the problem. In response to shortages, Chávez recently declared an electricity emergency and announced that severe rationing could continue for months. In a sign of desperation, state electricity company Edelca called on its workers to attend an hour-long prayer meeting to petition the Almighty for rain.

After a quick introduction to Henry's younger sister, Betzenia, we decided to go out and visit Coro's famed "mini Sahara Desert," which was an expanse of rolling sand dunes on the outer fringes of the city. After that, Henry suggested we attend a Tchaikovsky concert that a friend of his was playing in. On our way out the door, I got to see how popular Jay was with the rest of the family. He had a really interesting way of conversing with Henry's mother and grandmother, both of whom he would superficially speak to sternly but then finish off with his characteristic cheeky smile. They loved it and were fussing all over him. Outside the house, we stood for a group photo with Henry's brothers when an attractive girl in her twenties walked past. Jay was on heat and immediately tried to cajole her into joining us. She declined but gave him a suggestive smile for his troubles. He was certainly the ladies' man.

The desert began on the northeast fringes of the city in an area designated a national park. We took a cab there, coming to a halt along a wide avenue at the end of which was a large sculpture of a woman on her knees, situated on a yellow plinth in the middle of a fenced-off pool. It was a tribute to motherhood, aptly named Monumento a la Madre–monument to the mother.

Jay was convinced the cabby was trying to overcharge him and erupted into a heated remonstration over the fare. Henry stepped in as the diplomat, calming him down with soothing tones like a wise old sage. They were such different personalities but seemed to get on great. Jay was in-your-face and superenergized with a short fuse and darting attention, Henry calm and unassuming–a gentle giant–acting as a moderating force on Jay's manic enthusiasm.

Beyond the road, the desert began. We clambered up the first dune, rising from the park's entrance and blocking the horizon from view. For every step I took forward, I seemed to sink backwards by about a third as much, the sand warping around my feet and collapsing in miniature avalanches. On reaching the summit, I looked out onto a different world. A sprawling desiccated landscape stretched out into the distance, its rolling dunes casting vast curvaceous shadows in their wake. A soft wind created a light spray of sand that gently hissed over the terrain in soothing tones, feathering from the dune's peaks as if vapor from a breaking wave. It was a magical location with a peaceful yet playful atmosphere. Despite being lots of people about, the vastness of the dunes allowed for everyone to have their own space and solitude should they desire. I liked it immensely.

Henry and Jay began taking running leaps off the dunes' peaks, tumbling to an eventual laughter-inducing halt down below. Jay was pretty good at this and started to up the ante, doing backflips which Henry tried repeatedly to catch on camera. After every attempt, Jay would clamber back up to Henry's position with a cry of, "Did you get it? Did you get it?" Only to discover on checking the digital display that Henry had been a fraction of a second too early or too late, and that Jay would have to perform his acrobatics again.

I did nothing so strenuous and, after strolling through a section of dunes, perched myself atop one of their peaks to watch the disappearing sun. I picked up a handful of cool sand from the shady side of the dune and for a while studied its texture and sparkle in the low pink sunlight. We stayed until nightfall when a group of quad bikers took to the sands, their headlights illuminating their distant positions like ground-dwelling incandescent fireflies.

When we arrived at the concert hall in town, the power cut had taken its toll on proceedings, which were now cancelled. Milling around outside with the crowds, we met up with Henry's violinist friend who was part of the orchestra. He was disappointed not to be playing but didn't seem particularly surprised, having clearly experienced the same on previous occasions. He had learnt to play through El Sistema and would soon be trying out for the world-famous Simón Bolívar Youth Orchestra, where two of his friends were already members. I wished him luck.

With no concert and the streets pitch-black, Henry suggested we go to a "poetry house." This, essentially, was an artistic bohemian bar where poetry readings took place, located out the back of an art gallery in the historic quarter of town. Although a complete hassle for the locals, it's got to be said, the power cut provided an extremely atmospheric setting for the poetry house. To get in, we walked along a thin dark corridor leading to and through the art gallery, all of which was delicately lit by the inviting haloey light of flickering candles. Out the back was a courtyard with a small bar and several tables, on each of which a candle faintly accentuated the features of those around it with a warping orange glow. It seemed a very artistic crowd and the place even more so thanks to the sublime illuminations. It was my kind of venue.

All of a sudden the lights came on, providing a whole new perspective to the bar's surroundings and its occupants. The place erupted into cheers. I think I must have been the only one who was a little disappointed. Although it did, of course, mean the fridges were back on–and warm beer in this part of the world was a capital crime. We stuck around for an hour or so then strolled through the historic cobbled streets of Coro's Calle Zamora area, the buildings of which were painted a cheerful kaleidoscope of colors and visible now for the first time. Henry pointed out buildings of interest–including the oldest church in Venezuela (dating from the late 1500s) and the oldest Jewish cemetery on the continent (established in the early 1800s)–enlivening our stroll with a splattering of history from Coro's past.

Coro was one of the oldest of the New World's settlements, having been founded by the Spanish in 1527 to suppress slave hunting in the area. A year later, it became the first capital of Venezuela; and today, this modest port town of some two hundred thousand people is the capital of the Falcón State. The indigenous Caquetío people named the area "Curiana," or "place of winds." With cooling sea breezes blowing in off the Caribbean, it is an apt description for what is generally considered the most attractive and best preserved of Venezuela's colonial towns.

Coro's early history bares a heavy German influence, with the town, and much of present-day Venezuela, being leased in 1527 by King Charles V to the wealthy German banking and merchant family, the Welsers, to whom he was heavily indebted. His debts amounted to 6,600 pounds of gold–money he borrowed to trounce the candidacy of Francis I of France to be crowned by the pope as the next Holy Roman Emperor, a title Charles V was awarded in 1530. Over the following twenty years, German conquistadors used Coro as a base to explore the territory in search of riches, in particular, El Dorado, the mythical city of gold. The German lease was terminated in 1546 and the capital moved 125 miles inland to El Tocuyo, to protect it from pirate attack. (In 1577, the capital was moved to Caracas.) With the departure of the Germans, the town's importance and growth soon waned. In 1567, 1595, and 1659, it suffered crippling pirate raids and, in 1681, was devastated by a cyclone.

The good times returned in the 18th century, thanks to Coro becoming the chief supply center of livestock and farming produce for the nearby Dutch colonies of Bonaire and Curacao. The majority of the town's remaining historic architecture dates from this period, which in 1993 saw Coro designated a World Heritage Site by the United Nations Educational, Scientific, and Cultural Organization (UNESCO). By 2005, though, the effects of torrential rains had seen it added to UNESCO's List of World Heritage Sites in Danger.

In a 2009 interview with the Smithsonian Institute magazine, the restoration architect, Graziano Gasparini, who first nominated the town to become part of the heritage list, claimed that although UNESCO had made several recommendations on how the city could be preserved, nothing had been done, noting, "There was an allocation of $32 million on the part of the Venezuelan government to address Coro's problems, and no one knows where it went."

On our way back to Henry's place, we stopped off at a big outdoor courtyard where a band played and a large group of couples danced the night away. When the music stopped, a master of ceremonies with a microphone introduced two women in their thirties to the crowd. A "dance off" was about to ensue. The music struck up, and the crowd began clapping rhythmically. First up was a slim and beautiful brunette who exuded self-confidence from every pore and had the crowd eating out of the palm of her hand, wriggling about like an eel, bending her form like a contortionist. Jay turned to me with an agitated look as if his hormones were sending him insane.

"It is *too* much!" he said, shaking his head.

She finished off with a final dramatic flurry, eliciting a roar of delight from those watching. Her competition was going to have to pull something spectacular out of the bag to top this. She didn't. A blonde with slightly more meat on her bones danced into center stage, doing a nice-enough routine but without the wow factor of the girl before, who was unanimously pronounced the winner.

We carried on up the road, with Jay jumping up and grabbing hold of the metal window railings of several colonial buildings in order to haul himself up off the ground so Henry could take a photo of him spread-eagle in the frame. Around the corner from a historic church, we came upon a large banner suspended across a cloister-resembling red-tiled walkway. At either end of the banner was a depiction of the internationally recognized circular red prohibited sign with characteristic diagonal line cutting across it. Inside of this were four emblems: a skull and cross bones, the silhouette of a man with a bazooka, a helicopter, and a bomb. Scrawled across the middle of the banner was Spanish text, reading, "Let's repudiate the gringo interference!" and proclaiming "Popular bases of peace in our America." This, coupled with the emblems, was likely a reference to the planned unpopular acquisition of seven giant U.S. (gringo) military bases in neighboring Colombia, something which will take the total number of U.S. facilities there to ten.

Chávez has denounced this, warning that "the winds of war were beginning to blow across the region" and accusing Washington of wanting to use Colombia as a launchpad from which military interventions could be conducted throughout the continent. Officially, the Pentagon acknowledges approximately nine hundred[54] military facilities worldwide, although the actual figure is closer to a thousand with unacknowledged facilities in Israel, the

Philippines, Kuwait, and elsewhere. This constitutes a staggering 95 percent of all the world's military bases maintained by any nation on foreign soil.

The United States claims it wants to relocate its military bases from Ecuador to Colombia for counternarcotic and counterterrorism operations only–after the president of Ecuador, Rafael Correa, denied an extension to a previous agreement that permitted U.S. bases in his country. However, the installations are, in reality, desired for quite different objectives. An official 2009 document of the Department of the U.S. Air Force[55] makes clear that the proposed base in Palanquero will give the U.S. military "an opportunity for conducting full spectrum operations throughout South America" and specifically refers to the "constant threat" posed to the region by "anti–U.S. governments." To Washington's thinking, any government seeking to develop independently of U.S. interference fits this description, but there is little doubt it is primarily a reference to Venezuela and Bolivia, and to a lesser extent Ecuador and Paraguay. The document also states that the U.S. presence will "increase our capability to conduct Intelligence, Surveillance, and Reconnaissance (ISR), improve global reach . . . and expand expeditionary warfare capability." In addition to the new bases, the agreement between the United States and Colombia, signed in October 2009, grants the United States "access and use of all other installations and locations as necessary." This startling clause effectively grants the U.S. sovereignty over Colombian soil, allowing them to use even commercial airports for military purposes should they see fit.

All of this comes amid growing tensions between Venezuela and Colombia, something which the bases will only exacerbate. Colombia has, for well over a decade, been the largest recipient of U.S. military support in the Western Hemisphere and has South America's worst record on human rights, including a notorious record of backing death squads (ten thousand Colombian soldiers were trained in the United States at the infamous School of the

Americas in Georgia; notorious for its training of Central and South American death squads in assassination, interrogation, and torture techniques). Interestingly, despite Colombia having a far worse record of human rights abuses than Venezuela, it is Venezuela that is lambasted for this in the corporate media, with Colombia receiving something of a "get out of jail free" card simply because the nation is an ally of the United States. Jeff Cohen of American Media watchdog, Fairness and Accuracy in Reporting (FAIR), succinctly described the phenomenon, "[W]hen a foreign government is in favor with the United States, with the White House, its human rights record is basically off the mainstream media agenda, and when they do something that puts them out of favor with the US government, the foreign government's human rights abuses are, all of a sudden, major news."[56]

Imagine, if you will, the saturation coverage Venezuela would receive were a mass grave of two thousand people discovered within the country. But this is exactly what recently occurred in Colombia, and the corporate media silence has been deafening. In 2009, the largest mass grave to be unearthed in Colombia was discovered just outside a Colombian army base overseen by U.S. military advisors. The grave came to light when children became seriously ill after drinking water from a nearby stream contaminated by run off from the decomposing bodies. According to Colombian officials, the grave contains the bodies of approximately two thousand people, all of whom the army has admitted to killing, claiming that those buried are guerillas.[57] However, having previously been embroiled in the so-called false positive scandal–where Colombian soldiers received payment for the number of guerrillas killed but took instead to murdering civilians who they then dressed like guerrillas in order to justify increased U.S. aid–the immediate suspicion is that the new mass grave is further evidence of this repugnant practise. "False positive" killings have been so common in Colombia, that the UN high commissioner for human rights, Navi Pillay, described them as "systematic."[58]

With two thousand corpses discovered just outside a base overseen by U.S. military advisers, you might be forgiven for thinking this would be big news in the United States, and that serious questions would be asked in the media as to the activities of U.S. forces in Colombia as well as the justification for the gargantuan U.S. military aid the country receives. Nothing of the sort. As per usual, the corporate mainstream media has played useful idiot and almost completely ignored the story; and for many, if it isn't reported in the mainstream, then it simply didn't happen. But for many Venezuelans, the revelations of both the mass grave and the U.S. Air Force document that spells out the true motivations for appropriating the seven additional Colombian military bases have gone anything but unnoticed.

As Henry and I stepped out of his house into another gloriously sunny morning, I caught myself stating the absurdly obvious.

"Lovely sunny day today," I remarked to Henry, as if sunshine in the tropics was an unusual event, somehow worthy of comment.

"Err, yes," he responded, in the sort of confused agreement you might expect from someone you had just pointed out that the sun had risen again this morning.

I'd caught myself doing this all over the country, a typical British trait borne out of far too many conversations at home centered around the weather, where every sunny day did indeed merit a mention–old habits died hard.

With Coro possessing a rolling desert and historic quarter, it was a wonderful place to spend a couple of days, but while here, I also hoped to visit another nearby attraction, the peninsula of Paraguaná. This was a huge bulbous landmass that sat proudly in the Caribbean Sea between the nearby islands of the Dutch Antilles and the South American continent, which it was connected to by a thin stretch of sandy land. It was roughly forty miles from end to end and boasted flaming pink flamingos, crusty salt mines, and about two hundred miles of coastline, much of which was prime sandy beach. The peninsula had been a former haven for smugglers and pirates during colonial times and was now one of the country's top locations for kitesurfing and windsurfing. The majority of its terrain was sparsely populated parched desert plain, with the exception of a single mountain rising proudly in its center, which was visible all over the peninsula. I suggested going there to Henry.

He sighed with a gracious smile.

"I'd be happy to take you, but I went there with Jay the day before you arrived, so thought you might like to take a trip into the countryside instead."

I didn't have the heart to drag Henry along on an identical trip to the one he'd made a couple of days before with Jay–who had departed earlier this morning for Maracaibo en route to the Colombian border–neither did I feel I could really suggest me going solo to the peninsula, leaving him with no one to host. And so I told him it was a grand idea.

We caught a carrito heading to the rural town of Pueblo Nuevo de la Sierra, driving through a rugged landscape of rolling green hills peppered with typically lush vegetation.

Whenever a passenger in a car, I'm always scanning the landscape, trying to identify plants and especially trees on the hoof; but for a while in Venezuela, this had been a fruitless force of habit, with little past the easily identifiable and distinctive banana tree registering in my consciousness. Although I could identify all the trees in Britain and knew many of their edible and medicinal uses, when it came to the tropics, it was a different matter altogether. However, by now I was quietly pleased to be able to identify distant mango trees whizzing past from the briefest of glances, which had become my favorite tropical tree. I had really got into the study of trees recently, so much so that I'd qualified as a tree surgeon just months before and had worked for a while in this field prior to heading off traveling. The fun part about this, other than getting paid to be a big kid climbing trees for work, was that whenever I got asked, at dinner parties and the like, what I did for a living, I could respond with a big dose of intentional understatement, "Surgeon." This never failed to illicit the desired impressed response, and if then asked to elaborate on my area of specialization, I would reply solemnly, "Amputations" or "The removal of limbs." When one inquisitive individual probed further and asked what tools were used for this, I answered honestly, "Chainsaw."

As we drove through a remote rural village, a woman sharing our carrito informed Henry–who then translated for me–that the village had recently become home to a lot of Cubans.

"Are they doctors?" I asked, referring to a barter agreement in which Venezuela gives Cuba oil in exchange for teams of Cuba's world-renowned medical practitioners.

Henry asked then translated the answer, stating, in all seriousness, "No, they are masseuses." Having a rubdown with essential oils hardly seemed a crucial medical service to have specially imported from a foreign land to a sleepy hamlet in the middle of nowhere. As much as I didn't doubt Henry's translation, I did very much doubt that the woman who told him this was correct; otherwise, per capita, the villagers would have been the most pampered in the country.

The caritto reached the end of the line at Pueblo Nuevo de la Sierra. From here Henry and I set off on foot along a quiet country road surrounded by greenery and rugged hills, heading towards a forested area at the end of the road where the Crisóstomo Falcón National Park began. In the distance could be heard the sound of falling water. I pointed this out to Henry, who was surprised I could hear what he explained must be Hueque waterfall far up ahead. Being barely able to make out the sound himself, I got him to cup and point his ears in the sound's direction while also looking intently–something that can make a surprising difference and is the equivalent of "turning up the volume" of your ears.

"Wow, that's amazing," he said, lowering his hands down then raising them back up again to his ears as if checking that it still worked.

We arrived at the entrance of the national park and continued up a track until we reached a little park set amongst the shade of the forested hills. Here the waterfall was located. It was no Angel Falls, being about fifteen-foot high and about five times that in width. But it was a charming location nonetheless. Although just about deserted today, Henry said that during the holidays, the place was packed with families picnicking and cooling off under the water. I decided to give the latter a try and, after a bit of cajoling, got Henry to strip down to his shorts and join me under the water. Living in such a hot country, Henry found what I would consider delightfully cooling to be downright bloody freezing, and despite his towering stature and manly appearance, the water's temperature had him squealing like a girl.

Sorry, mate.

We made our way along the back of the waterfall, hugging the cool and slippery rocks as we went so that the curtain of water plunged over the top of us. On emerging at the far end, Henry spotted a guy approaching our clothing, shoes, and wallets with what he took, and I concurred, to be ill intent. On seeing us, the individual quickened his pace towards our belongings. We did the same, wading through the pool beneath the falls with large urgent strides in the direction of our possessions. When it became clear we'd get there first, the would-be thief abruptly changed his course, heading off into the trees. If he'd arrived before us and nabbed our shoes, there would have been no chance of catching up with him on this terrain.

We spent a good bit of the afternoon at the park chatting and taking in the scenery, during which time Henry told me about some translation work he was doing over the next few days. He would be working for a group of predominantly Baptist Christians from South Carolina in the United States, who were starting a tour of the surrounding area tomorrow, going into remote villages to try and evangelize the locals and convert the heathen savages to Christianity. The majority religion in Venezuela is Catholicism, which accounts for 95 percent of believers, but despite many indigenous groups having converted to this, and other branches of Christianity, there are still tribes that continue to practise their traditional beliefs. Other curious religious amalgamations exist, the most popular being the cult of revered nature goddess, Maria Lionza. This mixes elements from Catholicism, indigenous beliefs, and African voodoo, reflecting the three ethnic heritages that make up the country's population–European, indigenous, and African. The cult incorporates magic, trance dances, and esoteric rites and venerates a plethora of spirits, deities, and saints–of which even Simón Bolívar is included.

Although a Christian himself–and if forced to put myself into such a box would state likewise–Henry didn't seem in the slightest bit interested in trying to evangelize me like the aggressive Jehovah's Witness mob in Ciudad Guayana. As luck would have it, the group Henry was translating for tomorrow were heading for the town of Chichiriviche, next to the coastal national park of Morrocoy–exactly where I was going. They had hired a private bus for the trip and were leaving in the morning. Henry offered to arrange for me to tag along with them and get a free ride. I agreed.

A total of three power cuts occurred the following morning, making my attempts at using the house PC to check my e-mails difficult to say the least. The romance of flickering candlelight had, by now, fully worn off. It wasn't easy, but after a concerted effort, I managed to pick up an e-mail from Juan, who had messaged me with his brother's contact details so that I could get in touch with him regarding the Miss Venezuela School. I sent his brother an enthused message, expressing my desire to visit the place, and wrote that I'd call him when I returned to the capital. With Venezuela being the world's only self-styled "beauty superpower," the Miss Venezuela school's pink mansion was the beauty equivalent of the White House. I couldn't wait to go and try some of my suave British charm on the beauties.

Henry's mother was an absolute angel and had not only washed my dirty clothing but ironed and folded them all as well. She was unable to speak English, so I let it be known through Henry how much I appreciated her kindness. While killing time waiting to go off and meet the American missionaries, Henry and I got talking about Chávez. He was rather ambivalent either way about the president but told me that Chávez was always making dramatic promises–often during his marathon television appearances–that never came to anything. He gave two examples. Many of Venezuela's roads are potholed and in dire need of treating with asphalt, something Venezuela produces large quantities of as an offshoot of its oil industry. When Chávez learned that the country was exporting asphalt amid a dire domestic shortage, he promised that no more would go abroad until all Venezuelan roads were first covered. The country's roads remain in a poor state of repair and exports of asphalt continue aplenty. Henry's other example was that on the night of Chávez's first election victory, he had promised that if there were still street kids in Venezuela within three months, then he would officially change his name. There are still homeless children, and the president continues to go by the name of Hugo.

The American missionaries had selected a rendezvous spot renowned for its authentic Venezuelan cuisine–Subway. Even before we spoke to them, they were instantly recognizable as coming from the United States. It was hard to categorize, but there was something about their dress, supremely confident mannerisms, and characteristic "big boned" proportions that made their nationality immediately recognizable. In fact, you could almost tell they were Christians on an evangelical "mission from God" too, given their exaggerated smiles and "hey, buddy!" enthusiasm that to me seemed anything but sincere.

Henry introduced me around the group, which consisted of about thirty people ranging from a handful of young people in their late teens and early twenties to individuals in their fifties. I immediately felt out of place and wondered how on earth I had ended up hanging out with them. After the group had eaten enough Subway food for a fortnight on the road, we boarded the bus–its suspension groaning under the newfound weight.

Before we set off, the group's leader, Deisy, stood up and addressed the bus. Offering a prayer of thanksgiving, she praised the Lord for everything from the pilot who flew the group's plane the day before, to the tasty twelve-inch steak and double-cheese sub she'd just devoured for luncheon. She finished up by stressing the importance of their mission and of giving the people they contacted the message that "Jesus loves them."

I smiled inwardly, recalling a time I had seen a similar message scrawled on the inside of a toilet cubicle door in South Africa. In what is without doubt my favorite piece of WC graffiti, someone had written in big letters "Jesus loves you," under which somebody else had added the punch line "Everybody else thinks you're a cunt!"[59]

Ten minutes after hitting the road, Henry was called up front to speak to the leader, leaving the seat next to me free.

"Hey, mind if I join you?" said a thickly set man as he clambered over to join me. He sat down before I had a chance to answer.

"Henry tells me you've written a book, what's it called?"

"*Iranian Rappers and Persian Porn*."

He looked like he'd misheard. "I'm sorry, *Iranian* . . .?"

"*Rappers and Persian Porn*."

"Porn?"

"Yes, as in pornography."

"Uh . . . okay."

How did I always manage to bring porn up one way or another with Christians in Venezuela? The title didn't go down too well, so my new companion hastily changed the subject and, for the next twenty minutes, rambled on about everything from the perils of "socialized medicine" to how much he liked watching U.K. parliamentary debates and held a special place in his heart for Margaret Thatcher. I was all for trying to get along with the chap for the short period we would be sitting together but couldn't let that one go unchallenged.

"That's funny, because I hope there's a special place in hell for her," I responded, in all seriousness.

I steered us clear of politics and enquired as to how the group went about converting nonbelievers.

"We offer them free dentistry, and spread the word of our lord Jesus Christ at the same time."

"I thought you were against free health care."

"This is different. It's not provided by the government. All our dentists are private volunteers."

I can't say I particularly liked the notion of bribing locals in far-flung corners of the country with dental plans in exchange for conversion to their church. And so, in a moment of fleeting mischievous glee, I decided to mix things up a bit.

"Hey, what's the name of that extreme group of Christians in the U.S. that doesn't believe in the reality of evolution?" I asked him, as if surely his group wouldn't believe in such nonsense–knowing full well of course that they would.

"Well, I don't believe we come from monkeys!" he exclaimed, in a knee-jerk reaction, ready to launch into a well-rehearsed argument.

I ended up regretting my purposefully antagonist comment almost as soon as I'd made it and learnt quickly that there was no room for logic or reasoning with a true creationist believer. And what's more, what was I playing at? I was on a coach filled with missionaries who were giving me a free ride down the coast, so the last thing I needed was to get into this sort of debate. I made up my mind to shut up, enjoy the ride, and avoid controversy with the parishioners from now on.

Henry came back and retook his old seat next to me, sending the anti-Darwin away. Not long after, the group's leader came and joined us, standing in the aisle to lean over and talk to us. Henry had also told her about me writing a book, but this time when she inevitably asked me its title, I decided, in the interests of not offending her, to tell her a white lie. With a discreet nudge of Henry's leg, I told her the book had yet to come out and the title was undecided.

Sometime later, when I had access to a computer, I looked up the group (e3 Partners) and their website which, along with details on the cost of joining one of their evangelical tours of Venezuela (over two thousand dollars), had lots of faintly disguised disdain for President Chávez and plenty of out-and-out bullshit regarding him. It was a classic example of the typical misinformation widely written about Venezuela in the West, and of lying through omission:

> *In 2006, Venezuelan President Hugo Chavez expelled a church planting ministry that was reaching various tribal groups. A year later, he seized control of a major television station that questioned his policies. In 2008, his regime re-issued the national currency replacing the portraits of national heroes with those of leading cult figures. The government has also begun to seize private lands and to speak openly about nationalizing all private schools.*

Other nuggets on the website included

> *It is uncertain . . . how long followers of Christ will be permitted to preach freely* [in Venezuela].

Utter bollocks. Chávez is himself a Christian as are the vast majority of the population of Venezuela (over 95 percent), so to imply that somehow he or the government will outlaw the word of Christ is simply laughable. He has stated, rather aptly to my mind, that "the symbol of capitalism is Judas and of socialism it is Christ." As for Chávez expelling "a church planting ministry that was reaching various tribal groups," the group in question is in fact a notorious fundamentalist U.S. missionary group, New Tribes Mission, that has a sullied reputation amongst indigenous rights campaigners and has been accused of ignoring tribal people's rights in its desire to evangelize at all costs. According to indigenous rights organization, Survival International, when trying to convert the indigenous Ayoreo-Totobiegosode of Paraguay, the Florida-based missionaries "helped organize 'manhunts' in which large groups of Totobiegosode were forcibly brought out of the forest. Several Ayoreo died in these encounters, and others succumbed later to disease."

Other indictments of New Tribes Missions cited by Survival International include their activities in Brazil:

> *Members of the New Tribes Mission . . . carried out a clandestine mission to make contact with the Zo'é of Brazil to convert them to Christianity . . . Following their first real contact in 1987, 45 Zo'é died from epidemics of flu, malaria and respiratory diseases transmitted by the missionaries.*

Long before Chávez decided to expel a New Tribes Mission group, the government of Brazil took the lead, doing so in 1991.

As for e3 Partners' accusation that Chávez "seized control of a major television station that questioned his policies," as explained in a previous chapter, he did not "seize" anything but did not renew the station's licence after it had been caught directly assisting in a coup d'état against the elected government.

And with regard to "replacing portraits of national heroes with leading cult figures," if you look at the individuals on the two different sets of notes, the overriding theme of both those issued pre-2007 and post-2007 is people who fought or stood against Spanish colonialism.[60] The difference in the two is that those issued afterwards also include a woman, an indigenous Venezuelan, and an African Venezuelan (all of whom either fought the Spanish or played a role in the war of independence). With half the population being women, and 80 percent being "negro e indio" (that is black and indigenous), those featured are individuals whom the vast majority of Venezuelans can indeed identify with and so are not some sort of fringe "cult figures" as the e3 Partners missionaries would have readers of their website believe. They are very much "national heroes," only not necessarily to the country's white minority of 20 percent. This is, of course, ignoring the bigger question as to just what business is it of a group of foreign missionaries to criticize who an elected government decides to display on its national currency.

As to their charge that the Chávez government has "begun to seize private lands and to speak openly about nationalizing all private schools," what Chávez has actually said is that private schools need to admit school inspectors (as they do in Britain and many other countries) and follow a national curriculum, with those that refuse facing the threat of closure or nationalization. And finally, regarding Chávez "seizing private land," as explained earlier, it is only untilled land sitting idle that qualifies for redistribution to the landless. As Greg Palast states of the scheme, "It was a program long promised by Venezuelan politicians at the urging of John F. Kennedy as part of his Alliance for Progress. Progress waited for Chávez."

So much for an honest portrayal of Chávez and Venezuela from the e3 Partners missionaries. Other U.S. "people of God" have gone even further in their criticism of Chávez, with the Reverend Pat Robertson–whose father coincidently was the mentor of George W. Bush's grandfather, the U.S. senator, Prescott Bush–publicly calling on the Christian Broadcast Network's, *The 700 Club*, for Chávez to be assassinated:

> *[Hugo Chavez] thinks we're trying to assassinate him. I think that we really ought to go ahead and do it. It's a whole lot cheaper than starting a war, and I don't think any oil shipments will stop . . . We have the ability to take him out, and I think the time has come that we exercise that ability.*

CHAPTER 16

Smile, You're on Highjack Camera

"They don't look too friendly," observed Henry as we passed a group of locals staring at us as we made our way through the dusty unlit backstreets of Chichiriviche, in search of a posada where I could stay the night.

Half an hour earlier, we had arrived on the outskirts of town, where Henry and the missionaries were staying at a hotel which their group had filled to capacity. Even if there had been room, it was out of my price range anyway, so Henry had accompanied me into town–consisting of little more than a main high street leading to a quay with residential districts behind–where we'd been told there would be accommodation. I got a contact telephone number for a suitable place from the reception at Henry's hotel, and we stopped at a table in the street full of mobile phones for rent–something you see all over Venezuela. After renting one for a single phone call, Henry did the talking to avoid being charged a hefty foreigner price for the accommodation.

It was a modest traditional-looking one-storey house with a large veranda and front garden, set near the seafront behind a big security gate. Several dogs barked on our arrival. The posada's owner, who spoke fluent English with a slight American accent, came out to welcome us. Henry didn't stick around for long, and after saying our good-byes, he rather quaintly asked the owner to take good care of me. Although unnecessary, I thought it rather nice.

I turned out to be the only person staying at the posada, which doubled as the owner's family home. While making small talk with the proprietor, up popped Chávez on the television set in the corner of the room.

"Turn it over," he said to his wife in disgust, as if he couldn't stand being in the same room as an image of the president.

"We hate Chávez in this house!" he said.

"How come?"

"He is like Hitler."

Wow. I'd heard some Chávez bashing in Caracas, but this took the biscuit. Chávez may be many things, but a mass-murdering genocidal killer he most certainly was not. I couldn't be bothered to discuss it further if this was going to be the level of debate, so retired to my room.

It was a musty and basic setup located at the front of the house, containing three beds, a fan clogged with the thick sort of dust you get out of a Hoover bag and several old kitschy pictures–the type of thing your granny might have. In fact, the whole room was very grannyesque in both appearance and aroma. Off the main room was a small bathroom containing a toilet and shower, which could also be accessed from, and was shared with, the bedroom next door. On returning from the bathroom, I was greeted by the sight of one of the family's dogs lying on the bed nearest the door, scratching away furiously at a patch of mangy-looking fur. I shooed it outside and closed the door.

In the interests of getting a cooler night's sleep, I decided to abandon the room and rig up my hammock and mosquito net on the veranda instead. The owner was cool with this so long as he could lock the front door at night. Since he was unwilling to lend me a key, this would entail being shut out there until morning.

Having intended this anyway, I agreed. It proved to be a big mistake as despite being enclosed behind tightly weaved netting, this did nothing to prevent some minute rapacious sand flies giving me an almost identical night of tormented scratching as I'd experienced on arrival in Caracas.

The Morrocoy National Park boasts some of the finest desert islands, islets, coral reefs, coastal caves, mangroves, and diving locations in Venezuela. It encompasses an area of dramatically eroded mainland coastline and over thirty individual islands of varying sizes, many of which are surrounded by quintessential white sandy beaches and swaying coconut palms. It sounded the perfect place to spend my final day before completing my circle of the country and heading back to Caracas.

Boats left for the islands from the town's wharf with differing prices according to the distance the desired island was away. I had no idea which islands were the best to visit; but one thing was for sure, since the prices charged were per boat, not per passenger, if I was going to make this affordable, then I needed to tag along with a group. There were lots of Venezuelan tourists milling around at the wharf, but despite approaching several, I struggled to strike it lucky and find one willing to let me share their boat. I finally approached a young guy in his midthirties, making his way to a boat with his girlfriend and parents, having just paid for its hire. As luck would have it, the guy spoke reasonable English. Without any idea as to the island or islands they might be visiting, I asked if he'd mind if I tagged along. Without hesitation, he agreed. I asked how much I owed him for my share.

"Don't worry about it," he replied.

This was a very welcome, if wholly unexpected result. I clambered on board and now learnt that they were visiting one of the nearest and most popular of the islands, Cayo Sal. The boat would return to pick us up in the late afternoon.

It was a surprisingly choppy ride across to Cayo Sal, which was one of the national park's larger islands, in the heart of which was a giant pink-tinged lagoon. I had kind of been expecting a quiet deserted castaway affair, the sort of place where a bearded Tom Hanks would whisper sweet nothings to his beloved "Wilson," but as we approached the island, it became clear that large swathes of it were anything but. Lining the main beach were several bars and restaurants selling their wares to hundreds of Venezuelan tourists reclined on deck chairs and sun loungers, topping up their tans and sipping away at cocktails. Mr. Hanks might well have preferred to wash up on such a setting, but it was not what I was after today. As soon as we moored up on a little jetty and my feet touched down on terra firma, I immediately went exploring in search of a secluded spot elsewhere on the island.

The lagoon itself was nearly as big as the island and took up most of its central landmass where it was surrounded by palm trees and scrubland, which themselves led onto the white sandy beaches of the island's perimeter. I headed through the first set of trees to reach the lagoon and skirted along its outside edge to access the other side of the island. It didn't take long before the crowds had all but disappeared with only a handful of people bothering to walk beyond the main beach. I found a delightful little cove that was entirely deserted and sat down in the shade of a palm tree to take in the view. The crystal clear light blue water and deserted setting was tranquility itself.

I decided a leisurely swim was called for, so plunged into the bath-warm waters, lying back, and enjoying the serenity of drifting on the current. By the time I'd floated sufficiently far enough to warrant getting out of the water and walking back to where I'd hidden my shoes, wallet, and lunch in the bushes, two girls in their late teens had arrived in the cove. They began taking rather risqué photos of each other on their small digital camera–the sort of poses you'd expect from a swimsuit calendar. One minute, one of them was on all fours cavorting in the sea, the next straddling a piece of driftwood while looking at the camera. I had witnessed much the same on Margarita Island, and seen profile pictures of female

Venezuelan CouchSurfers taken in a similar vein. To me it seemed rather an odd thing to do but I guess in a nation obsessed with beauty pageants, it was considered normal.

I headed up the coast now to a far larger bay curving in a big crescent. It was a much nicer beach than the one containing all the bars but was virtually deserted, with just a young couple playing Frisbee. I continued on round the island to the next headland, beyond which the island changed dramatically–and not for the better. Mountains of old plastic bottles were washed up on the shore as far as I could see. There were literally thousands of them caught amongst the rocks and coastal vegetation. It was disgusting, and something I learnt later marred much of the national park. Other areas had suffered the effects of a severe chemical spill in the nineties that killed off up to half the area's coral, something which is still a long way from fully recovering.

I spent the remainder of the day on the near-deserted crescent bay which, thanks to its secluded orientation, avoided the curse of plastic suffered by the stretch of coast beyond. I savored the tranquillity while I could; tomorrow, I would be heading back to the chaos of Caracas.

Every now and again, Venezuela gives you pause for thought; something out of the ordinary happens, which serves as a reminder to the dangers lurking beneath the surface of everyday life in the country. So it was as I changed busses in Valencia on my way to Caracas. When everybody catching the bus was seated, a twitchy-looking bus company official came on board with a digital camera and proceeded to walk from seat to seat, taking close-up mug shots of every individual passenger, followed by one of the overall seating arrangement. Thanks to an e-mail I had received from my good friend Luke just weeks before I left for Venezuela, I knew this was a precaution against the bus being hijacked. Unfortunately, as Luke discovered, it was a precaution that didn't always work. Luke had been in Ecuador, not Venezuela, but as the Valencia bus company official finished taking our snaps, I couldn't help recall Luke's e-mail and hoped that in my case, the photos proved effective:

Jamie,

I spent last week on the beach with my girlfriend in the pacific surf town of Canoa where we spent an incredible week relaxing, drinking and romancing, it was paradise!

When we left Canoa we traveled to another town called Bahia where we took the night bus which was to take us back to Quito. When we arrived the bus company representative was noticeably agitated and insisted that everyone exit the bus, undergo a search and have a photo taken. Despite all this, ten minutes into the journey when I had popped my usual sleeping pill and had settled into the mediocre dubbed-in-Spanish movie, the man sitting next to us pulled out a gun and demanded all of our valuables whilst four other men at the front hijacked the bus and forced it off the road. Myself and the other male passengers were beaten to the ground, forced to take off our clothes and lie prostrated whilst the gunmen walked over us demanding that we give up everything or they would kill us. The smell of fear was palpable and throughout the ordeal I could hear the woman in the seat next to me praying for the lives of her children.

After the bus had come to a crashing stop we were subjected to an uncomfortably intimate frisking, followed by an interrogation as to our net worth; we were then led one-by-one off the bus and put into the luggage compartment beneath the bus. They attempted to jam eight or nine of us into the tiny rear compartment including the hysterical mother whose children were nowhere in sight. They eventually managed to fit just five of us into the compartment which they locked from the outside but not before threatening to rape my girlfriend, only stopping in their advances when she pleaded with them telling them that she was pregnant. The rest of the passengers were locked in the main compartments whilst the hijackers stripped the bus of all remaining items and took off on motorbikes and a car that had been tailing us since Bahia.

It was about half an hour before we were let out of that stifling metal box by the driver who had managed to escape from one of the other compartments. Packed in there together in the tropical humidity we were absolutely drenched with our own and each other's sweat and I can say for certain that at least one of my fellow captives was a fisherman.

Some of the passengers attempted to find their missing possessions in and around the bus but most efforts proved futile. The rest of us settled with picking up stray cigarettes and chain smoking them until the driver and his co-pilot managed to re-inflate the tires and get the bus back on the road.

We were left with nothing; they stole everything on the bus including even our clothes and shoes. Limping back into Bahia at 2am we managed to find a hotel that would take us in on good faith despite the fact that we turned up there penniless and practically naked.

Not a particularly fun experience but certainly a life-affirming one, just as well that I've never really been into owning stuff!

Peace, Luke

I'm pleased to say that the prejourney happy snaps did the trick for security on board my bus, and by late afternoon, I completed my circle of the country, with the bus arriving in the chaotic Caracas terminal on the outskirts of the city, thankfully, with all the passengers fully clothed.

Just like when I arrived in Caracas, I had initially struggled to find a CouchSurfer to put me up. This I had only succeeded in achieving late the night before when I received a confirmation from my first female host, a thirty-year-old called Christina, whose occupation she described on her profile as "webmistress." The mistress's instructions on how to meet up had simply been to arrive in Caracas and to give her a call. We would then agree a suitable location to rendezvous after she had finished work at 6:00 pm. I had no address for either her home or work. Needless to say, I wasn't too keen on this arrangement..

It was just noon so I headed towards the nearest subway station located close to a barrio rising up on a nearby hill and sprawling into the distance. I caught a metro train to the center of Caracas, getting off near the city's main park, Parque del Este, where I had spent my first day taking it easy. I did much the same again until it was time to call Christina. By now it was dark. Hiring a cell phone outside a subway station, I decided to first put a call through to Juan's brother to arrange a suitable time to visit the lovely beauty queens. It went to his answer phone, so after leaving a message, I dialed Christina. I got through first time, but was the recipient of bad news. She had to work late so would not be able to meet me until later on.

"Head to the subway station at Los Dos Caminos and call me again at seven pm," was the new instruction.

I jumped back on the subway, and after waiting around at Los Dos Caminos until the specified time, found another mobile for hire, and put in a call.

"I'll be there in fifteen minutes," she said.

After forty, there was still no sign of her. Was I being stood up? I called again. She apologized, telling me that some unexpected work was keeping her in the office and that I should make my own way to her place. Christina's mother would be there by now, so she could let me in. The problem was getting there as the directions were far from straightforward.

Christina asked if I could see a bus nearby with a specific color and markings.

I looked around at the buses in the vicinity. Only one type vaguely matched her description.

"Err, sort of," I told her.

"Great. Catch this and pay close attention to the following landmarks . . ."

"Hold on. They're going in both directions. Which one do I catch?"

"The one heading away from the mountain."

"I can't see the mountain. It's dark."

"Which side of the road are you on, left or right?"

"That depends which way I'm facing."

"If you're facing the mountain, is it left or right?"

"I can't see the mountain."

"Oh, yes. What's opposite you?"

"Los Dos Caminos subway station."

"Which exit are you facing?"

"I'm not sure."

"Is it the closest one to the mountain?"

This carried on for some time until Christina decided she'd established where I was and which bus I should take. The tricky bit was yet to come. She reeled off the most complicated list of micro landmarks I would have to look out for on board the bus in order to know when to get off. I didn't fancy my chances of spotting them as the bus twisted and turned up-and downhill through the city's confusing nighttime streets. An even more exhaustive set of directions followed on making the final leg on foot, something I felt far from confident of actually achieving. I could see this going sour and envisioned myself wandering around the notoriously dangerous streets of Caracas at night, carrying a dirty great tourist backpack without a clue where I was. This was not what I needed, and so decided to veto the suggestion of me making my own way there. In what was more of an assertion than a proposition, I stated that we should stick to the original plan and meet as arranged after she'd finished work. Christina agreed, and twenty minutes later, she arrived.

"Jamie?" enquired a big friendly woman dressed in professional office garb. She apologized for the earlier confusion and her unexpected delay. After the shortest of pleasantries, we jumped on a bus–heading in completely the opposite direction to the one suggested on the phone.

We arrived at her first-floor apartment situated on a main road up a steep hill in the east of the city. Even if I'd caught a bus going in the correct direction, I was dubious I could have made it here unaccompanied. Christina unlocked a thick padlocked security gate at the bottom of the apartment's stairs, setting off the excited barking of her energetic dog above, who ran out to join us at the top. Inside was a simple but homely flat with a large main sitting room in which Christina's mother sat, watching a subtitled version of the now notorious Charlie Sheen sitcom *Two and a Half Men*. Christina introduced me. After making a quick cup of herbal tea together in the kitchen, we sat down and joined her mum in front of the television.

CHAPTER 17

Venezuela's Indiana Jones

Another phone call to Juan's brother yielded the same results as the day before. I had sent him a second e-mail when in Chichiriviche but had yet to get a response. I was beginning to wonder whether I would get to see the beauty queens after all. With only today and tomorrow left in Venezuela, time was running out to so do.

Sadly, Christina would be working today, so had little available time to hang out. With no host or beauty queens yet to speak of, I planned to spend my time picking up some books that Austin had kindly let me leave at his place and to meet with someone whose exploits I had read about years before, Venezuela's most renowned outdoorsman, survivalist, and explorer, Charles Brewer-Carias. Charles was something of a legend in these fields and had explored more of Venezuela than anyone alive or dead. I had first become aware of Charles through a BBC documentary, which interviewed him regarding his time living with Venezuela's indigenous hunter-gather tribes and had subsequently read about him in the *National Geographic* article that had first so captured my imagination with its photograph of Roraima. Having no small interest in the natural world, survival, and so-called bushcraft skills myself, I was extremely interested to meet with someone who could teach me a little of these fields in a tropical environment–something I knew next to nothing about. We had exchanged a couple of e-mails prior to me arriving in the country, in which he had said to give him a call when I got here so that we could meet. The call didn't quite go according to plan.

After meeting up with Austin, he had kindly let me use his phone to contact Charles and was keen to meet the enigmatic explorer too. Although he wasn't certain, Austin thought he recognized the name Brewer-Carias, and that maybe he had previously met Charles's brother through his former work at the British Chambers of Commerce.

I tried Charles's home phone and got through to his wife. She informed me he was out but passed on his cell number. I called it.

"Hola, no hablo español," I struggled to say to the Spanish greeting I received–near exhausting my own Spanish in the process. I followed up with a more comfortable, at least for me, "Hello, is that Mr. Brewer-Carias?"

"Yes," he answered in a surprisingly cagy manner.

"It's Jamie Maslin here from England, we corresponded recently on the e-mail about meeting up."

"Oh really?" he responded in a sarcastic manner, following up with a triumphant, "But you're calling from a Caracas number!"

"Yes, that's where I am now," I replied in a state of significant confusion.

Bizarrely, he now claimed to only speak a tiny bit of English so couldn't understand me. This was very strange indeed, as not only had he spoken perfect English in the sentence beforehand but had corresponded well enough in the English written word when e-mailing.

"Hold on," I said, in a slow deliberate manner. "I'll get my friend who speaks Spanish." I marshaled Austin to the cause of conversing with Señor Brewer and handed over telephone duties to him. Despite beginning in Spanish, within a few seconds, Austin had reverted to English, casually discussing the details of where and when we were going to meet. On finishing the call, he hung up and told me that Charles could meet us later in El Hatillo. Charles's English had, apparently, been fine, so Austin didn't know why I'd had trouble communicating with him. This confused me to no end and put me slightly on edge about meeting the guy. I hoped for better luck face-to-face.

It turned out that Charles wanted to meet us in a bank in El Hatillo's main shopping mall. As we approached the bank's glass-fronted windows, I immediately recognized Charles inside from his photographs I'd seen online. Despite being seventy years old, he looked like a man in his midfifties, and a healthy one at that, being of muscular form with a back as straight as a flagpole, a thick moustache, and a full head of hair. I hoped to look that way when drawing my pension.

Austin and I introduced ourselves, receiving a charismatic warm smile and a firm handshake in return. Charles immediately apologized for his strange behavior on the phone this morning and explained that a friend of his was constantly playing telephone pranks on him by calling him up and affecting a French, Cockney, Indian, or other accent, followed by some tall story, which Charles invariably fell for. When he heard my English accent, he was sure it was his friend winding him up again, whom he had previously mentioned our planned meeting to. Since he had not given me his cell number over the e-mail, and had thought for some reason that I was arriving next week, when the Caracas number popped up on the display of his cell, he saw this as proof positive that he'd finally rumbled his friend. No such luck, I'm afraid, Charles.

I told him that I was familiar with the routine as my brother, Matt, was often doing likewise to me. More often than not, I could see through his feeble accent from the inception of the call, but one of his friends, Simon, was constantly getting suckered in. His best telephone windup, which I recalled now for Charles and Austin, was when he phoned Simon just after he'd become the proud owner of a small boat.

Now Simon could ill afford the purchase, despite it being little more than a glorified bathtub with a sail; but it was his, and he was damned proud of that little dinghy. But woe betide anyone who called it such; to him it was a "compact yacht," thank you very much. As far as he was concerned, to own a boat was the height of sophistication. Sailing, after all, was a rich man's hobby, so for him to be able to hobnob with the great and the good at the yacht club meant he'd arrived–even if it had been by way of public transport. Despite the cost, he concluded the purchase was money well spent.

My brother was used to Simon's completely blatant attempts at social one-upmanship, so when Simon let slip that he had yet to arrange insurance for the boat, a light went on in Matt's head.

"Hello, is that Simon?" a cut-glass accent asked on the telephone, interrupting Simon's work meeting.

"Yes, speaking."

"Hello, Simon, it's Roger from the yacht club."

"Hello, Roger, how are you?!" exclaimed an enthusiastic Simon in his poshest voice, faking familiarity with the fictional "yachty" in order to effect a bit of nifty social ladder climbing at the club.

Matt hastily moved the phone from his mouth to divert an involuntary snigger. He composed himself.

"Well, not too bad, Simon, but unfortunately, I've got a little bit of bad news for you."

"Oh."

"Yes, I'm afraid the sea cadets had their annual barbeque party last night and, well, things got a little out of hand. There were high jinks all round and one thing led to another, culminating with them setting fire to your"–Matt twisted the knife–"little dinghy."

Silence.

"Unfortunately, because it occurred away from the clubhouse itself, our insurance won't cover it, but I shouldn't worry, I'm sure your policy will sort everything out."

Silence.

"Hello, Simon?"

Charles and Austin both had a good laugh.

Charles, it seemed, was experiencing some sort of problem with the bank in getting his yearly allowance of foreign currency–something the government limits in order to prevent people taking advantage of the artificially high official exchange rate, and capital fleeing the country. For some reason, things weren't going smoothly in the state-run bank. Charles attributed this to the notoriety of his family name, and in particular his brother Allan, a legal professor who had fled the country for the United States after being accused of drafting the decree that had been used during the failed coup in 2002 to abolish the constituted branches of the government.

Austin now confirmed that he had in fact met Allan a couple of times.

A few minutes of mutual Chávez bashing followed between Austin and Charles, and since it was clear I wasn't going to see eye to eye with either of them politically, I decided to stay well out of it. I knew before meeting Charles that we were poles apart in this respect after reading an interview he did for *The New York Times* in which he stated, "I am for an oligarchy, an oligarchy of the well prepared." Since I was here to learn from his wide-ranging botanical knowledge, fascinating explorations, and highly honed bushcraft skills, I thought it best to avoid getting into any emotive political discussions, at least at this stage, which might have put a wrench in the works for me.

While waiting to see the bank manager in an attempt to rectify the problem, Charles told us of a harrowing experience he'd had not too long ago, which he mentioned in the casual manner of making polite conversation with strangers. When at home with his wife, an armed gang had broken in to burgle the place. Fearing for their lives, Charles decided to tackle the burglars. He'd managed to shoot one of them dead with a shotgun, leading the others to make a hasty run for it. In the process, Charles was shot in the shoulder with an explosive round, fragments of which still remained.

Shit. In England, we chatted about the weather when passing the time in queues with someone we were unacquainted.

After speaking to the bank manager and, I think, sorting everything out, we headed to Charles's home. I rode with Charles while Austin followed behind. Despite our age gap, and difference of opinion on matters political, Charles and I immediately hit it off. On the way there, Charles would spot an interesting tree or plant out of the corner of his eye and pull the car over to give me an impromptu biology or survival lesson. One plant we stopped at was so poisonous that if you ingested the flowers, you'd soon be deader than a burglar at the Brewer-Carias residence. We stopped at another, which was related to the Northern Hemisphere's sweet chestnut, to collect nuts for roasting.

To get to Charles's house, we had to pass a manned security booth and car barrier, which led on to a twisting private mountain road that contained but a handful of residences staggered up the forested peak, of which Charles's was the highest. At the base was a sign warning would-be intruders that there were armed patrols in operation.

It was one hell of a location to live in. On the way up the meandering road, we drove through tropical woodland, making the residences here seem removed from the city below, of which they had the most glorious views. Looking down from here was deceptive; Caracas, framed by more mountains in the distance, seemed so very peaceful and calm.

We pulled into Charles's place up an insanely steep driveway and entered through an automatic security gate. His home was not quite how I'd expected. Given that this must have been one of the finest pieces of residential real estate in the whole city, with unquestionably one of the best views, I had expected something akin to the tasteless opulence I had seen before in Caracas, but the house itself was rather modest, charming, and rustic with real character. It was painted a subtle pastel yellow, had huge twisting wooden pillars, a spacious open veranda, and was constructed, primarily, over just one level. Its design had been done from a plan by Charles and his wife based on rural Andean homes and had been built, in large part, by them. The pillars, Charles explained, were made from a super hard tree wood known as guayacan, which would last for hundreds of years. Traditionally, shavings of the wood had been boiled in water to treat syphilis.

The garden led directly into the forest. Here, majestic birds perched on nearby trees, while others soared high above. Flowers of myriad colors glowed in the radiant midday light, swaying gently in a whisper of breeze as cirrus clouds drifted idly by on the wind above. I liked it up here immensely and imagined that Charles, as a botanist and all-round nature guru, was in his element.

We were introduced to Charles's delightful wife Fanny, who was significantly younger than him, and shown around inside. The sitting room was part natural history museum, part living area, part bushcraft shrine. On the wall were framed specimens of all manner of weird and wonderful creatures, ranging from giant spiders to beetles, from butterflies to scorpions. Several indigenous blowpipes of colossal proportions hung on display. A table with every imaginable design of machete was the centerpiece of the room. Bowls, carvings, trinkets, fossils, and fascinating artifacts were everywhere.

Even in the kitchen's fridge were signs this was the house of a naturalist. Charles pulled a frozen rattlesnake from the freezer section–something he had found near the house. In the kitchen were also several hand-carved wooden bowls called totuma and a giant midsection of an araguaney tree, which was being used as a huge chopping board. The wood from this was incredibly hard and dense, so much so that Charles said it sank in water.

We headed now to the library. To get there, we squeezed down a thin hallway laden with traditional bows and arrows, handmade hammocks, natural rope, and mountains of books and documents.

In here we settled down, and Charles told us about his life and exploits.

In many respects, Charles is an explorer from a bygone age, an adventurer in the Victorian tradition, skilled in multiple disciplines. Among his many fields of expertise are botany, anthropology, geology, survival skills, and zoology.

He was born in 1938 into a prominent Caracas family of Spanish and English descent. His grandfather was a British diplomat, and on his mother's side of the family are descendants of a Spanish general sent from Madrid to fight Simón Bolívar's army. In 1960, he qualified as a dentist and soon after become active in the field of dental anthropology. Through this work, he traveled to the remote rainforests of the Orinoco basin where he stayed with the Ye'kuana tribe of hunter-gatherers. In photos from that time, you don't see Charles in the white robes of an external dental professional but in the scant traditional garb of the indigenous population themselves, whom he lived with in the jungle as if one of them. He is fluent in their language and understands that of the Yanomami–in addition to speaking four European languages.

For the next twenty years, he worked as a dentist, during which time he began to study biology in earnest, a subject that he would leave a significant mark upon. To date, his discoveries in this field have led to twenty-five species being named after him, including reptiles, insects, plants, and a scorpion. A whole new genus of bromeliad plants bears the name–*Brewcaria.* The New York Botanical Gardens made him an honorary research associate in recognition of his work cataloguing plant use among the Yanomami.

Perhaps most of all, though, he is renowned for the many expeditions, totalling over two hundred to date, which he has led into Venezuela's wildest regions, the tepuis in particular. Despite being over seventy, although he hardly seems that age, Charles shows no sign of hanging up his khaki expedition kit for a quiet life in front of the fire with a pipe and a pair of slippers anytime soon. His notable expeditions have included one of monumental length to the "Mountain of the Mists" on the Venezuelan-Brazilian border, the duration of which was a staggering four years, running from 1983 to '87. Hundreds of new species were discovered during this colossal scientific voyage that was described as the "largest biological expedition carried out in the world." Other expeditions have resulted in the discovery of the world's largest quartzite cave, and the biggest sinkholes on earth–both of which are located on tepuis. In 1974, he coined the phrase "islands in time" to describe their isolated nature, something which has since become common parlance.

In addition to exploration, he served as cabinet minister for youth and sports affairs from 1979 to 1982, and arranged "frontier camps" for youngsters to visit remote natural areas of the country. During this time, he organized a clandestine surveillance expedition deep into the disputed neighboring territory of Guayana Esequiba, which is claimed by Venezuela but within the current borders of Guyana. For this, Charles was awarded the Land Army by Cross and the Navy Award from the military, and the Liberator Award from the government, its highest commendation.

One of Charles's other areas of expertise was photography. To say that his photographs were good would be a gross understatement, they were exceptional. For the next couple of hours, we were treated to a slide-show adventure around Venezuela's back country with its many varied flora and fauna, accompanied by Charles's vivid descriptions of the locations, the strenuous journeys undertaken to get there, and the significance of the discoveries made.

Some of his photos were of the grandest of vistas, capturing towering waterfalls cascading down from atop cloud-covered tepuis; others of more delicate and diminutive curiosities, including a collection of tiny sand flies photographed in extreme close-up on Charles's arm. Visible in rear cavity of one of the flies was a fresh cache of Charles's bright red blood (reproduced in this book). One picture in particular really caught my attention. It was from the Canaima National Park where I had previously visited Angel Falls and Roraima. The picture (also reproduced here) was taken within a tepuis's giant teardrop-shaped cave, looking outwards past an internal waterfall towards the expanse of jungle beyond. It brought to mind a tropical version of the famous picture taken on Scott of the Antarctic's ill-fated second voyage to the South Pole, in which two of his compatriots stood inside a similar-shaped cave, this time within a berg, with their ship *Terra Nova* in the background amid an expanse of ice.

"Look closely," Charles instructed with a wry smile.

Down at the bottom of the picture were what looked like tiny insects on the floor of the cave. On closer inspection, it became apparent that they were in fact helicopters.

"Bigger than you thought?"

It was indeed.

For lunch on my penultimate day in the country, Charles kindly offered to take Austin and me to Venezuela's most exclusive venue, the *Country Club*. We accepted.

Before setting off, Charles led us into the undergrowth near his house to show us some plants and to collect some bamboo. Although a stone's throw from the city itself, the house was surrounded by lush forest. For an area so close to such a vast urban sprawl, it contained a staggering diversity of life. One of Charles's latest discoveries was made, not in some far-flung, never-visited corner of the country, but in his own backyard. Here he discovered a curious type of frog that was recently confirmed by taxonomists as a completely new species. Charles named it *Mannophryne vulcano*, a reference to the mountain on which he lives, Cerro El Volcán.

Wading through the bush, Charles stopped by a tree and, with his machete, began peeling off a thin strip of bark. The tree began to bleed, bloodred. This was the Sangre de Drago (dragon's blood) tree, traditionally used to stop bleeding and act as a coagulate.

"Taste it," Charles instructed.

Daubing some on my fingers, I tentatively raised it to my mouth. It had an extremely bitter taste and astringent affect.

"One of its other traditional uses is to shrink haemorrhoids," he said with a wry smile. Another traditional use, Charles explained, was for girls to bath their genitals in the liquid in order to tighten them.

Not twenty feet from the roadside was a towering stand of bamboo, some of it as thick as my thigh. Looking at its staggering size and thick woody structure, it was easy to forget that bamboo is in fact a grass. With some deft swipes of his machete, Charles harvested several suitable pieces. We took these back to his place and dropped them off in his backyard then set off in Charles's car for a spot of lunch at the *Country Club.*

It was located in an area of the same name comprising opulent old colonial mansions and a splattering of modern monstrosities–one of which had giant fortresslike sheet metal gating, giving the place a wholly unattractive bombproof bunker appearance. Seeing such staggering wealth again hit home how different life was for the haves and the have-nots in Venezuela. On the way there, plenty of general anti-Chávez rhetoric flowed between Charles and Austin. It was interesting to hear this again as with the exception of the posada owner in Chichiriviche, I had not heard such talk outside Caracas.

We pulled into a car park next to a beautifully maintained exquisite old colonial building with an arched bell tower, red roof tiles, and opulent connecting buildings. Next to it was an expansive golf course. After parking up, we headed into the club, walking through an elegant arched entrance porch, and in doing, stepped into an oasis of old money and privilege. Charles pointed out the club's coat of arms proudly positioned on the wall and showed us around some of the many lavish rooms. Some were arranged for fine dining with tables set with pressed white cloths, freshly cut flowers, and sparkling finery; others sported beautiful dark wooden beamed ceilings carved with ornamental embellishments from which hung decorative stained glass lanterns and candled chandeliers. It was quite the place to have come for lunch.

Charles had planned to meet up with a friend of his in the club's gym to do a brief workout before eating. On entering the gym's changing rooms, he was greeted with enthusiastic cries of "Charlie!" from those standing around in towels, combing their slick wet hair in the mirror, and getting changed into polo shirts, blazers, and the like. After meeting up with his training partner, Charles took us through to the gym itself, not that Austin or I had any intentions of working out or were suitably dressed, but ever the showman, Charles was keen to show us his prowess with the gym's equipment. Watching him complete multiple chin-ups, squats, and other exercises, it was easy to forget he was in fact in his seventies. I felt tired just watching.

Austin and I adjourned to a sun-drenched courtyard outside, where a bar and inviting pool were located nearby. We took a table in the shade and were attentively served by one of the many waiters floating from table to table, delivering cool drinks to the rich, lighter-skinned club members. Looking around, it was hard to believe that I was in the heart of Caracas and that just a few miles down the road was the most appalling poverty. With such a sharp dichotomy between the rich and the poor, and such a huge difference in their numbers, it was hardly surprising that crime in Venezuela was out of control.

Two freshly squeezed, tangy pineapple juices later and Charles joined us at our table with his friend, Federico "Kiko" Mayoral, who had previously joined him on, as well as helped finance, several expeditions. We all headed for lunch in a separate building in another part of the complex. While strolling through this epitome of old money and tradition, Charles stopped by a large gnarled tree to give an impromptu bushcraft lesson.

"This is the guacimo tree that in 1546, historian Fernández de Oviedo reported the Indians using to start their hand-drill fires."

Charles flicked out his pocketknife and began cutting off suitable "suckers," or basal shoots, from the tree to use later as hand-drill friction fire lighters. The tree, Charles explained, had also been described by Sir Walter Raleigh–although Raleigh had not given the tree's name–and was the same tree as depicted in a 16th-century illustration from Sir Francis Drake's manuscript that Charles had shown me earlier. The round fruits of the tree had medicinal qualities and were used to treat the kidneys. The bark was used to make a refreshing, although slightly gluey, drink.

It was a funny sight, really; here we were amongst the quiet civility of the sports-jacketed brigade of Venezuela's elite, and Charles was still ever the explorer and outdoorsman.

"You can dry the wood out with the heat of your body by putting the stick in your sleeping bag. After just one night, it will be dry enough to use."

At the entrance of the restaurant, Charles propped the wood up against one of the inner walls with the nonchalance of someone leaving an umbrella. I wondered what the other well-to-do diners thought of his collection of sticks.

Lunch was a three-course meal of onion soup, filet steak in a mushroom sauce, and a tangy guava pie. While eating, Charles told us of a tantalizing future expedition he planned. Charles believes he has pinpointed a lake, now dry, which is the location for the legendary El Dorado, or city of gold, mentioned in the writings of such explorative luminaries as Sir Walter Raleigh. In 1990, Charles found relics of clay and pottery mixed with gold dust at the site, which he hopes to explore further to prove his hypothesis.

I told him there and then, that if he ever needed volunteers, or simply someone to act as a porter, then I'd love to be involved. Months later, after a bit of pestering from me, he e-mailed over scans of old Indiana Jones-style parchment maps of the area in question, and recommended that I read two books on the subject, before discussing his theory further. They were *In Search of El Dorado* by Sir John Hemmings and *The Discoverie* (old-English spelling) by Sir Walter Raleigh.

When we arrived back at Charles's house, his daughter Karen was hanging out in the garden, observing an eagle perched on a nearby tree. It took to the air and circled above. In a mimicked bird call, Karen let out a highly convincing shrieking cry in its direction. She was Charles's daughter all right and shared his love of wildlife and the natural world. Karen had joined him on previous expeditions, including one to the world's largest quartzite cave, in which the biggest hall measures an estimated four hundred thousand cubic metres and now bears her and her mother's name.

Austin and I stuck around until late into the evening when we were treated to a traditional meal of *hallaca*–chicken, beef, olives, onions, pickles, and almonds enclosed inside a cornmeal wrap, which was itself wrapped up inside a smoked plantain leaf. The package was then boiled before serving. Karen explained that it was a customary meal to eat at Christmastime. Over our meal, I quizzed her on life as a young person in such a dangerous city and her plans for the future. They weren't to stay in Venezuela. She intended to go to Europe after finishing her degree.

"It is so dangerous, I haven't been to the theatre in years," she told me.

Karen could fire a pistol and carried pepper spray around for protection, something her boyfriend knew all too well. She recounted a time they'd been driving and stuck in traffic. For some reason, an irate and burly driver nearby had taken exception to Karen's fella, grabbing him through the car's open window with ill intent. Karen came to his rescue, or at least attempted to, by retrieving her pepper spray, which she unloaded with a big extended squirt. Unfortunately, she hadn't checked which way the nozzle faced and ended up sending a fine jet of the noxious liquid directly into her boyfriend's face–not really what he needed under the circumstances. A hasty realignment, and the second squirt did the job, sending the attacker packing, but not after ruining her boyfriend's afternoon.

Austin and I laughed.

We both stayed at the Brewer-Carias residence until long after dark. When it was finally time to leave, I thanked Charles and his family for their generosity and for such a wonderful day. Before departing, I quickly popped to the bathroom. Outside of here was something that needed no explanation. It was a metal sign taken from the triple point atop Roraima, designating the territory of Guyana–it seemed Charles and Chávez had something in common after all.

Being my final morning in the country, it was with a degree of regret that after another unsuccessful call to Juan's brother, I reluctantly concluded that the queens and I were just not destined to meet. It was a shame that I wouldn't get to visit their quirky pink mansion headquarters–the epicentre of the world's only beauty superpower–and meet their eccentric surgery-advocating headmaster, but by the sounds of it, the school didn't really represent typical Venezuelan beauty anyway. Charles described it to me as "some kind of American European values," with the real darker-skinned Venezuelan beauties found elsewhere–i.e., everyday Venezuelan life. When out strolling with Austin, a typical Venezuelan woman–a runway model in other parts of the world–elegantly sauntered by. "I think they must drown the ugly ones at birth," he remarked. He had a point. Maybe it is something in the water, as Venezuela certainly possesses an uncannily high proportion of everyday stunners–the country's real beauty queens.

And so with no hillside mansion to visit, I spent an easy day readying myself for my imminent departure–chilling out with Christina and her mother in front of more U.S. television programs. I would be leaving the country in the early the morning, so decided to get my head down early. Before I did, Christina and her mother went through the required security procedure I needed to follow in the morning to get out of the apartment, politely stressing the importance of me doing this quietly so as not to wake them. I had to unlock the padlocked security gate at the bottom of the stairs then secure it again when outside, before throwing the key a sufficient distance back into the apartment so that it could not be reached from the street. After going through the plan, I thanked them for their kindness in letting me stay then crashed out in bed.

The next morning, things didn't quite go according to plan. Getting out and locking up sounded simple enough as I crept down the thin dark staircase to get to my waiting taxi outside. My only concern was paying close attention to the creaking floorboards–lest I wake Christina or her mother sleeping above. With the same delicate maneuvering I carefully unlocked the clanking barred metal security gate at the bottom of the stairs, muffling its sounds as best I could to prevent my hosts from stirring. Stepping outside into the street, I stealthily began securing the padlock back onto the gate, but with the sky still pitch-black, and little in the way of light coming my way from nearby street lamps, I struggled to see what I was doing. I made a fatal error. Spotting what I assumed was a light switch just inside the security gate, I flicked it on.

A loud unmistakable sound rang out, making me jump. It was no light switch but a bloody doorbell.

Shit!

Of all the things I wanted to avoid doing at 4:00 am, ringing the frigging doorbell had to be number one on the list–especially after having received specific instructions to be as quiet as possible. For a second or two, I hoped forlornly that maybe, just maybe, they hadn't heard me. I was wishing in vain. Moments later a confused and sleepy-eyed Christina and her mother came downstairs to see what all the commotion was about. Apologizing profusely, I sheepishly dropped the padlock into Christina's mother's hand then turned about heel and slinked off to the taxi, cringing all the way to the airport.

Sorry.

As the tires of my plane lifted off the tarmac of Caracas's international airport and the South American continent slowly disappeared from sight, I looked back on my trip with mixed emotions. Venezuela was without doubt one of the most beautiful places I had visited, possessing no shortage of spellbinding world-class scenery worthy of multiple visits. It was a place where I had made some great friends and a country where exciting and dynamic social developments were reshaping the nation for the betterment of the poor majority, empowering once-marginalized people and setting free their democratic hopes for a better life. But to be flying out, especially from Caracas, was also something of a relief. With such a crazy crime rate in the country at large, and Caracas in particular, there were times when I had sensed a palpable underlying danger, a difficult-to-define presence not necessarily worthy of mention at the time, but real nonetheless, especially in retrospect when compared to other countries. All too often, I had found myself acutely scanning my surroundings to an unhealthy degree, not a paranoid red alert as such, but a highly unwelcome state of constant surveillance greater than should be required in everyday normal life. Being used to strolling as the whim takes me through my home city's central streets and parks at all hours, I found such a reality extremely confining. Not so much in what I did or where I went, but in the mental state in which I did it, something which robs you of a sense of freedom–one of my primary motivations for traveling in the first place.

It had been a fascinating trip, but was it, I wondered, somewhere I would particularly like to return? Certainly not Caracas. Before leaving Europe and setting off on my journey, I had asked a good friend who had previously been to Venezuela whether he had any recommendations for me. "Yeah," he replied. "Go to Guyana instead!" From a strictly tourist point of view, he had a point. Neighboring Guyana possesses similar towering waterfalls, flat-topped tepuis, and a picturesque Caribbean coastline. But I hadn't come here just to have a romp around spectacular landscapes or to lie on sun-drenched beaches. I'd wanted to get a feel for the place and its people. To discover their attitude to the changes being made to the country by Hugo Chávez's "Bolivarian Revolution" and the "participatory democracy" he had introduced.

Venezuela is a country where the politics of oil, social revolution, and elite resistance are never far from the surface. Where the country goes in the next few years will be fascinating. Will Chávez's support continue to remain high enough for him to remain in power? If so, will another coup be launched to replace him with a stooge of the United States and a corporate power so vehemently opposed to his policies of popular empowerment? Will Chávez survive with his life at all? Will Venezuela continue its reign as beauty queen supremos? Only time will tell.

But one thing is for sure. Whatever the future holds for this tropical nation sitting atop the largest reserves of oil in the world, it will have ramifications that extend far beyond its borders.

Would I return? Maybe.

But then, there were so many other places I intended to explore first.

Notes and References

1. In 2008 *Foreign Policy* listed Caracas as the world's murder capital in article: *The List: Murder Capitals of the World:* http://www.foreignpolicy.com/articles/2008/09/28/the_list_murder_capitals_of_the_world
2. Palast, Greg, (2006) *Armed Madhouse*, London, Penguin, Page 183
3. Wilpert, Gregory (2007) *Changing Venezuela by Taking Power: The History and Politics of the Chavez Government*, London, Verso, page 72–73.
4. Soon after I left the country, Chávez announced (in early 2010) that the bolivar would be devalued, with the currency's previous fixed official rate of 2.15 being replaced with a multi-tiered exchange rate of 2.6 for essential imported items, and 4.3 for other goods. This was done in an attempt to boost local production of nonoil exports, replace imports, control inflation, and kick-start the economy which, like much of the world, was currently suffering from a recession.
5. Figure quoted by director of the Venezuelan Observatory of Violence, Roberto Briceño-León, to *The New York Times*.

6. *The New York Times*, (28 December 2009) *New York on Track for Fewest Homicides on Record*: http://www.nytimes.com/2009/12/29/nyregion/29murder.html?_r=1

7. Carroll, Rory, (7 September 2009) *The Guardian, Deadly force: Venezuela's police have become a law unto themselves*: http://www.guardian.co.uk/world/2009/sep/06/venezuela-police-law-themselves

8. Ibid.

9. Wilpert, Gregory (2007) *Changing Venezuela by Taking Power: The History and Politics of the Chavez Government*, London, verso, page 17.

10. The fourteen out of fifteen elections over a twelve-year period are: 1998, presidential election (1) 1999, referendum on constitutional assembly; (2) election of members to constitutional assembly; (3) referendum on new constitution; (4) 2000 "mega-elections" of president, national assembly, governors, and mayors; (5) local elections; (6) roughly five months later, 2004 recall referendum; (7) governors; (8) 2004 recall referendum; (9); governors; (10) about four months later, 2005 national assembly; (11) and local elections; (12) 2006 president; (13) 2007 constitutional reform referendum (LOST) 2008 governors and mayors; (14) 2010 constitutional amendment referendum; (15) 2010 national assembly; (16) Details kindly provided in email from Gregory Wilpert.

11. Statistics provided by the Ministry of Planning and Finance which is the data used by the World Bank and different UN institutions: http://www.sisov.mpd.gob.ve/indicadores/IG0000180000000/

12. *Blum, William (2004) Killing Hope: US military & CIA Interventions since World War II, London, Zed Books*

13. Golinger, Eva, (13 April 2010) Coup and Countercoup, Revolution: http://venezuelanalysis.com/analysis/5274

14. Wilpert, Gregory (2007) *Changing Venezuela by Taking Power: The History and Politics of the Chavez Government*, London, Verso. From the notes section "In some of Venezuela's poorer states establishment candidate Henrique Salas Römer beat Chávez 54–44, and in Apure 60–39. Chávez, though, beat Salas Römer in wealthier states, such as Carabobo (Salas's home state), by 53–44, in Miranda 51–43, and in Zulia 55–41."

15. Ibid. Page 19

16. Palast, Greg, (2006) Armed Madhouse, London, Penguin, page 178

17. Clip shown in documentary, *The Revolution Will Not Be Televised*, by Kim Bartley and Donnacha O'Briain: http://video.google.com/videoplay?docid=5832390545689805144#

18. White House news release: www.whitehouse.gov/news/releases/2002/04/20020412-1.html

19. Campbell, Duncan, (April 29, 2002) *The Guardian, American navy 'helped Venezuelan coup'.* : http://www.guardian.co.uk/world/2002/apr/29/venezuela.duncancampbell

20. Chávez told this to a gathering of international journalists in September 2003

21. Wilpert, Gregory, (2007) *The 47-Hour Coup That Changed Everything*, http://venezuelanalysis.com/analysis/2336)

22. Cited in, Palast, Greg, (2002) *The Best Democracy Money Can Buy*, London, Robinson, page 191.

23. *Agence France-Presse*, (28 November, 2004)

24. Blum, William, (April 14 2002), *The CIA and the Venezuelan Coup. Hugo Chavez: A Servant Not Knowing His Place*, http://www.counterpunch.org/blum0414.html

25. Strictly speaking, "Latin America" is comprised of those countries in the Americas where languages derived from Latin are spoken (known as romance languages), primarily Spanish and Portuguese. I have also included the countries Suriname, Guyana, Haiti, and Grenada in this list where other languages are spoken due to their geographical proximity to the others.

26. Edwards, David & Cromwell, David (2009), *Newspeak in the 21st Century*, London, Pluto Press, page 193

27. Number cited in, Palast, Greg, (2002) *The Best Democracy Money Can Buy*, London, Robinson. Page 195

28. Pilger, John, (13 May 2006) *The Guardian*, Chávez is using oil revenues to liberate the poor: http://www.guardian.co.uk/commentisfree/2006/may/13/venezuela

29. To avoid encountering the same hair-splitting pedantry that Oliver Stone's film *South of the Border* was subjected to from *The New York Times'* Larry Rohter, who took Stone's cowriter Tariq Ali to task for stating that Bolivia's government decided "to sell" the water system, I should, perhaps, point out that a company called, International Waters Ltd. (an affiliate of Bechtel Corporation), was granted control over the city's water system for forty years. Since they got, as Ali succinctly put it, "control over the city's water supply and the revenue that can be gained from selling it," and therefore his description was accurate, the deal also qualifies as a "privatisation" in my book (literally), and so my description of it as such remains–as does mine here of Rohter as a plonker.

30. *United Nations University International Network on Water Environment and Health (UNU-INWEH), (2008), Safe Water as the Key to Global Health.*

31. World Bank, (August 1997) *Confidential Assessment Corrupted Bank Funds: Summary of RSI staff views regarding the problem of "leakage" from World Bank project budgets*, Jakarta.

32. Mark Curtis, (2003) *Web of Deceit: Britain's Real Role in the World,* London, Vintage.

33. World Bank reports, (September 1997 and March 1998), cited in, *Focus,* on the Global South, CUSRI, Chulalongkorn University, Bangkok, Thailand

34. Palast, Greg, (2006) Armed Madhouse, London, Penguin, page 175

35. In 1998 ,the IMF demanded that Indonesia raise interest rates to 80 percent.

36. See film, *Life and Debt* (2001) by Stephanie Black, Tuff Gong Pictures

37. Palast, Greg, (2006) Armed Madhouse, London, Penguin, page 174

38. Ibid

39. Ibid. page 176

40. As stated by IMF spokesman, Thomas Dawson.

41. Note – On March 02, 2006, then Senator Obama voted for the renewal of the Orwellian named Patriot Act. See U.S. Senate Legislation and records: http://www.senate.gov/legislative/LIS/roll_call_lists/roll_call_vote_cfm.cfm?congress=109&session=2&vote=00029. In February, 2010 Obama signed an extension to several of the law's provisions: http://www.washingtontimes.com/news/2010/feb/27/obama-signs-one-year-extension-patriot-act/

42. Since torturing is in violation of both U.S. and international law, and both President George W. Bush and Vice President Dick Cheney gave the green light for its use (as revealed in the forced release of redacted memos of the Justice Department), the refusal of Obama to prosecute anyone involved

in the practise is a refusal of him to carry out his constitutional duty to "take care that laws be faithfully executed" and, as such, is an excuse of the practise itself. As Obama's head of the CIA, Leon Panetta, has made clear, his and the president's preferred excuse for torture is that of the Nazi defense, i.e., that those involved were only following orders, "What I have expressed as a concern, as has the president, is that those who operated under the rules that were provided by the Attorney General in the interpretation of the law [concerning torture] and followed those rules ought not to be penalized. And . . . I would not support, obviously, an investigation or a prosecution of those individuals. I think they did their job." Neither has Obama "banned torture" as is routinely parroted by his followers, for big loopholes exist in the cleverly worded executive orders which actually permit the practise but still provide a deceptive veneer of the opposite, enabling warm and fuzzy public relation's driven headlines claiming its prohibition. Semantically deceptive examples within the orders include them only being applicable "in any armed conflict," leaving the door open for "counter terrorism" operations; their authorization of the CIA to extrajudicially abduct and transfer civilians without due process to other countries; their banning of Americans from directly torturing but saying nothing of those in their employ, effectively approving torture's outsourcing; their supposed banning of secret prisons but noting that this did "not refer to facilities used only to hold people on a short-term, transitory basis," but crucially leaving out a definition as to what "short-term" or "transitory" actually mean; and although calling for interrogations to coincide with guidelines set out in the *Army Field Manual*, Obama's former director of national intelligence, Admiral Dennis Blair, has stated that new types of "harsh interrogation," may be added to the manual and kept classified.

43. This is where the rank whiff of Obama's hypocrisy is truly overpowering. In 2006, the then senator Obama stated of Bush's military Commissions act, which denied habeas corpus to detainees imprisoned in Guantánamo, "As a parent, I can also imagine the terror I would feel if one of my family members were rounded up in the middle of the night and sent to Guantánamo Bay without even getting one chance to ask why they were being held and being able to prove their innocence . . . By giving suspects a chance, even one chance to challenge the terms of their detention in court, to have a judge confirm that the government has detained the right person for the right suspicions, we could solve this problem without harming our efforts in the war on terror one bit." And after the Supreme Court ruled during the 2008 presidential campaign that those imprisoned at Guantánamo were entitled to habeas corpus, Obama praised the decision, stating it was "a rejection of the Bush Administration's attempt to create a legal black hole at Guantánamo," and that they had rejected "a false choice between fighting terrorism and respecting habeas corpus" and were "protecting our core values." In order to sidestep the ruling the Bush administration simply took prisoners to the notorious Bagram airbase in Afghanistan instead, which was seen as somewhere outside the court's jurisdiction. So what do you think happened when detainees from Bagram challenged the now president Obama on their right to habeas corpus? Did he back up his earlier rhetoric of "giving suspects a chance . . . to challenge the terms of the detention"? Did he hell. Obama fought tooth and nail in court to preserve his right to abduct, transfer and hold civilians without due process for as long as he deems fit. In February 2009, *The New York Times* noted that Obama's legal team had "told a federal judge that military detainees in Afghanistan have no legal right to challenge their imprisonment there, embracing a key argument of former President Bush's legal team." (http://www.nytimes.com/2009/02/22/washington/22bagram.

html?_r=1&scp=2&sq=bagram&st=cse). Despite the presiding judge's decision going against the Obama administration, they appealed; a decision *The New York Times* described as "signal[ing] that the administration was not backing down in its effort to maintain the power to imprison terrorism suspects for extended periods without judicial oversight." (http://www.nytimes.com/2009/04/11/world/asia/11bagram.html?_r=3&partner=rss&emc=rsshttp://www.nytimes.com/2009/04/11/world/asia/11bagram.html?_r=1&partner=rss&emc=rss). Obama, the man who described the right to habeas corpus as "protecting our core values," won the appeal and with it the right to decimate such values.

44. Milne, Seumas, (5 August, 2010) *The Guardian: The US isn't leaving Iraq, it's rebranding the occupation.*

45. Pakistan Body Count, (www.pakistanbodycount.org)

46. Press TV, (14 March, 2010) *The Real Deal*, interview with George Galloway

47. www.ae911truth.org

48. See DVD, *9/11 Blueprint for Truth; The Architecture of Destruction, (2008)* available on *Google Video*: http://video.google.com/videoplay?docid=-4617650616903609314#.

49. Given such a perplexing occurrence, you'd have thought the collapse of 7 WTC would have warranted an exhaustive explanation in the official *9/11 Commission Report*, but in a startling omission, the 571-page document fails to mention 7 WTC with a single solitary word. Despite there being, for several years after 9/11, no official position on what happened to 7 WTC, the generally accepted version in both media and government circles was that debris from the collapse of the twin towers started small fires within the building which grew throughout the day until the structure could take no more, and so collapsed.

Such an explanation was finally endorsed as the official position in late 2008 by the U.S. Department of Commerce's, National Institute of Standards and Technology (*NIST Final Report on the Collapse of World Trade Center Building 7, [20 Nov 2008]*: http://wtc.nist.gov/NCSTAR1/PDF/NCSTAR%201A.pdf), which despite its independent sounding name is very much a government agency, the directors of whom were all Bush appointees (Griffin, David Ray, [2007], *Debunking 9/11 Debunking: An Answer to the Defenders of the Official Conspiracy Theory*, Moreton-in-Marsh, Aris Books, page 143). However, such a position raises serious problems, especially for architects and engineers. If they accept its conclusions as true, then it follows they must also accept that much of what they have come to know about the behavior of steel framed buildings is simply incorrect, and that existing building codes will have to be thrown out and rewritten. Before 9/11 no steel framed high-rise had ever collapsed due to fire, despite over a hundred examples of fires from around the world–Caracas included–that have raged in steel structures, many of which were towering infernos burning far longer and hotter than 7 WCT. (Three prominent examples: On 23 February, 1991, a thirty-eight-storey skyscraper, 1 Meridian Plaza, in Philadelphia caught fire, burning across eight floors for eighteen hours. Officials described the fire as the "most significant fire of the century." On 17 October, 2004, a fire in a fifty-six-storey Caracas skyscraper raged across twenty-six floors for over seventeen hours. On 12 February 2005, a thirty-two-storey skyscraper, the Windsor Building, in Madrid, caught ablaze, engulfing the top ten stories in a fire that burned uncontrollably and lasted nearly twenty-four hours. None of these buildings collapsed). And there is a good and elementary reason why. Steel melts at around 2,800 degrees Fahrenheit, whereas a hydrocarbon fire fuelled by office contents, which is what 7 WTC was, is only capable, under absolutely perfect conditions, of reaching around 1,800 degrees Fahrenheit. (In an interview with NOVA for, *The Collapse: An Engineer's Perspective,* Engineer Thomas Eagar, who is a supporter of the official version, stated that, "The maximum temperature [of the World Trade Center fires] would have been 1,600°F or 1,700°F. It's impossible to generate temperatures much above that in most cases with just normal fuel, in pure air. In fact, I think the World Trade Center fire was probably only 1,200°F or 1,300°F. [www.pbs.org/wdbh/nova/wtc/collapse.html].) The small isolated pockets of smoke rich–and therefore inefficient–fire on a few floors of 7 WCT would have been nowhere near that temperature. A common counter argument to this fact by defenders of the official story is that the steel would not need to melt but simply lose enough of its strength through heating to collapse. It's an argument that has no historical examples to back it up. Were it valid, you would expect numerous instances of steel buildings from around the world that have caught on fire and subsequently collapsed after their steel heated to the requisite temperature. There are none. Not one single example. What's more, in the nineties several giant experiments were carried out at Cardington in the U.K. to test how steel buildings behave when on fire, the results of which rubbish this flawed "strength loss" hypothesis. The experiments involved constructing an eight-storey steel-frame building that was filled with office furniture and fittings then purposefully set ablaze. Despite temperatures reaching as high as 1,800 degrees Fahrenheit–far hotter than the localized fires in 7 WTC–in none of the experiments did the building's steel give up the ghost and collapse, but instead remained solid and standing, albeit with a minor sag. The other major problem for the official version is the speed and symmetry at which 7 WTC came down. If one watches footage of the event, it is clear that the neat symmetrical collapse takes about 6.5 seconds. This is approximately the rate of free fall experienced when there is *zero* resistance. Having jumped out of numerous planes in my life, I can attest that the first one thousand feet take roughly 10 seconds to descend at free fall–an average of about a hundred feet per second until terminal velocity is reached. Since 7 WTC was nearly six hundred feet tall, the 6.5 seconds it took to collapse averaged, just like skydiving, about a second for every hundred foot of tower. Despite this time frame being easily observable and obvious from video footage of the collapse, NIST originally tried to deny that 7 WTC descended at free fall, only later to backtrack on this and finally acknowledge–for the first hundred feet at least–that 7 WTC had indeed experienced free-fall speeds. The speed of decent is highly significant. For the only way that 7 WTC could have fallen at free-fall speeds–the rate a bowling ball would descend through air were it dropped from the building's roof–is if it suddenly encountered zero resistance from the forty thousand tons of structural steel designed to resist its weight. For this to happen, all of the building's eighty-one structural support columns would need to give way at exactly the same time. The only means of achieving such an unnatural state is through the use of explosives in a controlled demolition–something even the staunchest defenders of the official account would have to admit 7 WTC at least *appears* identical to. When controlled-demolition expert Danny Jowenko was shown footage of 7 WTC by a film crew, he concluded, without hesitation or doubt, "This is a controlled demolition," stating it was "performed by a team of experts" and was "without a doubt a professional job."(Interview conducted by Dutch television news program, *Zembia Investigates 9/11 Theories*, 2006. To watch a compilation of footage of 7 WTC's collapse, including Danny Jowenko's comments, see: http://video.google.com/videoplay?docid=2073592843640256739#). Commenting on the collapse the evening it occurred, Dan Rather stated on CBS news that 7 WTC's collapse was "reminiscent of those pictures we've all seen too much on television before when a building was deliberately destroyed by well-placed dynamite to knock it down." If, as a growing number of engineers and architects who are analyzing the event with their own critical intelligence believe, it wasn't just "reminiscent" of a controlled demolition but actually was one, then this has huge ramifications for the whole of the government's official 9/11 narrative. For you cannot rig a building, especially one on fire, with explosives in a matter of hours, meaning it had to have been planned way in advance of 9/11. To achieve such an end, you would need high-level security access to the building in order to attack the core columns, something a group of terrorists organized from a cave in Afghanistan would have been unable to obtain, especially since the building was a highly secure facility with many unusual occupants. These included the Secret Service, the Department of Defense, and the CIA, which housed its clandestine New York station there. Other interesting tenants and facilities within 7 WTC included the mayor of New York's sealed-off emergency bunker and the Security and Exchange Commission, which was using the building to store thousands of files relating to ongoing Wall Street fraud investigations into companies such as Enron and WorldCom. With the building's destruction numerous ongoing cases had to be closed. Another problem for the official account is the presence of huge pools of molten steel in the rubble of both the twin towers and 7 WTC, something that was observable weeks after the collapses and described by fire fighters as being "like lava" and resembling "a foundry."(Numerous eyewitnesses spoke of seeing molten steel at the WTC. Since this is a huge problem for NIST's official version of events, NIST simply denies the molten steel and the witness's existence. To watch their farcical denial juxtaposed against examples of witness testimony to the molten metal's presence, see DVD, *9/11 Blueprint for Truth; The Architecture of Destruction, at 27.22–34:55 mins;* on *Google Video*: http://video.google.com/videoplay?docid=-4617650616903609314#). Not only would 7 WTC's standard open-air fires fuelled by office contents have been incapable of melting this steel, neither would any hydrocarbon fire, including the kerosene (jet fuel) initiated fires of the twin towers–the maximum temperature of which is 1,800 degrees Fahrenheit when burning under absolutely optimum conditions. This leaves an inescapable shortfall of at least 1,000 degrees, which has to be found from somewhere to account for the abundance of molten steel and is the simple reason kerosene-burning heaters constructed of steel don't suddenly melt into squishy inconvenient pools on the ground. So what could have melted the steel into vast rivers of molten metal? Compelling forensic evidence has emerged that an incendiary known as thermite, and the closely related nano-thermite, were responsible. Thermite can reach temperatures in excess of 4,500 degrees, and slice effortlessly through steel by liquefying it on contact, thus bringing down the building. It can burn underwater just as easily as in air, containing its own supply of oxygen–a likely reason why the lake of water pumped into the site had so little effect on the fires, the last of which was extinguished three months after 9/11. Any thermite reaction leaves behind by-products of its use providing unique chemical evidence, a signature or fingerprint if you will, of its presence that would be unobservable had it not been used. This unique signature is something that was first discovered by physics professor Dr. Steven E. Jones through analysis of partially evaporated steel from the towers and of dust samples from the cloud of debris that carpeted Manhattan. His findings have since been confirmed by numerous other scientists in studies published in peer reviewed journals. (*The Open Chemical Physics Journal, Active Thermitic Material Discovered in Dust from the 9/11 World Trade Center Catastrophe,* (2009) http://www.bentham-open.org/pages/content.php?TOCPJ/2009/00000002/00000001/7TOCPJ.SGM). An argument sometimes raised against this irrefutable forensic evidence, is that maybe a thermite cutter torch of some description was used in the clean up, which left behind the unique chemical signature. This, however, completely ignores the fact that the by-products of a thermite reaction were discovered not just on pieces of WTC steel but in dust samples that were collected long before any cleanup took place–from locations including apartments pelted with debris, and a layer that blanketed the surface of the Brooklyn Bridge. Although Farrin, unlike Chávez, refused to get drawn into speculation as to who might have been responsible for the towers' implosion, or how it could have been accomplished–stressing instead the need for a proper independent investigation–from my experience, even if you are unwilling to speculate beyond the physical evidence, when you present such evidence to someone for the first time, you encounter several of the same questions, all but demanding you speculate. The most common being: How could someone rig an office building with explosives without anyone noticing? Since the only way to bring the towers down was by attacking their huge core columns, the question should more actually be How could someone access the core columns without anybody noticing? Mechanical engineer Gordon Ross has addressed this by pointing out that the core columns were, "accessible from inside the elevator shafts. And I believe that gets around the argument that's put forward by some people that says how could you plant explosives in an office building that was being used every day [without anybody noticing]. Well there's your answer: From inside the elevator shafts." (Quote taken from a presentation by Gordon Ross given at the Indian YMCA, London, 8 June 2007.) And it just so happens that the largest elevator modernisation in history was being carried out in the towers in the nine months prior to 9/11. (As documented in magazine, *Elevator World*, [March 2001], *Drive to the Top*. The article describes the work being carried out to the WTC elevator systems as "one of the largest, most sophisticated elevator modernization programs in the industry's history.") Coincidently, the company that provided security for 7 WTC, and indeed the whole of the World Trade Center complex, was Stratesec (formerly known as Securacom), a company George W Bush's brother, Marvin P. Bush, was a principle in from 1993 to 2000, and Bush's cousin Wirt D Walker III was CEO of from 1999 until Jan. 2002. (See Burns, Margi, [20 January 2003] American Reporter, Secrecy Surrounds a Bush Brother's Role in 9/11 Security. Also, Unger, Craig, [2004] House of Bush, House of Saud: The Secret Relationship between the World's Two Most Powerful Dynasties, New York, Scribner, page 249.

50. Palast, Greg, (3 December, 2007), *Fear of Chavez is Fear of Democracy*, cites "The US Department of Energy documents I obtained indicate . . . that Venezuela is sitting on 1.36 *trillion* barrels of crude, *five times* the reserves of Saudi Arabia." http://www.gregpalast.com/fear-of-chavez-is-fear-of-democracy/

51. Figure cited in Palast, Greg, (2006) *Armed Madhouse*, London, Penguin, page 183

52. Ibid., page 183

53. Raby, D.L. (2006) *Democracy and Revolution: Latin America and Socialism Today*, London, Pluto Press & Boudin, Chesa, Gabriel González, and Wilmer Rumbos, (2006) *The Venezuelan Revolution: 100 Questions - 100 Answers*. New York, Thunder's Mouth Press

54. See U.S. Department of Defense Base structure report: http://www.defense.gov/pubs/BSR_2007_Baseline.pdf & Cooley, Alexander (2008) *Base Politics: Democratic Change and the U.S. military Overseas*, Cornell University Press, Ithaca (US)

55. The official government document, which was submitted to Congress in May 2009 as part of a budget justification for the following year, can be viewed here: http://www.centrodealerta.

org/documentos_desclasificados/original_in_english_air_for.pdf

56. Quoted in Edwards, David, Cromwell, David, (2009) *Newspeak in the 21st Century*, London, Pluto Press, page 187.

57. Kovalik, Dan, (1 April, 2010) Huffington Post, *U.S. and Colombia Cover Up Atrocities Through Mass Graves Human and Labor Rights Lawyer*: http://www.huffingtonpost.com/dan-kovalik/us-colombia-cover-up-atro_b_521402.html

58. Vieira Constanza, (19 July, 2009) *UN Confirms 'Systematic Killings of Civilians by Soldiers'* http://ipsnews.net/news.asp?idnews=47300

59. Sorry, Mother.

60. The notes issued pre 2007 feature Simón Bolívar (liberator from Spanish colonialism), Andrés Bello (humanist and poet), Francisco de Miranda (freedom fighter against Spanish colonialism), Antonio José de Sucre y Alcalá (independence leader in fight against Spanish colonialism), Simon Rodriguez (Bolivar's mentor and tutor) and José María Vargas (Venezuela's fifth president). Those issued in 2007 also feature Simón Bolívar, Simon Rodriguez, and Francisco de Miranda, in addition to Maria Luisa Cáceres Diaz de Arismendi (a heroine of the war of independence), Cacique Guaicaipuro (an indigenous hero who fought against Spain's conquest of Venezuela) and Pedro Camejo (a renowned solider of African descent who obtained the rank of lieutenant fighting against Spain in the war of independence).